face2face

Elementary Student's Book

Chris Redston & Gillie Cunningham

CAMBRIDGE
UNIVERSITY PRESS

Welcome to the class!

Vocabulary colours; the alphabet and spelling; days of the week

Real World saying hello and goodbye; introducing yourself; classroom instructions

1 TEACHER Hello. What's your name, please?
CLAIRE My name's Claire Dupont.
TEACHER I'm Sarah Taylor. Welcome to the class.
CLAIRE Thank you.

Welcome to the class!

Hello!

1 a) **R0.1** Look at conversation 1 and listen.

b) Practise conversation 1 with your teacher. Use your name.

2 a) **R0.2** Look at conversation 2 and listen.

b) Practise conversation 2 with six students. Use your name.

Colours

3 Match the words to the colours.

red   green   blue   yellow
white   black   grey

3 PABLO Hello. Sorry I'm late.
TEACHER No problem.

The alphabet

4 a) **R0.3** **P** Listen and say the alphabet.

TIP! • **P** = pronunciation.

Aa Bb Cc Dd Ee
Ff Gg Hh Ii Jj Kk
Ll Mm Nn Oo Pp
Qq Rr Ss Tt Uu
Vv Ww Xx Yy Zz

b) Work in pairs. How do we say these letters?

1 the ▨▨▨ letters   4 the ▨▨▨ letters

2 the ▨▨▨ letters   5 the ▨▨▨ letters

3 the ▨▨▨ letters   6 the ▨▨▨ and ▨▨▨ letters

c) **R0.4** **P** Listen and practise.

d) **R0.5** Listen and write the words.

TIP! • ee = *double e*

2

MARCO	Hello, my name's Marco.
LIN	Hi, I'm Lin.
MARCO	Nice to meet you.
LIN	Nice to meet you too.

Classroom instructions

5 **a)** Tick (✓) the instructions you understand. Then do the exercise in Language Summary Welcome **RW0.2** p121.

Look at page ten.
Answer the questions.
Fill in the gaps.
Open your book.
Read the article.
Match the words to the pictures.
Check your answers.
Work in pairs.
Work in groups.
Listen and practise.
Don't write.
Close your book.

b) **R0.6** Listen and underline the instructions in **5a)** when you hear them.

Spelling

6 **a)** Look at conversation 3. Then match the teacher's questions to Pablo's answers.

1	TEACHER	What's your first name?	a)	PABLO	R–U–A–N–O.
2	TEACHER	What's your surname?	b)	PABLO	Ruano.
3	TEACHER	How do you spell that?	c)	PABLO	It's Pablo.

b) **R0.7** Listen and check.

c) **R0.8** Listen to two conversations, A and B. Write the names.

d) Look at R0.8, p148. Listen again and check your answers.

7 **a)** **R0.9** **P** Listen and practise the questions in **6a)**.

b) Ask four students these questions and write the names.

Goodbye!

8 **a)** Put the days of the week in order.

> Friday   Tuesday   Thursday   Monday *1*
> Wednesday   Saturday   Sunday

b) **R0.10** **P** Listen and check. Then listen again and practise. What day is it today? What day is it tomorrow?

9 **R0.11** Listen and write the day. Practise with other students.

PABLO	Bye, Lin.
LIN	Goodbye! See you on ....
PABLO	Yes, see you.

Progress Portfolio

10 Tick (✓) the things you can do in English. You can check this language in Language Summary Welcome, p121.

- ☐ I can say hello and goodbye.
- ☐ I can introduce myself.
- ☐ I can say colours.
- ☐ I can say the alphabet.
- ☐ I can understand instructions.
- ☐ I can spell my name.
- ☐ I can say the days of the week.

11 Work in pairs. Close your book. Tell your partner three things you can do in English.

1 Meeting people

1A Where are you from?

QUICK REVIEW ●●●
Write six words in English. Work in pairs. Spell the words to your partner. He/She writes them down. Are they correct?

> **Vocabulary** countries and nationalities
> **Grammar** *be* (1): positive and *Wh-* questions; subject pronouns and possessive adjectives
> **Real World** introducing people
> **Help with Listening** word stress
> **Review** saying hello; the alphabet

Introducing people

1 a) R1.1 P Read and listen to conversation 1. Listen again and practise.

b) Practise conversation 1 with four other students. Use your name.

2 a) R1.2 P Read and listen to conversation 2. Listen again and practise.

b) Work in groups of six. Take turns to introduce students to each other.

Help with Listening Word stress

4 R1.3 Listen and notice the word stress (•) in the countries and nationalities in **3a)**.

5 R1.3 P Listen again and practise. Copy the word stress.

Brazil   Brazilian

Vocabulary
Countries and nationalities

3 a) Tick (✓) the countries you know.

countries I'm from ...	nationalities I'm ...
Brazil	Brazili _a n_
Australia	Australi _ _
Argentina	Argentini _ _
the USA	Americ _ _
Germany	Germ _ _
Italy	Itali _ _
Mexico	Mexic _ _
Russia	Russi _ _
the UK	Brit _i s h_
Spain	Span _ _ _
Poland	Pol _ _ _
Turkey	Turk _ _ _
China	Chin _e s e_
Japan	Japan _ _ _
France	French

b) Write the missing letters in the nationalities. Check in Language Summary 1 V1.1 p122.

①
CAROL Hello, John.
JOHN Hi, Carol. How are you?
CAROL I'm fine, thanks. And you?
JOHN I'm OK, thanks.

③
RECEPTIONIST Good morning. What's your name, please?
MARIA It's Maria Favia.
RECEPTIONIST And where are you from?
MARIA I'm from ....

②
MONICA Elena, this is Roberto.
ROBERTO Hello, Elena. Nice to meet you.
ELENA And you.

Listening and Grammar

6 R1.4 Read and listen to conversations 3, 4 and 5. Write the countries.

Help with Grammar
be: positive and *Wh-* questions

7 **a)** Fill in the gaps with '*m*, '*re* or '*s*.

POSITIVE

1 I'_____ from Italy.	(= I am)
2 You'_____ in room C.	(= you are)
3 He'_____ from Mexico.	(= he is)
4 She'_____ from Australia.	(= she is)
5 It'_____ Maria Favia.	(= it is)
6 We'_____ from the USA.	(= we are)
7 They'_____ from Spain.	(= they are)

b) Fill in the gaps with *are* or '*s*.

WH- QUESTIONS

1 Where _____ you from?
2 Where'_____ he from?
3 Where'_____ she from?
4 What'_____ your name?
5 What _____ your names?
6 Where _____ they from?

c) Check in G1.1 p123.

4

RECEPTIONIST	What are your names, please?
JOE	My name's Joe Hill and this is Susan West.
RECEPTIONIST	Where are you from?
JOE	We're from _____ .
RECEPTIONIST	Welcome to the conference. You're in room C.

5

MOLLY	Where's he from?
DAVID	He's from _____ .
MOLLY	OK. And where's she from?
DAVID	She's from _____ .
MOLLY	Right. And where are they from?
DAVID	They're from _____ , I think.

8 **a)** R1.5 P Listen and practise the sentences in 7a).

b) R1.6 P Listen and practise the questions in 7b).

c) Work in pairs. Practise conversations 3, 4 and 5.

9 Fill in the gaps with '*m*, '*re*, *are* or '*s*.

DAVID Where ¹*are* they from?
MOLLY They ²_____ both from Germany.
DAVID What ³_____ **their** names?
MOLLY **His** name ⁴_____ Tomás and **her** name ⁵_____ Verena.

RECEPTIONIST What ⁶_____ **your** names?
BARBARA **Our** names ⁷_____ Barbara Petit and Pedro Moreno.
RECEPTIONIST Where ⁸_____ you from?
BARBARA I ⁹_____ from France and he ¹⁰_____ from Mexico.

Help with Grammar
Subject pronouns and possessive adjectives

10 **a)** Fill in the table with the words in **bold** in 9.

subject pronouns	I	you	he	she	it	we	they
possessive adjectives	my	_____	_____	_____	its	_____	_____

b) Check in G1.2 p123.

11 R1.7 P Listen and practise.

My name's Carol.

12 R1.8 Listen and fill in the gaps on the name cards.

A
Name: Karen
Country:

Name: Peter
Country:

B
Name: Murat
Country:

C
Name: Dorota
Country:

Get ready ... Get it right!

13 Work in pairs. Student A → p104.
Student B → p112. Follow the instructions.

1B In the coffee break

Vocabulary numbers 0–20;
phone numbers; jobs; *a* and *an*
Grammar *be* (2): negative, *yes/no*
questions and short answers
Review *be*: positive; countries

QUICK REVIEW ● ● ●
Work in pairs. Take turns to ask your partner the names of other students
in the class: *What's his name? It's Mario, I think. / I can't remember!*

Vocabulary Numbers 0–20

1 Work in pairs. Can you say these numbers?
Check in **V1.2** p122.

0 1 **2** 3 **4** 5 **6** 7 8 **9** 10
11 12 13 **14** 15 16 **17** 18 19 **20**

2 a) **R1.9** Listen to five conversations A–E. Write
the hotel room numbers.

b) Work in pairs. Take turns to say five numbers.
Your partner writes the numbers. Are they correct?

3 a) How do we say these phone numbers?

TIP! ● In phone numbers 0 = *oh* and 22 = *double two*.

a) Hotel 020 8695 7322
b) Peter 01279 567390
c) Barbara 07949 274118
d) Maria 0034 93 2867 746

b) **R1.10** **P** Listen and check. Then listen again
and practise.

4 a) **R1.11** Listen and write the phone numbers.

b) Ask three students their phone numbers. You
can invent numbers if you like!

What's your phone number?

It's ...

What's your mobile number?

Vocabulary Jobs; *a* and *an*

5 a) Tick the words you know. Then do the exercise
in **V1.3** p122.

a doctor   a musician   an engineer   a shop assistant
a cleaner   a police officer   a waiter/a waitress
an accountant   an actor/an actress   a builder
a teacher   a manager   a housewife   a lawyer
unemployed   retired

TIP! ● In these vocabulary boxes we only show the
main stress.

b) **R1.12** **P** Listen and practise. Copy the stress.

Help with Vocabulary *a* and *an*

6 a) Look at the jobs in 5a). Then complete the
rules with *a* or *an*.

● We use .... with nouns that begin with
a consonant sound. (The consonants are
b, c, d, f, etc.)

● We use .... with nouns that begin with
a vowel sound. (The vowels are *a, e, i, o, u.*)

b) Fill in the gaps with *a* or *an*.

1 .... job   4 .... room
2 .... student   5 .... English book
3 .... answer   6 .... number

7 a) Look again at the pictures in **V1.3** p122. Take
turns to cover the words and test your partner.

What's his job?   He's an actor.

What's her job?   She's a doctor.

b) What's your job? Ask other students.

What's your job?   I'm a manager.

What do you do?   I'm an engineer.

Listening and Grammar

8 **a)** R1.13 Read and listen. Fill in the gaps.

1

A   Are you from Sydney?

B   No, we aren't from Australia. We're from South Africa.

A   Oh, really? And what do you do?

B   Well, I'm an _____ and Connie's a _____ .

2

A   Who's he?

B   His name's John Palmer.

A   Is he a _____ ?

B   Yes, he is. But he isn't famous.

3

A   And what do you do?

B   I'm a _____ .

A   Oh, really? I'm a _____ .

B   Are you from Spain?

A   No, I'm not. I'm from Argentina.

b) Look at the photo. Match the conversations to the groups of people A–C.

Help with Grammar   *be*: negative, *yes/no* questions and short answers

9 **a)** Look again at **8a)**. Find the parts of *be* in the conversations.

b) Fill in the gaps in these negative sentences with *'m*, *aren't* and *isn't*.

1   I'_____ not a teacher.

2   You/We/They _____ from Australia. (= are not)

3   He/She/It _____ famous. (= is not)

c) Fill in the gaps in these questions and answers with *'m*, *Is*, *Are*, *isn't* or *aren't*.

1   __*Are*__ you from Spain?
    Yes, I am./No, I _____ not.

2   _____ he a musician?
    Yes, he is./No, he _____ .

3   _____ you from Sydney?
    Yes, we are./No, we _____ .

d) Check in G1.3 p123.

10 R1.14 P Listen and practise.

I'm not a teacher.
We aren't from Australia.

11 **a)** Tick the sentences that are true for you. Make the other sentences negative. Write the correct sentences.

1   I'm from France.
    I'm not from France. I'm from Germany.

2   My English class is in room 17.

3   I'm a doctor.

4   My teacher's from Canada.

5   My language school is in England.

6   My English lessons are on Wednesdays and Fridays.

7   The students in my class are all from my country.

b) Work in groups. Compare sentences.

Get ready ... Get it right!

12 Work in pairs. Student A → p104. Student B → p112. Follow the instructions.

1C Personal details

Real World asking for and giving personal details; asking people to repeat things
Vocabulary numbers 20–100; age
Help with Listening numbers with -teen and -ty; sentence stress (1)
Review be; phone numbers

QUICK REVIEW ● ● ●
Work in pairs. Write all the jobs you know.
Which pair has the most words?

What number is it?

1 How do we say these numbers? Check in **V1.5** p122.

**20 30 40 50 60
70 80 90 100**

2 Work in pairs. Say these numbers.

| 28 | 34 | 47 | 51 | 63 | 75 | 86 | 92 | 100 |

Help with Listening Numbers with -teen and -ty

3 **a)** **R1.15** Listen to these numbers and notice the stress.

thirteen   thirty   fifteen   fifty   nineteen   ninety

b) Where is the stress in these numbers?

forty   seventeen   eighty   sixty   eighteen
fourteen   sixteen   seventy

c) **R1.16** Listen and check.

4 **a)** **R1.16** **P** Listen again and practise the numbers in 3b).

b) Work in pairs. Say a number between 1 and 100. Your partner says the next three numbers.

thirty-seven   thirty-eight, thirty-nine, forty

Hiring a car

5 **a)** Molly and David are at a car hire office. Look at the photo. Match these words to Molly's things 1–4.

a credit card   a passport   a business card   a letter

b) Answer these questions about Molly.

1 Is she Australian?   3 Is she married or single?
2 What's her job?   4 How old is she?

United Kingdom of Great Britain and Northern Ireland
Passport Passeport
Surname
BLACKWELL (a)
Given names
MOLLY JANE
Nationality
BRITISH CITIZEN (b)
Date of birth
23 JUN 80
Sex Place of birth
F   LONDON
Date of issue
15 MAY 04   Authority   UKPA
Date of expiry   Signature
15 MAY 14   MJ Blackwell

P<GBRBLACKWELL<<MOLLY<JANE<<<<<<<<<<<<
<<<<<<<<<<<<<<<<<<<<<<<<<<<<<<<<<<<<

6 **a)** Match these words to the letters a)–j) in the pictures.

1 first name g)   6 mobile number
2 surname   7 home address
3 nationality   8 postcode at work
4 home phone number   9 email address
5 work number   10 credit card number

b) Check your answers in pairs.

What's her first name?   It's Molly.

2

(c) 22 Harris Street
London SE6 1GY

(d) Tel: 020 8566 7821
(e) Mobile: 03342 678922

22nd March

Dear Jenny,

Hi! How are you? Thanks very much for the book.
It's very good.

3 EUROBANK
CREDIT CARD

(f) 4550 7690 7172 3059
4550

VALID FROM 02/05   EXPIRES END 01/10

MRS MOLLY J BLACKWELL

4 WOLF & JONES LTD

63 Bank Street
London
(h) EC2Y 6HD

(g) Molly Blackwell
Company Lawyer

(i) TEL: 020 7544 3219
FAX: 020 7544 8735
(j) EMAIL: molly.blackwell@wjl.com

Help with Listening Sentence stress (1)

7 a) R1.17 Listen to these questions and notice the sentence stress. We stress the important words.

1 What's your surname, please?
2 What's your first name?
3 And what's your nationality?
4 What's your address?
5 What's your home phone number?
6 And what's your mobile number?
7 What's your email address?

b) Listen again. Notice how we say *your* /jə/ and *and* /ən/ in these sentences.

---

8 a) R1.18 Listen to David's conversation and fill in the gaps on the form.

CCH452

Car Hire Form
Customer ref. 000237

CITY CAR HIRE

Surname	....
First name	*David*
Nationality	....
Address	.... *Road*
	Birmingham ....
Home phone number	....
Mobile phone number	*07810* ....
email address	*dholmes@webmail.com*

b) Look at R1.18, p148. Listen again and notice the sentence stress on the woman's sentences.

Real World Asking people to repeat things

9 a) R1.19 Listen to the sentences from the conversation in 8a). Fill in the gaps with these words. Then check in RW1.2 p123.

say	repeat	again	could	sorry

1 Could you .... that .... , please?
2 I'm .... ?
3 Sorry, ... you .... that, please?

b) P Listen again and practise. Copy the polite intonation.

---

10 a) R1.20 P Listen and practise the questions in 7a).

b) Work in pairs. Interview your partner and fill in the form.

CCH452

Car Hire Form
Customer ref. 000238

CITY CAR HIRE

Surname	....
First name	....
Nationality	....
Address	....
	....
Home phone number	....
Mobile phone number	....
email address	....

1D Lost property

Vocabulary personal possessions (1); plurals; *this*, *that*, *these*, *those*
Review *be*

QUICK REVIEW ● ● ●
Work in pairs. Count from 0 to 51 in threes. (*0, 3, 6, 9*, etc.). Take turns to say the numbers. Now count from 0 to 98 in sevens. (*0, 7, 14*, etc.).

1 Look at the picture of the lost property room in the hotel. Match these words to 1–14.

> diaries *14*   suitcases   wallets   shoes
> coats   an umbrella   a CD player
> ID (identity) cards   watches   a camera
> dresses   bags   a bike/bicycle   false teeth

Help with Vocabulary   Plurals

2 **a)** Write the missing letters. When do we add *-s*, *-es* and *-ies*? Which plurals are irregular?

singular	plural
a bag	bag _
a shoe	shoe _
a suitcase	suitcase _
a wat**ch**	watch _ _
a dre**ss**	dress _ _
a diar**y**	diar _ _ _
a man	m _ n
a woman	wom _ n
a child	childr _ n
a person	p _ ople
a tooth	t _ _ th

b) Check in **V1.7** p122.

3 **R1.21** **P** Listen and practise the plurals in **2a)**.

4 Write the plurals.

a) bike *bikes*   e) country
b) credit card   f) address
c) nationality   g) camera
d) waitress   h) colour

5 Work in pairs. Take turns to test each other on 1–14.

> Number 14.   They're diaries.

> Number 9.   It's an umbrella.

6 Eva's got a job at the hotel. Look at the pictures and fill in the gaps with words from **1**.

1 What's this in English?
It's an _____ .

2 What are these in English?
They're _____ .

3 What's that in English?
It's a _____ .

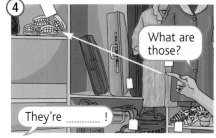

4 What are those?
They're _____ !

Help with Vocabulary
this, that, these, those

7 Fill in the table with *this*, *that*, *these*, *those*. Then check in V1.8 p122.

	here ↓	there ↗
singular		
plural		

8 a) R1.22 P Listen and practise Eva's questions in **6**.

b) Choose three things in the classroom or from your bag. Ask your teacher what they are in English.

---

1 a) Find ten countries. V1.1

R	E	B	R	A	Z	I	L
G	E	R	M	A	N	Y	R
U	P	S	E	D	F	P	U
K	I	T	A	L	Y	O	S
F	R	A	N	C	E	L	S
L	A	R	U	S	A	A	I
L	O	N	C	H	I	N	A
T	U	R	K	E	Y	D	W

b) Write the nationalities.

Brazil → Brazilian

c) Work in pairs. Where is the stress on the countries and nationalities?

Brazil   Brazilian

2 a) Put an apostrophe (') in these sentences. G1.1

1 His names Boris.
2 Theyre from Italy.
3 Im from England.
4 Her surnames Owen.
5 My names Amanda.
6 Hes from Germany.

b) Write questions for the answers in **2a)**.

1 What's his name?

3 Fill in the gaps in these jobs with the vowels *a, e, i, o, u*. Then put *a* or *an* in the boxes. V1.3 V1.4

1 [a] l a wy e r
2 [   ] _ ct _ r
3 [   ] m _ s _ c _ _ n
4 [   ] w _ _ tr _ ss
5 [   ] _ cc _ _ nt _ nt
6 [   ] m _ n _ g _ r
7 [   ] _ ng _ n _ _ r
8 [   ] p _ l _ ce _ ff _ c _ r

4 a) Choose a new nationality and a new job for you. Don't tell other students.

b) Work in groups. Take turns to ask each student *yes/no* questions to find out his/her new nationality and job. G1.3

---

5 a) Make these sentences negative. Write correct sentences. G1.3

1 Sydney is in England.
Sydney isn't in England.
It's in Australia.
2 Brad Pitt is an accountant.
3 Venus and Serena Williams are from Spain.
4 Nike and Ford are British companies.
5 Ferraris are German cars.

b) Write three more incorrect sentences.

c) Work in pairs. Swap sentences. Correct your partner's sentences.

6 a) Write questions with *you* or *your* for these answers. RW1.3

1 Smith. *What's your surname?*
2 It's Jane.
3 I'm British.
4 It's 01865 568004.
5 jane22@webmail.com
6 28 New Road, Leeds.
7 I'm 26.
8 No, I'm single.

b) Work in pairs. Ask your partner five questions from **6a)**. Write the answers.

c) Check your partner's information about you. Is it correct?

Progress Portfolio

a) Tick the things you can do in English.

- [ ] I can introduce people.
- [ ] I can say countries and nationalities.
- [ ] I can say and understand the numbers 1–100.
- [ ] I can talk about jobs.
- [ ] I can ask for, give and understand personal information (name, address, etc.).
- [ ] I can ask people to repeat things.

b) What do you need to study again? See CD-ROM ⦿ 1A–D.

2 People and possessions

2A What's important to you?

QUICK REVIEW ●●●
What's in the lost property room at the hotel? Write all the things you can remember. Compare your lists in pairs. Then check on p12.

> **Vocabulary** adjectives (1); adjectives with *very*; personal possessions (2)
> **Grammar** *have got*
> **Review** *be*; possessive adjectives

Vocabulary Adjectives (1)

1 Tick the adjectives you know. Then do the exercise in Language Summary 2 **V2.1** p124.

new	old	big	small
good	bad	long	short
cheap	expensive	fast	slow
beautiful	ugly	young	old
easy	difficult	right	wrong

nice	important	great	favourite

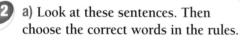

Help with Vocabulary
Adjectives with *very*

2 a) Look at these sentences. Then choose the correct words in the rules.

She's old.   *He's a very **happy** child.*
*It's a **small** bag.*   *Those are my **new** shoes.*

● We put adjectives *before/after* the verb *be*.
● We put adjectives *before/after* a noun.
● We put *very before/after* adjectives.
● Adjectives *are/aren't* plural with plural nouns.

b) Check in **V2.2** p124.

3 a) Make sentences with these words.

1 expensive / It / isn't . *It isn't expensive.*
2 camera / old / It / 's / my .
3 very / are / The / dresses / beautiful .
4 cheap / a / It / very / watch / 's .
5 your / They / new / 're / books .

b) Work in pairs. Check your sentences.

Reading, Listening and Grammar

4 a) **R2.1** Read and listen to Sally and her grandfather, Bill. Find four things that are important to each person.

> **SALLY** What's important in my life? Well, I've got a great CD player. I haven't got lots of CDs, but my friend Ian is a musician and he's got hundreds! And I've got an old bike – that's very important to me. What else? Well, I've got a beautiful long dress. It's red, my favourite colour, and I love it. Oh, and my new mobile phone is very important to me – it's got all my friends' phone numbers in it!

> **BILL** What things are important to me? Well, I've got a very old Toyota. It's not very fast but it's important to us – my wife, Pat, hasn't got a car. And we've got a dog. His name's Fred and he's twelve years old. He's very important to us. Oh, and I've got an expensive digital camera. It's very small but the pictures are great. And I've got a very good DVD player and hundreds of DVDs – we love old films. The problem is, we haven't got a very good TV!

b) Read the texts again. Are these sentences true (T) or false (F)?

1 Sally's friend Ian is a doctor. *F*
2 Her favourite colour is red.
3 Her mobile phone is very old.
4 Bill's camera is very cheap.
5 His dog is called Fred.
6 His DVD player isn't very good.

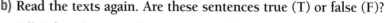

Help with Grammar
have got: positive and negative

5 **a)** Look again at the texts in **4a)**. Find all the positive and negative examples of *have got* and *has got*.

b) Fill in the gaps with *'ve*, *'s*, *haven't* and *hasn't*.

POSITIVE
I/you/we/they'............ got (= have got)
he/she/it'............ got (= has got)

NEGATIVE
I/you/we/they .... got (= have not got)
he/she/it .... got (= has not got)

c) Check in **G2.1** p125.

6 **R2.2** **P** Listen and practise. Copy the stress and contractions (*I've*, *he's*, etc.).

I've got an old car.

7 **a)** Fill in the gaps with the correct form of *have got*.

1 I __haven't got__ a car, but I'............
   an expensive bike.
2 Oh, you'............ a blue dress!
3 We'............ a black cat.
4 They'............ a big house in
   France. It's very nice.
5 He'............ lots of CDs, but
   he............ a CD player!

b) Think of four things that are important to you. Then compare ideas in groups.

> I've got a lot of old books.

> Really? What's your favourite?

Vocabulary
Personal possessions (2)

8 Work in pairs. Tick the words you know. Check new words in **V2.3** p124.

> a mobile (phone) [US: a cell phone]
> CDs   a CD player   videos
> a video recorder [US: a VCR]
> a TV/television   a computer
> a personal stereo   a DVD player
> DVDs   a laptop   a digital camera
> a radio

Listening and Grammar

9 **a)** Bill and Sally answer questions for a survey. Work in pairs. Guess which things they've got. Write *yes* or *no* in the *your guess* columns.

Customer name	Bill Robinson		Sally Robinson	
Product	your guess	his answer	your guess	her answer
computer				
mobile phone				
digital camera				
personal stereo				
DVD player				

b) **R2.3** Listen and write *yes* or *no* in Bill and Sally's answer columns. Are your guesses correct?

Help with Grammar *have got*: questions and short answers

10 **a)** Fill in the gaps with *have*, *has*, *haven't* or *hasn't*.

QUESTIONS   SHORT ANSWERS
Have you got a computer?   Yes, I __have__ ./No, I ....
.... he/she got a DVD player?   Yes, he/she ..../No, he/she ....
.... they got any cheap TVs?   Yes, they ..../No, they ....
What .... you got in your bag?

b) Check in **G2.2** p125.

11 **R2.4** **P** Listen and practise the questions and short answers in **10a)**.
Have you got a computer?   Yes, I have.   No, I haven't.

12 Work in pairs. Take turns to ask and answer questions about Bill and Sally.

> Has Bill got a new car?

> No, he hasn't.

Get ready ... Get it right!

13 Work in pairs. Student A → p105. Student B → p113. Follow the instructions.

Meet the Robinsons

Vocabulary family; *How many ...*
Help with Listening the schwa
in words and sentences
Grammar possessive *'s*
Review *be*; *have got*; jobs

QUICK REVIEW ● ● ●

Work in pairs. Ask questions with *have got*. Find five things you've got but your partner hasn't got.

BILL

PAT

husband ~~daughter~~ son father
mother brother children

LISA   We're a typical British family, I think. My
¹ *husband* 's name is Tom and we've got two ² .... ,
a girl and a boy. Our ³ *daughter* 's name is Emma and
Chris is our ⁴ .... – he's just a baby. And my parents?
Well, Bill is my ⁵ .... and Pat is my ⁶ .... I've got
one ⁷ .... , his name's Max, and one sister, Kate.

~~wife~~ ~~parents~~ sisters grandson
granddaughters grandchildren

MAX   My ⁸ *wife* 's name is Anna and we've got one
daughter, Sally. She's sixteen years old now. I've got two
⁹ .... , Lisa and Kate. Lisa's married with two kids
and Kate's divorced. My ¹⁰ *parents'* names are Pat and
Bill. They've got three children and three ¹¹ .... :
two ¹² .... , Sally and Emma, and a ¹³ .... , Chris.

 TOM

LISA

KATE

MAX

 ANNA

~~aunts~~ ~~grandparents~~ cousins grandmother grandfather uncle

SALLY   My mum and dad's names are Anna and Max. I've got
two ¹⁴ *aunts* , Lisa and Kate, and one ¹⁵ .... His name's
Tom and he's a musician. I've also got two ¹⁶ .... , Emma
and Chris. My ¹⁷*grandparents'* names are Bill – he's my
¹⁸ .... – and Pat, my ¹⁹ ....

 EMMA

 CHRIS

 SALLY

Vocabulary Family

1 a) Look at the family tree. Then read about the family. Fill in the gaps with the words in the boxes.

b) R2.5 Listen and check your answers.

2 Look again at the family tree. Put the words in the boxes in three groups. Then check in V2.4 p124.

1 ♂ male *father/dad*

2 ♀ female *mother/mum*

3 ♂♀ male and female *parents*

Help with Listening The schwa /ə/ in words

3 a) R2.6 The schwa /ə/ is very common in English. Listen to these words. Is the schwa stressed?

parents	daughter	children	brother	uncle	cousin
/ə/	/ə/	/ə/	/ə/	/ə/	/ə/

b) R2.7 Listen to these words. Where are the schwas?

doctor	address	woman	musician	manager

4 Work in pairs. Look at the family tree. Ask and answer six questions with *How many ...?* about the people.

How many brothers and sisters has Lisa got?
How many children have Pat and Bill got?

Grammar and Listening

5 Tick the correct sentences. Change the words in **bold** in the incorrect sentences.

1 Kate is Lisa's ~~cousin~~. *sister*
2 Bill is Pat's **husband**. ✓
3 Lisa and Tom are Chris's **parents**.
4 Pat is Emma and Chris's **grandmother**.
5 Kate is Sally's **cousin**.
6 Sally is Anna's **daughter**.

Help with Grammar Possessive *'s*

6 **a)** Look again at **5**. Then complete the rule.

- We use *name* + _____ for the possessive.

b) *'s* can mean *is*, *has* or the possessive. Match 1–3 to a)–c).

1 Bill is Lisa's father.   a) *'s = is*
2 Kate's her sister.   b) *'s = has*
3 She's got a brother.   c) *'s = possessive*

c) Check in **G2.3** p125.

7 Make sentences about these people.

1 Lisa / Sally *Lisa is Sally's aunt.*
2 Max / Anna
3 Pat / Bill
4 Chris / Bill and Pat
5 Emma / Chris
6 Sally / Anna and Max

8 **R2.8** **P** Listen and practise.

Sǎlly's → Lisa is Sǎlly's aǔnt.

9 **a)** Kate wants to show her new boyfriend, Tim, some photos. Look at photos A–C. Who are the people?

b) **R2.9** Listen to their conversation. Put the photos in order.

c) Listen again and choose the correct words.

1 Kate's sister Lisa is a ⟨doctor⟩ / lawyer.
2 Lisa's husband Tom is a *teacher / musician*.
3 Their daughter Emma is *six / seven*.
4 Kate's brother Max is a *musician / lawyer*.
5 His wife Anna is *Spanish / Italian*.
6 Kate's mother is *retired / a teacher*.
7 Kate's father is *sixty-three / seventy-three*.

Help with Listening The schwa /ə/ in sentences

10 **a)** **R2.9** In sentences we often say small words like *and*, *are*, *a*, *of*, *to*, *the* with a schwa /ə/. Listen to the first sentence again and notice the schwas. Are they stressed?

Cŏme and /ən/ loŏk at /ət/ thĕse phŏtos of /əv/ my fǎmily.

b) Look at R2.9, p149. Listen and notice the stressed words and the schwas.

Get ready ... Get it right!

11 **a)** Write your name and the names of five people in your family on a piece of paper. Think what you can say about these people (age, job, married, etc.). Don't write this information.

b) Choose a partner, but don't talk to him/her. Swap papers. Make questions to ask about your partner's family.

Who's (Johann)?   Is he married?   Has he got any children?

12 **a)** Work with your partner. Take turns to ask questions about his/her family. Make notes on your partner's answers.

b) Tell another student about your partner's family.

2C Time and money

Real World talking about times and prices; buying tickets

Vocabulary time words (*minute, year*, etc.); *How much ...?*

Review numbers

QUICK REVIEW ●●●

Work in pairs. Write all the family words you know. Which words are for men/boys, women/girls, or both?

What's the time?

1 Put these words in order. Then check in **V2.5** p124.

a minute   a year   a day   a week
an hour   a second   *1*   a month

2 a) Work in pairs. Look at photos A–F. What are these things, do you think?

a cooker   a laptop   a radio
a mobile (phone)   a TV   a digital camera

I think E is a mobile.

Me too.

I don't. I think it's a digital camera.

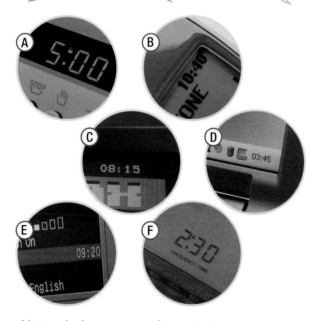

b) Match the times to photos A–F.

five o'clock A   eight fifteen   nine twenty
two thirty   ten forty   three forty-five

c) We can say times in a different way. Match these times to photos B–F.

quarter to four   twenty past nine   half past two
quarter past eight   twenty to eleven

3 Write the times. Then check in **RW2.1** p125.

1 five past _____   2 twenty-five to _____   3 ten _____

4 _____ _____ twelve   5 _____-five   6 _____ _____

4 **R2.10** Listen and match conversations 1–3 to three of the photos A–F in **2a)**.

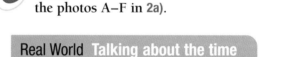

Real World Talking about the time

5 a) Fill in the gaps in the questions and answers.

What time ¹ _____ it?   It's five o'² _____ .

What's the ³ _____ , please?   It's about half ⁴ _____ two.

Excuse me. Have you ⁵ _____ the time, please?   Yes, it's eight fifteen.

b) Fill in the gaps with *to, from* or *at*.

1 My English class is _____ ten.
2 My son's class is _____ seven _____ nine thirty.

c) Check in **RW2.2** p125.

6 a) **R2.11** **P** Listen and practise the questions and answers in **5a)**. Copy the polite intonation.

b) Write six times. Work in pairs. Take turns to ask and answer the questions in **5a)**. Write your partner's times. Are they correct?

An evening out

7 **a)** Look at adverts A–C. Which is for:

1 a cinema?   2 a concert?   3 an exhibition?

b) R2.12 Listen and write the missing times 1–5 on the adverts.

A

The Lewisham Gallery

Molesworth St, Lewisham SE13
Modern Art in Europe
April 2nd–May 25th

Opening times:
10.00–¹_____ Mon–Fri
10.00–²_____ Sat & Sun
ᵃ⁾£_____
(Students/Children ᵇ⁾£_____)

Ticket office: 020 8960 2424
www.lewishamgallery.org.uk

B

Mary Colgan
at the Camden Apollo

Thursday 4th/Friday 5th April
at ³_____ p.m.

Tickets ᶜ⁾£_____ and
ᵈ⁾£_____ (plus booking fee)

From the box office or by
credit card on 0870 636 3200
or book online at
www.ticketstoday.co.uk

C

The Ritz

Catford, London SE6
Films for all the family   April 5th–11th

Sons and Daughters (12)
3.25, ⁴_____ , 8.50

Good Times, Bad Times (15)
⁵_____ , 5.10, 8.30

Tickets: ᵉ⁾£_____ adults, ᶠ⁾£_____ children.

For more information phone 0870 505 2000
www.ritzcatford.co.uk

8 **a)** Work in pairs. How do we say these prices?

£20   £7.50   40p   £29.99   €9   €6.50 $35   50c

b) R2.13 P Listen and check. Listen again and practise.

c) R2.14 Listen and write the ticket prices a)–f) on the adverts.

9 **a)** Kate is at the cinema. Match the ticket seller's part of the conversation a)–d) to Kate's sentences 1–4.

KATE
1 Two tickets for *Sons and Daughters*, please.
2 Yes, please. How much is that?
3 Here you are. What time is the film?
4 Right. Thanks a lot.

TICKET SELLER
a) £13, please.
b) You're welcome. Enjoy the film.
c) Two adults?
d) Ten to nine.

b) R2.15 Listen and check.

c) Practise the conversation in pairs.

Real World Asking about prices

10 **a)** Write *is* or *are* in the gaps.

1 How much _____ that?
2 How much _____ the tickets?
3 How much _____ the concert?
4 How much _____ these books?

b) Check in RW2.3 p125.

11 Work in pairs. Student A → p105.
Student B → p113. Follow the instructions.

VOCABULARY IN CONTEXT

2D Where's the baby?

Vocabulary things in a house; prepositions of place; *Whose ...?*
Review possessive *'s*; possessive adjectives; personal possessions

QUICK REVIEW ● ● ●
Write four times and four prices. Work in pairs. Say them to your partner. He/She writes them down. Are they correct?

1 Work in pairs. Tick the words you know. Then do the exercise in V2.6 p124.

a table   a chair   a desk   a sofa   a carpet   a door
a window   the floor   a plant   a coffee table

Help with Vocabulary Prepositions of place

2 Match the prepositions to pictures 1–6. Then check in V2.7 p124.

in   on   by
under   behind
in front of

3 Look at the picture. Work in pairs. Where are these things?

Lisa's DVDs
Tom's suitcase
Tom's keys
Tom's mobile phone
the DVD player
Lisa's coat
Emma's new shoes
the cat
Emma's bag
Emma's books
Tom's passport
Emma's personal stereo

Lisa's DVDs are on the floor, by the TV.

Lisa

Emma

Tom

20

4 Work in pairs. Cover the box in **3**. Point to the picture and ask questions with *Whose ...?*

> Whose mobile phone is it?

> It's Tom's.

> Whose shoes are they?

> They're Emma's.

5 **a)** **R2.16** Listen and tick the things in the box in **3** that the family talk about.

b) Listen again. Three things are in the wrong place in the picture. What are they?

c) Where's the baby?!

6 **R2.16** Look at R2.16, p149. Listen again and <u>underline</u> all the prepositions of place.

7 Look at the picture for two minutes. Cover the picture. Work in pairs. Take turns to ask where things are in the living room.

> Where's Emma's personal stereo?

> It's on the coffee table.

> Where are Lisa's DVDs?

> I can't remember!

2 Review   Language Summary 2, p124

1 **a)** Write the adjectives. **V2.1**

1	**ewn**	n *ew*
2	**epahc**	c_____
3	**lamls**	s_____
4	**swol**	s_____
5	**teubaulfi**	b_____
6	**ysea**	e_____
7	**uogny**	y_____
8	**dogo**	g_____

b) Work in pairs. What are the opposites of the adjectives?

1 new *old*

2 **a)** Write four sentences with the adjectives in **1a)** and *have got*. **G2.1**

My sister's got a new car.
I've got a very old laptop.

b) Work in groups. Compare your sentences.

3 **a)** Fill in the gaps with *Have* or *Has*. **G2.2**

1 __*Have*__ you got a bike?
2 _____ your mother got a car?
3 _____ you got a mobile phone with you?
4 _____ your parents got a DVD player?
5 _____ you got a laptop?

b) Work in pairs. Take turns to ask and answer the questions.

4 Work in pairs. Complete the sentences. **V2.4**

1 Your mother's son is ...
   ... your brother.
2 Your mother's daughter is ...
3 Your son's children are ...
4 Your mother's brother is ...
5 Your sister's grandfather is ...
6 Your father's sister is ...
7 Your father's parents are ...
8 Your mother's brother's daughter is ...

5 Look at these sentences. Does *'s* mean *is*, *has* or *possessive*? **G2.3**

1 John**'s** got a camera. *'s* = *has*
2 He**'s** got a computer.
3 Mark**'s** unemployed.
4 This is Jo**'s** baby.
5 She**'s** from Moscow.
6 That**'s** Kim**'s** husband.

6 **a)** Put these times in order. **RW2.1**

twenty to ten *1*	five to ten
quarter past ten	ten past ten
quarter to ten	ten to ten
twenty-five past ten	half past ten

b) Work in pairs. Say the times a different way.

twenty to ten → *nine forty*

7 **a)** Write three true sentences and three false sentences about the picture on p20. Use *in, on, by, under, behind* and *in front of*. **V2.7**

The books are in the bag. (true)
The bag is by the TV. (false)

b) Work in pairs. Close your book. Take turns to say the sentences to your partner. Are they true or false?

Progress Portfolio

a) Tick the things you can do in English.

☐ I can use adjectives with *very* to describe things.

☐ I can talk about personal possessions.

☐ I can talk about families.

☐ I can talk about times and prices.

☐ I can find important information in adverts for concerts, exhibitions, etc.

☐ I can say where things are in a room.

b) What do you need to study again? ● **2A–D**

3 Daily life

3A A glamorous life?

Vocabulary daily routines
Grammar Present Simple (1): positive and *Wh-* questions (*I/you/we/they*)
Review the time

QUICK REVIEW ● ● ●
Work in pairs. Say where something is in the classroom: *It's on the floor behind the desk.* Your partner guesses what it is: *Is it a bag?* and you answer: *Yes, it is./No, it isn't.*

Behind the camera – an actor's life

Beautiful clothes, expensive restaurants, all-night parties, holidays in the Caribbean. This is the glamorous life of a film actor. Or is it? We talk to Sam Dane, star of *Good Times, Bad Times*, about his daily routine.

Q Sam, tell us about your life as a film actor.
A Well, a typical film is about three months' work. We work very long days and a lot of the actors live in a hotel, not at home.

Q What time do you get up?
A I get up at five o'clock in the morning. The people from the studio phone us then.

Vocabulary Daily routines

1 **a)** Tick the words/phrases you know. Then do the exercise in Language Summary 3 **V3.1** p126.

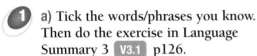

get up   go to bed   leave home   get home
have breakfast   have lunch   have dinner
start work/classes   finish work/classes
work   study   sleep   live

TIP! ● In these vocabulary boxes we only show the main stress in phrases.

b) Match words/phrases from **1a)** to these times of day.

1 in the morning *get up*   3 in the evening
2 in the afternoon   4 at night

Reading and Grammar

2 **a)** Look at the photos of Sam Dane. What's his job?

b) Guess the times that film actors do these things.

1 get up   3 start work
2 have breakfast   4 have lunch

c) Read the interview and check your answers.

3 Read the interview again. Are these sentences true (T) or false (F)? Correct the false sentences.

1 A lot of the actors live at home. *F*
   A lot of the actors live in a hotel.
2 They get up late.
3 The actors have breakfast at the studio.
4 They have 45 minutes for breakfast.
5 After breakfast, they work for four hours before lunch.
6 They have an hour for lunch.

Help with Grammar
Present Simple: positive (*I/you/we/they*)

4 **a)** Find the verbs in these sentences. They are in the Present Simple.

1 I get up at five o'clock.
2 You get up very early.
3 We start work at about 5.45.
4 They have an hour for lunch.

b) Is the form of the Present Simple the same or different after *I*, *you*, *we* and *they*?

c) Check in **G3.1** p127.

5   **R3.1** **P** Listen and practise the sentences in **4a)**.
I get up at five o'clock.

Help with Grammar
Present Simple: *Wh- questions (I/you/we/they)*

8 **a)** Look at the table. Notice the word order in questions.

question word	auxiliary	subject	infinitive	
Where	do	they	have	dinner?
What time	do	you	go	to bed?

b) Write questions 1–3 in the table.

1 When do you get back to the hotel?
2 What time do they finish work?
3 When do we start work?

c) Check in `G3.2` p127.

9 **a)** Make questions with these words.

1 Where / live / you / do ?
2 you / do / Where / work ?
3 What time / get up / you / do ?
4 start / When / do / you / work or classes ?
5 do / What time / get / you / home ?
6 dinner / do / When / you / have ?

b) `R3.3` `P` Listen and check. Then listen again and practise.

Where do you /dʒə/ live?

c) Work in pairs. Take turns to ask and answer the questions in **9a)**.

Get ready ... Get it right!

10 Write eight questions about people's routines in the week or at the weekend. Use words/phrases from **1a)**.

What time do you go to bed in the week?
When do you get up at the weekend?

11 **a)** Ask other students your questions. For each question, find one student who does this at the same time as you.

b) Tell the class two things that you and other students do at the same time.

(Petra and I both get up at seven o'clock.)

Q You get up very early!
A Yes and I'm not a morning person, so it's always difficult! We leave the hotel at 5.15 and I get to the studio at about 5.30. That's when I have my first coffee of the day. Then we start work at about 5.45.

Q What about breakfast?
A We have breakfast at the studio at about 7.30. But that's only for half an hour.

Q And lunch?
A We have lunch at twelve and we start work again at about one o'clock.

6 Write six sentences about your daily routine. Use words/phrases from **1a)**.

I start classes at half past nine.

7 **a)** Read about Sam's afternoon and evening routine. Which answers are correct, do you think?

1 Most days we finish at about *9/11* o'clock.
2 But some days I sleep for *four hours/an hour or two* in the afternoon.
3 We have dinner at the studio at *9.30/11.30* p.m.
4 I get back to the hotel at *10.30/12* o'clock.
5 Then I sleep for *seven/six* hours.

b) `R3.2` Listen to the end of the interview and check your answers.

c) Look at R3.2, p150. Listen again and find all the questions.

3B Evenings and weekends

Vocabulary free time activities (1); time phrases with *on*, *in*, *at*, *every*
Grammar Present Simple (2): negative and *yes/no* questions (*I/you/we/they*)
Help with Listening questions with *do you ...?*
Review Present Simple: positive

QUICK REVIEW ●●●
Write your daily routine and the times you do these things: *get up – 8.30, have breakfast – 9.00*, etc. Work in pairs. Compare your daily routines. Are the times the same or different?

Vocabulary Free time activities (1)

1 a) Tick the phrases you know. Then do the exercise in **V3.2** p126.

> go out   stay in   eat out   go for a drink
> go to the cinema   go to concerts   go shopping
> phone friends/my family   visit friends/my family
> have coffee with friends   do sport   watch TV

b) Work in pairs. What are your five favourite things to do on Saturdays?

Listening and Grammar

2 Look at the photo of Tanya and Robert. Where are they? Are they good friends, do you think?

Help with Listening Questions with *do you ...?*

3 a) **R3.4** Listen to Robert's questions. Fill in the gaps.

1 Do you __*go*__ for a __*drink*__ after work?
2 What do you _____ in the_____ ?
3 Do you _____ out?
4 And what do you _____ at the _____ ?
5 Do you _____ to _____ ?

b) Listen again. Notice how we say *do you* /dʒə/ in questions.

4 a) **R3.5** Listen to the conversation. Tick the true sentences.

1 Robert and Tanya work in the same office.
2 Tanya stays in a lot in the week.
3 She goes out on Saturday evenings.
4 Robert and Tanya want to go to a concert together.
5 They're both single.

b) Listen again. Choose Tanya's answers to Robert's questions in 3a).

1 a) Yes, I do.   b) (No, I don't.)
2 a) I visit friends.   b) I don't go out very much.
3 a) Yes, I do.   b) No, I don't.
4 a) I go shopping.   b) I have coffee with friends.
5 a) Yes, I do.   b) No, I don't.

Help with Grammar Present Simple: negative (*I/you/we/they*)

5 a) Look at the table. Notice the word order.

subject	auxiliary	infinitive	
I	don't (= do not)	go	out in the week.

b) Write sentences 1 and 2 in the table.

1 We don't stay in at the weekend.
2 They don't watch TV in the day.

c) Check in **G3.3** p127.

6 **a)** Tick the sentences that are true for you. Make the other sentences negative.

1 I phone my family every day.
   I don't phone my family every day.
2 I go shopping on Saturdays.
3 I watch TV every evening.
4 I eat out with my friends a lot.
5 I live near this school.
6 I have lunch at 12.00 every day.
7 I work at the weekends.

b) Work in pairs. Compare your sentences.

> I go shopping on Saturdays. Me too./I don't.

> I don't watch TV every evening. Me neither./Oh, I do.

Help with Grammar Present Simple:
yes/no questions and short answers (*I/you/we/they*)

7 **a)** Look at the table. Notice the word order.

YES/NO QUESTIONS				SHORT ANSWERS
auxiliary	subject	infinitive		
Do	you	eat	out a lot?	Yes, I do. No, I don't.
				Yes, we do. No, we don't.
				Yes, they do. No, they don't.

b) Write questions 1 and 2 in the table.

1 Do you go to concerts?   2 Do they watch TV a lot?

c) Check in G3.4 p127.

8 **a)** Fill in the gaps with *do*, *don't* or an infinitive from the box.

go (x 3)   have   stay   visit   watch   do

1 A .... you .... out in the week?
  B Yes, sometimes. We .... friends.
2 A .... you .... coffee with friends at the weekends?
  B Yes, sometimes.
3 A .... you .... to the cinema every week?
  B Yes, I ....
4 A .... your friends .... out a lot?
  B No, they .... They .... in and .... TV!
5 A .... you .... sport at the weekends?
  B No, we ....

b) R3.6 **P** Listen and check. Then listen again and practise.
Do you go out in the week?

c) Work in pairs. Take turns to ask A's questions in **8a)**. Answer for you.

Vocabulary Time phrases

9 **a)** Write these words and phrases in the correct circle. Some words/phrases can go in more than one circle. Then check in V3.3 p126.

> ~~Saturday~~   ~~the morning~~   ~~nine o'clock~~   ~~week~~
> Thursday   the afternoon   day   the evening
> month   half past three   night   the week
> Mondays   Monday mornings   the weekend
> Sunday afternoon   morning

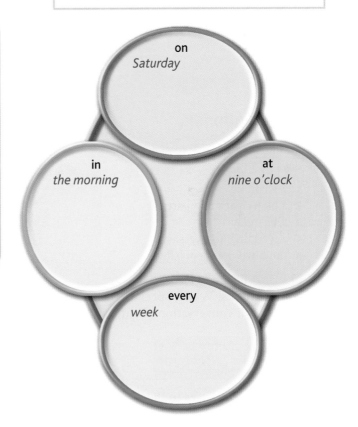

on
Saturday

in
the morning

at
nine o'clock

every
week

b) Work in pairs. Test your partner.

> the weekend   at the weekend

10 Work in three groups. Group A → p106. Group B → p114. Group C → p120. Follow the instructions.

3C Special days

Real World phrases for special days; suggestions
Vocabulary months and dates
Help with Listening dates
Review *be*; Present Simple

QUICK REVIEW ●●●
Write four ways to end this sentence: *On a perfect day I ...* (*get up in the afternoon/don't go to work*). Work in pairs. Compare your days.

Congratulations!

1 **a)** Match cards A–E to special days 1–5.

1 a wedding
2 a New Year's Eve party
3 a birthday
4 a wedding anniversary
5 the birth of a new baby

b) **R3.7** Listen to five conversations. Which special day is each conversation about?

Real World Phrases for special days

2 Match these phrases to the special days in **1a**.

Happy birthday!
Happy New Year!
Congratulations!
Happy anniversary!

3 **a)** **R3.8** **P** Listen and practise the phrases in **2**.

b) **R3.9** Listen and answer with the correct phrase.

When's your birthday?

4 **a)** Put the months in the correct order.

July	March	December	January *1*	April	October
August	June	February	November	May	September

b) **R3.10** **P** Listen and check. Then listen again and practise.

5 **a)** Match the dates with the words. Notice the two letters at the end of each number and word. Then check in **V3.5** p126.

1st	second	13th	twenty-second
2nd	fourth	20th	thirteenth
3rd	first	22nd	thirty-first
4th	fifth	23rd	twentieth
5th	third	31st	twenty-third

b) **R3.11** **P** Listen and practise the dates in **5a**).

Help with Listening Dates

6 **a)** **R3.12** Listen and fill in the gaps.

1 A What's the date today? B It's the fifth of ....
2 A What's the date tomorrow? B It's .... the sixth.
3 A When's your birthday? B It's on the twentieth of ....

b) Listen again. Notice how we say *the* /ðə/ and *of* /əv/.

7 **a)** R3.13 Listen. Which date do you hear?

1 ~~September 5th~~/September 15th   4 *July 22nd/July 2nd*
2 *December 30th/December 13th*   5 *October 12th/October 20th*
3 *March 4th/March 14th*   6 *February 1st/February 3rd*

b) R3.14 P Listen and practise the dates in **7a)**.

8 **a)** Write four dates that are important to you.

b) Work in pairs. Say all your dates to your partner. Write your partner's dates. Then ask why they are important.

> Why is May 20th important?

> Because it's my birthday.

What shall we get him?

9 **a)** R3.15 Listen to Tanya and her husband, Simon, talk about their friend Tom's birthday. What do they decide to buy?

b) Listen again and fill in the gaps.

TANYA   What's the date today?
SIMON   The ¹_____ . Why?
TANYA   It's Tom's ²_____ tomorrow. What shall we get him?
SIMON   Let's get him a ³_____ .
TANYA   I'm not sure.
SIMON   OK. I know! He's got a new ⁴_____ player. Let's buy him a ⁵_____ .
TANYA   That's a ⁶_____ idea. What about a Star Trek DVD?
SIMON   Yes, or the Simpsons.
TANYA   Oh yes. Let's give him the new Simpsons DVD. Then we can ⁷_____ it first!

Real World Suggestions

10 **a)** Look at the conversation in **9b)**. Then fill in the gaps in the table.

asking for suggestions

What	_____ we	get him? buy him? give her?

making suggestions

_____	get him a book. buy him a DVD. give her a CD.
_____ about	a DVD?

responding to suggestions

✓   That's a good _____ .
✓✗ I'm not _____ .
✗   No, I don't think so.

b) Check in RW3.2 p127.

11 **a)** R3.16 P Listen and practise.

What shall we get him for his birthday?
Let's get him a book.

b) Work in pairs. Practise the conversation in **9b)** until you remember it. Use today's date.

c) Close your book. Practise the conversation again.

12 **a)** Work in groups of four. Make a list of typical birthday presents.

b) Choose one birthday present from your list for each student in another group. Draw the presents on four pieces of paper.

c) Work with the other group. Take turns to give your presents and say thank you.

> Happy birthday, Maria. This is for you.

> Oh, thank you. It's great/lovely.

3D Early bird or night owl?

Vocabulary frequency adverbs
Grammar subject and object pronouns
Review Present Simple; routines

QUICK REVIEW ● ● ●
Your class wants to go out tonight. Work in groups of four. Ask for and make suggestions. Then decide what to do and where to go. Tell the class your group's plan. Which plan is the best?

1 Put these frequency adverbs on the line. Check in **V3.6** p126.

hardly ever   never   always   sometimes   often   usually

hardly ever

100%   0%

2 a) Read the questionnaire. Tick your answers.

b) Look at p158. What's your score? Are you an early bird or a night owl?

c) Work in groups. Compare scores. How many of your answers are the same?

Help with Vocabulary
Word order of frequency adverbs

3 a) Find the frequency adverbs (*often*, etc.) in the questionnaire.

b) Choose the correct words in the rules.

- Frequency adverbs go *before/after* the verb *be*.
- Frequency adverbs go *before/after* other verbs.

c) Check in **V3.7** p126.

4 a) Put a frequency adverb in these sentences and make them true for you.

1 I get up at eight in the morning.
I never get up at eight in the morning.
2 I have breakfast before 9 a.m.
3 I'm tired on Friday evenings.
4 I study English in the evening.
5 I'm happy on Monday mornings.
6 I'm late for class.

b) Work in pairs. Compare sentences. How many are the same?

Are you an early bird or a night owl?

Do the questionnaire to find out!

1 When I get up in the morning …
a) I'm always happy and I have a lot of energy.
b) I'm sometimes happy, but I don't have a lot of energy.
c) I'm not very happy and I never have a lot of energy.

2 At the weekend …
a) I sometimes get up before 9 a.m.
b) I always get up before 9 a.m.
c) I hardly ever get up before 9 a.m.

3 When there's a good film on TV late at night …
a) I always watch it to the end.
b) I usually record it and go to bed.
c) I often watch the beginning but I never see the end.

4 When I go to a party …
a) I always stay to the end.
b) I sometimes stay to the end.
c) I never stay to the end.

5 When I see friends at the weekend …
a) I usually see them in the afternoon.
b) I sometimes have coffee with them in the morning.
c) I hardly ever see them before 9 p.m.

6 When a friend phones me before 8 a.m. …
a) I'm always happy to talk to him/her.
b) I'm sometimes happy to talk to him/her.
c) I never answer the phone.

Help with Grammar
Subject and object pronouns

5 **a)** Look at the words in **bold** in these sentences. Which are the subject pronouns? Which are the object pronouns?

*I often phone **her** at 11 p.m.*
*We usually see **him** in the week.*

b) Fill in the table with these object pronouns.

| me you her us |
| them him it |

subject pronouns	object pronouns
I	me
you	
he	
she	
it	
we	
they	

c) Check in **G3.5** p127.

6 Find the object pronouns in the questionnaire. What do they refer to?

*When there's a good **film** on TV …*
*I always watch **it** to the end.*

7 **a)** **R3.17** Listen to Tanya do the questionnaire. Write *T* by her answers.

b) Check your answers in pairs. What's Tanya's score? What kind of person is she?

3 Review
Language Summary 3, p126

1 **a)** Write questions with *you* for the words in **bold**. **V3.1** **G3.2**

1 I live **in London**.
   Where do you live?
2 I get up **at 7.00**.
3 I work **in a school**.
4 I start work **at 9.00**.
5 I have lunch **at 1.30**.
6 I finish work **at 4.45**.
7 I have dinner **at home**.
8 I go to bed **at 11.30**.

b) Work in pairs. Take turns to ask and answer your questions.

2 Match a verb in A to a word/phrase in B. **V3.2**

A	B
eat	your family
have	TV
watch	shopping
go	out
go	coffee with friends
visit	to the cinema
stay	sport
do	in

3 **a)** Fill in the gaps with *in*, *on* or *at*. **V3.3**

1 __in__ the week
2 _____ the weekend
3 _____ Friday evenings
4 _____ Saturdays
5 _____ night
6 _____ Sunday afternoons
7 _____ the morning
8 _____ two o'clock

b) Write three true sentences and three false sentences about your free time. Use phrases from **2** and **3a)** or your own ideas. **G3.1** **G3.3**

I go out at the weekend.
I don't work on Saturdays.

c) Work in pairs. Swap sentences. Guess your partner's false sentences.

4 **a)** Put the dates in order. **V3.5**

Jan 1st 1	Nov 30th	Sept 10th
Dec 25th	June 19th	Apr 7th
Aug 22nd	July 13th	Oct 4th
May 31st	Mar 16th	Feb 28th

b) Work in pairs. Take turns to say the dates in **4a)**. Your partner says the next two dates.

c) Ask seven people when their birthday is. Write the dates.

5 **a)** Make sentences with these words. **V3.6** **V3.7**

1 Sundays / work / don't / I / usually / on
   I don't usually work on Sundays.
2 I / in / hardly ever / the afternoons / sleep
3 on / I / Friday / at home / sometimes / 'm / evenings
4 don't often / go / friends / the week / out / My / in
5 always / My / birthday / remember / friends / my

b) Which of these sentences are true for you? Compare with a partner.

4 Time off

Away from home

> **Vocabulary** free time activities (2)
> **Grammar** Present Simple (3): positive and negative (*he/she/it*)
> **Help with Listening** linking (1)
> **Review** Present Simple (*I/you/we/they*); frequency adverbs

QUICK REVIEW ●●●
Write sentences about things you: never, sometimes, always, often do on Sundays. Compare sentences in pairs. Are any of your sentences the same?

To Alison and Erin with lots of love, Paul/Dad

Vocabulary
Free time activities (2)

1 a) Tick the phrases you know. Then do the exercise in Language Summary 4 **V4.1** p128.

> read books/magazines
> watch DVDs/videos   play tennis
> take photos   go skiing
> go swimming   go running
> go dancing   listen to music
> listen to the radio
> watch sport on TV

b) Work in pairs. Take turns to ask and answer questions about the free time activities.

> Do you watch sport on TV?
> No, never.
> Yes, every weekend.

Listening and Grammar

2 a) Look at the photo. Where is Paul? Who are Alison and Erin, do you think?

b) **R4.1** Listen to Alison talk about Paul to her friend, Vicky. Choose the correct answers.

1 Paul is in *the Arctic /(Antarctica)/ Canada*.
2 He's *a doctor / an engineer / a pilot*.
3 People at the weather station work *five / six / seven* days a week.
4 They have *two / three / four* months off a year.

3 a) Work in pairs. What does Paul do in his free time, do you think? Choose four activities from **1a)**.

b) **R4.2** Listen and check. Are your guesses correct?

Help with Listening Linking (1)

4 a) **R4.2** Look at R4.2, p150. Listen again and follow Alison's part of the conversation. Notice the linking between consonant (*b, c, d, f*, etc.) sounds and vowel (*a, e, i, o, u*) sounds.

The people_at the weather station_all work six days_a week.

b) Work in pairs. Find four examples of consonant-vowel linking in Vicky's part of the conversation.

Help with Grammar Present Simple: positive and negative (*he/she/it*)

5 **a)** Look at these sentences. Then complete the rules.

*Paul **works** in Antarctica.*
*He **watches** a lot of sport on TV.*

*He **doesn't like** the job very much.*
*She **doesn't talk** to him very often.*

- In positive sentences with *he/she/it* we add _____ or _____ to the infinitive.
- In negative sentences with *he/she/it* we use _____ + infinitive.

TIP! • *have* is irregular: *he/she/it* **has** …

b) When do we use *doesn't* in negative sentences? When do we use *don't*?

c) Check in **G4.1** p130.

6 **a)** Check the spelling rules in **G4.2** p130. What are the *he/she/it* forms of these verbs?

play	watch	get	go	write	phone
finish	have	study	live	do	start

b) **R4.3** **P** Listen and practise the *he/she/it* forms of the verbs in **6a)**. Which verbs have the sound /ɪz/ at the end?

7 Fill in the gaps with the correct form of the verbs in brackets.

Alison, Paul and Erin ¹ *live* (live) in Toronto, Canada. Alison ² _____ (work) at the airport and she always ³ _____ (meet) Paul when he ⁴ _____ (get) home from Antarctica. Erin is always very happy when her father ⁵ _____ (come) home. He ⁶ _____ (buy) her a lot of presents and they ⁷ _____ (go) to the cinema or ⁸ _____ (play) tennis in the evenings. When her husband is away Alison ⁹ _____ (watch) TV all the time, but she ¹⁰ _____ (not watch) it when he's at home. Alison ¹¹ _____ (not have) a lot of holiday, but they usually ¹² _____ (go) to a hot country for two weeks before Paul ¹³ _____ (go) back to Antarctica.

8 **R4.4** **P** Listen and practise the consonant-vowel linking.

live in → *They live in Toronto.*

Get ready … Get it right!

9 **a)** Choose a partner, but don't talk to him/her. Look at the sentences in the box. Guess what your partner does/doesn't do. Complete the sentences.

How active is your partner?

_____ tennis. (play)
He/She plays/doesn't play tennis.
_____ to work/school every day. (walk)
_____ a lot of sport. (do)
_____ a lot of sport on TV. (watch)
_____ running. (go)
_____ a lot of DVDs or videos. (watch)
_____ dancing at the weekend. (go)
_____ swimming. (go)
_____ early at the weekend. (get up)
_____ out with friends a lot. (go)

b) Make questions with *you* for each sentence in the box.
Do you play tennis?

10 **a)** Work with your partner. Take turns to ask and answer your questions. How many of your guesses are correct?

Yes, I do.

Do you play tennis?   Yes, sometimes.

No, I don't.

b) Is your partner very active, quite active or not very active?

c) Tell another student about your partner.

First Date!

Vocabulary things you like and don't like; verb+*ing*
Grammar Present Simple (4): questions and short answers (*he/she/it*)
Review free time activities

QUICK REVIEW ●●●
Write ten free time activities. Work in pairs. Tell your partner when you do the things on your list: *I play tennis on Fridays. I watch sport on TV at the weekend.*

Vocabulary
Things you like and don't like

1 Tick the words/phrases you know. Then do the exercise in **V4.2** p128.

> reading   football   travelling
> cats   shopping for clothes
> computer games   animals
> dancing   cooking   dance music
> rock music   jazz   Italian food
> Chinese food   fast food

2 Put these phrases in order 1–7. Check in **V4.3** p128.

> I love ...   *1*   I hate ...   *7*   I like ...
> ... is/are OK.   I don't like ...
> I really like ...   I quite like ...

Help with Vocabulary **Verb + *ing***

3 **a)** With the phrases in **2** we can use verb+*ing* or a noun. Look at these sentences.

I love reading. (verb+*ing*)
I like books. (noun)

b) Find all the verb+*ing* words in **1**.

4 Work in pairs. Talk about the things in **1** and your own ideas. Do you like the same things?

> I really like computer games.

> Me too./I don't. I hate them!

> Do you like dance music?

> Yes, I love it./It's OK./No, not really.

Hello and welcome to *First Date!*. Tonight you choose a date for Mark Skipper. Mark is 28 years old and he's a teacher. In his free time he watches TV and plays computer games. He also goes to the cinema a lot and he plays football and tennis every weekend. He loves rock music and Chinese food, but he hates shopping for clothes! He also likes animals – he's got a dog and three cats. So, Mark – who do you want to ask about first?

Kim

Susie

Jo

Er, Kim, please.

OK. Remember, you can only ask six questions.

Reading and Grammar

5 **R4.5** Read and listen to the TV game show, *First Date!*. Find four things Mark likes and one thing he doesn't like.

6 **a)** Match Mark's questions about Kim to the presenter's answers.

1 What does she do in her free time?
2 Does she watch TV a lot?
3 Does she like films?
4 What music does she like?
5 Does she like animals?
6 And what does she do?

a) Yes, she does. She's got two dogs.
b) Yes, she goes to the cinema every Saturday evening.
c) She loves dance music, but she doesn't like rock.
d) She plays tennis and she eats out a lot. She loves Italian food.
e) No, she doesn't. She hates watching TV!
f) She's a vet.

b) **R4.6** Listen and check.

Help with Grammar Present Simple: questions and short answers (*he/she/it*)

7 **a)** Look at **6a)**. Then fill in the gaps with *does* or *doesn't*.

QUESTIONS

1 .... she **like** animals?
2 .... she **watch** TV a lot?
3 What .... she **do** in her free time?

SHORT ANSWERS

Yes, she ....
No, she ....

b) Look at the table. Notice the word order in questions. Then write questions 3 and 4 from **6a)** in the table.

question word	auxiliary	subject	infinitive	
What	does	she	do	in her free time?
	Does	she	watch	TV a lot?

c) When do we use *does* in questions? When do we use *do*?

d) Check in G4.3 p130. Then read G4.4 .

8 **a)** Write questions with *she*.

1 What / do? *What does she do?*
2 / like rock music?
3 What food / like?
4 / like sport?
5 / have any animals?
6 What / do on Saturday evenings?

b) R4.7 P Listen and check. Then listen again and practise.

What does she do?

c) Work in pairs. Take turns to ask and answer the questions in **8a)** about Kim. Find her answers in **6a)**.

9 **a)** Work in pairs. Student A, read about Jo on p104. Student B, read about Susie on p112. Find the answers to the questions in **8a)**.

b) Work with your partner. Take turns to ask and answer the questions in **8a)** about Jo or Susie.

c) Tell your partner three more things about Jo or Susie.

10 **a)** Work in groups. Which woman do you want to choose for Mark's first date – Kim, Jo or Susie? Why?

b) Tell the class which woman your group wants for Mark's first date and why. The class must agree on one person!

c) Read about Mark's date with the woman the class chose. (Kim → p109, Jo → p117, Susie → p120). Answer these questions.

1 Does Mark like her? Why?/Why not?
2 Does she like Mark? Why?/Why not?
3 Do they want to see each other again?

Get ready ... Get it right!

11 **a)** Work in pairs, but don't talk to your partner. Choose a friend to introduce to your partner. Tick the things in the box that your friend does or likes.

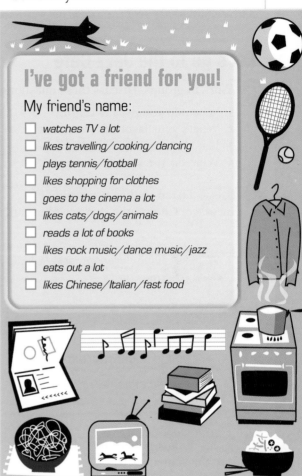

I've got a friend for you!

My friend's name: ....

☐ *watches TV a lot*
☐ *likes travelling/cooking/dancing*
☐ *plays tennis/football*
☐ *likes shopping for clothes*
☐ *goes to the cinema a lot*
☐ *likes cats/dogs/animals*
☐ *reads a lot of books*
☐ *likes rock music/dance music/jazz*
☐ *eats out a lot*
☐ *likes Chinese/Italian/fast food*

b) Choose eight things you do or like from the box. Make questions with *he/she*.

Does he/she watch TV a lot?
Does he/she like Italian food?

12 **a)** Work with your partner. Take turns to ask and answer questions about your friends. First, ask about the friend's name, age, job and where he/she lives. Then ask your questions from **11b)**.

b) Do you and your partner's friend do or like the same things? Tell another student.

We both eat out a lot.

He likes rock music, but I don't.

4C Eating out

Real World requests and offers with *Can I/we have ...?, I'd/We'd like ...* , *Would you like ...?*
Vocabulary food and drink (1)
Help with Listening questions with *Would you like ...?*
Review *How much ...?*; prices; Present Simple

QUICK REVIEW ●●●
Write the names of three people in your family. Work in pairs. Ask questions about the people on your partner's list: *What does Lucia do in her free time?*

Let's go to the Jazz Café

1 Work in groups. Discuss these questions.

1 When do you usually eat out?
2 What's your favourite restaurant?
3 Is it cheap or expensive?
4 What do you usually eat there?

2 R4.8 Listen to the answerphone message. Choose the correct information.

📞 FROM Henry/Jack/John
TIME 4/6/8 o'clock

MESSAGE:
1 *I'm at/Meet me at* the airport.
2 See you in about *two/three* hours.
3 We can *eat at home/eat out*.

3 R4.9 Emma phones Jack. Listen. Are the sentences true (T) or false (F)?

1 Jack is at the airport.
2 Jack wants to go to the Chinese restaurant.
3 There's a new restaurant on Queen Street.
4 The Jazz Café is an expensive place to eat.
5 Emma doesn't want to go to the Jazz Café.

4 a) Match photos 1–10 to food and drink on the menu. Check in V4.5 p129.

1 Chicken salad

b) Work in pairs. Take turns to point to a photo and test your partner.

(What's that?) (A cheese and tomato sandwich.)

5 Work in pairs. Take turns to choose something to eat and drink from the menu. Ask your partner questions with *How much ...?*

(How much is a tuna salad and a bottle of mineral water?) (Nine pounds.)

Help with Listening Questions with *Would you like ...?*

6 a) R4.10 Listen and fill in the gaps in questions 1–4 with these words.

anything	drink	order	red

1 Would you like _____ or white?
2 Would you like _____ else?
3 Would you like to _____ now?
4 What would you like to _____ ?

b) Listen again. Notice how we say *would you* /wʊdʒə/.

JAZZ CAFÉ

Open from 12 noon to 11 p.m.

PIZZAS

Margherita	£7.50
Neapolitan	£8.50

BURGERS

Burger & chips	£5.50
Cheeseburger & chips	£6.25

SANDWICHES

Cheese & tomato	£4.95
Tuna mayonnaise	£5.50

SALADS

Tuna	£6.50
Chicken	£7.25
Mixed	£3.90

DRINKS

Red/White wine	Glass	£3.95
	Bottle	£10.50
Bottle of beer		£2.50
Bottle of mineral water (still or sparkling)		£2.50
Coffee		£2.00

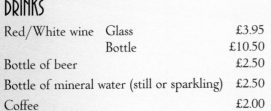

7 a) Read Jack and Emma's conversation with the waiter. Then fill in the gaps with questions 1–4 from **6a).**

WAITER	¹..?
EMMA	Yes. I'd like a tuna salad, please.
JACK	And can I have a cheeseburger and chips, please?
WAITER	²..?
JACK	Can we have a bottle of wine?
WAITER	³..?
JACK	White, please.
EMMA	And we'd like a bottle of sparkling mineral water, please.
WAITER	Yes, of course.
JACK	Excuse me.
WAITER	Yes, sir. ⁴..?
JACK	No, thank you, but can we have the bill, please?
WAITER	Certainly.

b) R4.11 Listen and check. What do Emma and Jack order?

Real World
Requests and offers

8 a) Look at these sentences. Then complete the rules with the phrases in **bold.**

Would you like to order now?
I'd/We'd like a bottle of water, please.
Can I/we have the bill, please?

- We use .... and .... for **requests** (we want something).
- We use .... for **offers** (we want to give something or help someone).

b) Check in **RW4.1** p130.

c) Look at the conversation in **7a)** again. Find three more requests.

9 a) R4.12 Listen and notice the stress and polite intonation.

Would you like to order now?

b) R4.13 Listen to these requests and offers. Which is polite, a) or b)?

1 (a) b)	**3** a) b)	**5** a) b)
2 a) b)	**4** a) b)	**6** a) b)

c) R4.14 P Listen and practise the polite sentences in **9b).** Copy the stress and intonation.

10 a) Work in groups of three. Practise the conversation in **7a)** until you remember it.

b) Close your book. Practise the conversation again.

11 a) Work in the same groups. Look at the menu. Write a conversation between a waiter and two customers.

b) Swap conversations with another group. Correct any mistakes.

c) Practise the new conversation. Then role-play it for the other group.

Vocabulary food and drink (2); countable and uncountable nouns
Review Present Simple; likes and dislikes; frequency adverbs

VOCABULARY IN CONTEXT

QUICK REVIEW ● ● ●
Work in pairs. What is on the Jazz Café menu? Which pair has the most things? Check on p35.

1 Tick the food and drink you know. Then do the exercise in **V4.6** p129.

> biscuits   milk   an apple   rice   toast
> bread   sausages   fish   eggs   coffee
> soup   cheese   vegetables   a banana
> orange juice   tea   jam   meat   fruit
> cereal

2 Which of the things in **1** do you usually have for breakfast? Is this typical for your country? Compare answers in groups.

3 **a)** What is a typical breakfast in Japan, Brazil, Spain and England, do you think? Work in pairs and make four lists. Use words from **1**.

b) **R4.15** Listen to two cooks at an international language school. Tick the food and drink on your lists that they talk about.

c) Listen again. Complete your lists of the four breakfast menus.

4 **a)** Look at the pictures in the table. Then choose the correct words.

1 We *can / can't* count biscuits and apples.
2 We *can / can't* count milk and rice.

COUNTABLE NOUNS		UNCOUNTABLE NOUNS	
singular	plural		
a biscuit	biscuit**s**	milk	rice
an apple	apple**s**		

b) Write the words from **1** in the table. Write the singular and plural if possible.

Help with Vocabulary
Countable and uncountable nouns

5 **a)** Look at the table in **4a)**. Choose the correct words in these rules.

COUNTABLE NOUNS
● Countable nouns *can / can't* be plural.
● We *use / don't use* **a** or **an** with singular countable nouns.
● We *use / don't use* **a** or **an** with plural countable nouns.

UNCOUNTABLE NOUNS
● Uncountable nouns *are / aren't* usually plural.
● We *use / don't use* **a** or **an** with uncountable nouns.

b) Check in **V4.7** p129.

6 a) Fill in the gaps with *a*, *an* or – .

1 I often have __–__ rice with my main meal.
2 My friends and I often go out for _____ burger.
3 I always have _____ toast and _____ jam for breakfast.
4 My family hardly ever eats _____ soup.
5 We don't eat _____ vegetables every day.
6 I sometimes have _____ apple in my break.
7 I usually have _____ cheese sandwich for lunch.

b) Make the sentences in **6a)** true for you. Change the underlined words if necessary.

*I often have **chips** with my main meal.*

c) Work in pairs. Compare your sentences.

7 Work in groups. Tell the other students which food and drink you like/don't like.

I really like eggs. | Oh, I hate them.

I hate cheese! | Me, too.

I love coffee. | Oh, I hate it.

8 a) Imagine your perfect breakfast. Where are you? What time is it? Who are you with? What do you have for breakfast?

b) Work in groups. Tell the other students about your perfect breakfast.

1 a) Match the verbs to the words/phrases. **V4.1**

play — running/dancing
listen to — tennis/football
watch — photos
take — books/magazines
go — music/the radio
read — DVDs/sport on TV

b) Work in pairs. Tell your partner which things in **1a)** you: always, sometimes, never do at the weekend.

2 a) Add *-s*, *-es* or – to the verbs in these sentences. **G4.2**

1 My kids watch _–_ TV a lot.
2 Ed play_____ golf on Sundays.
3 My sister live_____ in the USA.
4 Jo and Liz work_____ at home.
5 She go_____ out a lot.
6 Tim's parents like_____ jazz.
7 Our class start_____ at 6.

b) Make the sentences negative. **G3.3** **G4.1**

My kids don't watch TV a lot.

3 a) Write sentences for you with these phrases. **V4.2** **V4.3**

1 I love …
   I love cats/reading.
2 I really like …
3 I like …
4 I quite like …
5 … is OK.
6 I don't like …
7 I hate …

b) Work in groups. Compare sentences. Are any the same?

4 a) Make questions about Mark from the TV programme *First Date!*. **G4.3**

1 What / do / does / he ?
   What does he do?
2 What / like / he / does / food ?
3 like / Does / shopping for clothes / he ?
4 What / he / at the weekend / does / do ?
5 like / does / What / he / music ?
6 he / like / Does / animals ?

b) Work in pairs. Take turns to ask and answer the questions. Don't look at p32.

c) Check your answers on p32.

5 a) Work in pairs. You have a restaurant. Choose a name for it and write the menu. **V4.5**

b) Work in groups. Compare menus. Which restaurant has got the best food, do you think?

6 a) Find fifteen words for food and drink. **V4.6**

A	B	R	E	A	D	O	V
S	A	C	H	E	E	S	E
A	N	A	P	P	L	E	G
U	A	S	W	C	A	M	E
S	N	O	T	O	A	S	T
A	A	U	E	F	M	R	A
G	K	P	A	F	I	M	B
E	G	G	S	E	L	E	L
S	R	I	C	E	K	A	E
B	I	S	C	U	I	T	S

b) Work in pairs. Which words are countable (C)? Which are uncountable (U)? **V4.7**

bread (U)   sausages (C)

Progress Portfolio

a) Tick the things you can do in English.

☐ I can talk about other people's routines and free time activities.
☐ I can say what I like and don't like.
☐ I can ask and answer questions about people I don't know.
☐ I can say and understand words for food and drink.
☐ I can order something to eat and drink in a restaurant.
☐ I can offer things to people.

b) What do you need to study again? **4A–D**

5 Homes and shops

5A My kind of place

Vocabulary places in a town/the country
Grammar *there is/there are*
Help with Listening sentence stress (2)
Review adjectives

QUICK REVIEW ●●●
Work in pairs. Write all the words for food and drink you know.
Which pair has the most? Which words are countable/uncountable?

Vocabulary Places in a town/the country

1 **a)** Tick the words you know. Then do the exercise in **V5.1** p131.

> a square   a park   a market
> a bus station   a station   a lake
> a beach   the sea   a river   a museum
> an airport   mountains   a road   a café
> a bar   a shop   a flat [US: an apartment]
> a house   a hotel   a bed and breakfast

b) Which four things from **1a)** are important to you where you live and where you go on holiday?

Listening and Grammar

2 Look at the photos. Which is a big city, a small town, a village, do you think? Which things from **1a)** can you see in the photos?

Help with Listening Sentence stress (2)

3 **a)** **R5.1** Listen to these sentences from three conversations about the places in the photos. Notice the stressed words.

1 There's a beautiful lake near the town.
2 There's only one road.
3 There are lots of things to do in the evening.
4 Is there a hotel?
5 There are lots of mountains.
6 And there aren't any restaurants.
7 There's a nice beach.
8 Are there any cheap places to stay?
9 There isn't a park near our flat.

b) Are nouns, verbs, adjectives and negatives usually stressed or unstressed in sentences?

Auckland

Keswick

4 **R5.2** Listen to three conversations A–C and match them to the photos. Which person talks about:

1 where he/she lives now?
2 where his/her family lives?
3 where he/she goes on holiday?

5 **a)** Work in pairs. Look again at sentences 1–9 in **3a)**. Are they about Auckland, Keswick or Eyeries? (There are three sentences for each place.)

b) **R5.2** Listen again and check your answers.

6 **a)** Work in groups. Which place would you like to visit: Auckland, Keswick or Eyeries? Why?

b) Compare answers with the class. Which place is the most popular?

Eyeries

Help with Grammar *there is / there are*

7 **a)** Fill in the gaps in the tables with *'s, is, are, isn't* or *aren't*.

	singular
POSITIVE	There .... a beautiful lake.
NEGATIVE	There .... a park near our flat.
QUESTIONS	.... there a hotel?
SHORT ANSWERS	Yes, there .... / No, there ....

	plural
POSITIVE	There .... lots of things to do.
NEGATIVE	There .... any restaurants.
QUESTIONS	.... there any cheap places to stay?
SHORT ANSWERS	Yes, there .... / No, there ....

TIP! • We use *any* in negatives and questions with *there are*.

b) Check in G5.1 p133.

8 **a)** Look at these sentences about Keswick. Fill in the gaps with *'s, are, isn't* or *aren't*.

1 (✓) There __are__ lots of good shops.
2 (✗) There __isn't__ a station.
3 (✓) There .... a big theatre by the lake.
4 (✗) There .... any five-star hotels.
5 (✓) There .... three interesting museums.
6 (✓) There .... a nice old cinema.
7 (✗) There .... an airport near the town.
8 (✓) There .... two lovely parks.

b) R5.3 P Listen and practise the sentences in **8a)**. Notice how we say *there's* /ðəz/ and *there are* /ðeərə/.

9 **a)** Look at the table. Complete questions 1–8 with *Is there* or *Are there*.

places near my home	me	my partner
1 .... a park?		
2 .... any shops?		
3 .... any good restaurants?		
4 .... a station?		
5 .... any nice cafés?		
6 .... a market?		
7 .... any nice hotels?		
8 .... a cinema or a theatre?		

b) R5.4 P Listen and practise the questions in **9a)** and the short answers.

Is there a park?   Are there any shops?

c) Think about places near your home. Put *yes* or *no* in the *me* column.

d) Work in pairs. Take turns to ask and answer the questions in **9a)**. For each question, put *yes* or *no* in the *my partner* column. Give more information if possible. Do you live in similar places?

Is there a park near your home?

Yes, there is. It's only five minutes away.

Get ready ... Get it right!

10 Choose a favourite place (a town/city/village in your country or a holiday place you know). Tick/Cross the things in the box that are/aren't in this place.

My favourite place is: ....

nice parks   interesting markets   an airport
a beach   mountains   a river   beautiful squares
a university   good hotels   interesting shops
museums   interesting streets   a station
a lake   cheap/expensive restaurants   nice cafés
good places to go at night   big hotels

11 **a)** Work in groups of three or four. Tell the other students about your favourite place.

There isn't an airport.   There are lots of nice cafés.

b) Choose one of your group's places you would like to visit. Tell the class why you want to go there.

39

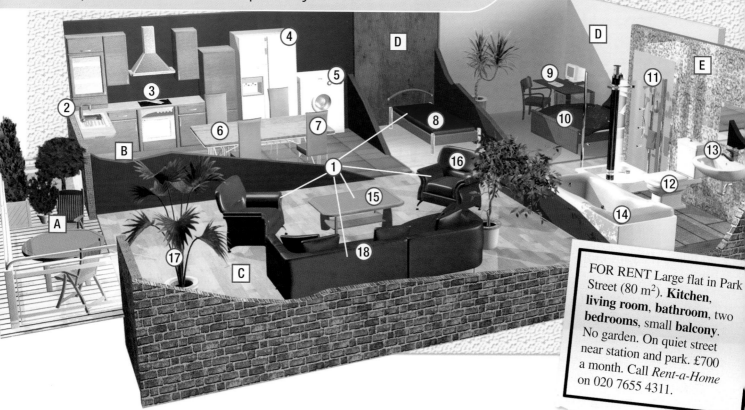

Vocabulary rooms and things
in a house
Grammar *How much ...?/
How many ... ?*; *some, any, a*
Review *there is/there are*; *have got*

QUICK REVIEW ●●●
Work in pairs. Make three true sentences and three false sentences
about places near your school. Use *there is/are* and *there isn't/aren't*.
Compare sentences with another pair. Can you find the false sentences?

> FOR RENT Large flat in Park
> Street (80 m²). **Kitchen,
> living room, bathroom,** two
> **bedrooms,** small **balcony.**
> No garden. On quiet street
> near station and park. £700
> a month. Call *Rent-a-Home*
> on 020 7655 4311.

Vocabulary Rooms and things in a house

1 Alex and his wife, Martina, want to find a flat. Read the advert and
match the words in **bold** to A–E on the plan of the flat.

2 Match these words with 1–18 on the plan of the flat.

> furniture *1*   a double bed *10*   a single bed   a fridge   a coffee table
> a bath   a chair   a shower   a cooker   a toilet   a sink   an armchair
> a desk   a plant   a sofa   a washing machine   a washbasin   a table

Grammar and Listening

3 Look again at the plan of the flat and the advert. Answer these
questions. You have two minutes!

1 Where is the flat?
2 How much is the rent every month?
3 How many bedrooms are there in the flat?
4 How much space is there in the flat?
5 How many chairs are there in the flat?
6 How much furniture is there in the living room?
7 How do you get more information about the flat?

Help with Grammar
How much … ?/How many … ?

4 **a)** Which of these nouns are
countable (C)? Which are
uncountable (U)?

> table *C*   bedroom   furniture
> people   money   chair
> space   time   phone

b) Look again at the questions in
3. Then complete the rules with
How much …? or *How many …?*.

● We use _____ with plural
countable nouns.
● We use _____ with
uncountable nouns.

c) Check in **G5.2** p133.

6 **a)** Read the advert again. Find two things you think are good about the flat.

b) [R5.5] Listen to Alex talk to an estate agent about the flat. Put the things they talk about in order.

a) the furniture *1*   c) the kitchen   e) the rent
b) the bathroom   d) the bedrooms   f) shops

7 [R5.5] Listen again. Are these sentences true (T) or false (F)?

1 There's some furniture in the flat. *T*
2 There isn't a TV in the flat.
3 The estate agent says both bedrooms are big.
4 Alex hasn't got any children.
5 The estate agent says there isn't a cooker.
6 There aren't any shops near the flat.
7 The rent is £700 a month.
8 Alex wants to see the flat.

Help with Grammar *some, any, a*

8 **a)** Fill in the gaps in the table with *some*, *any* or *a*.

	singular countable nouns	plural countable nouns	uncountable nouns
POSITIVE	There's __*a*__ cooker.	There are __*some*__ chairs.	I'd like _____ information.
NEGATIVE	There isn't _____ TV.	We haven't got _____ children.	I haven't got __*any*__ money.
QUESTIONS	Has it got _____ shower?	Are there __*any*__ shops?	Is there _____ furniture?

b) When do we use *some* and *any*?

c) Check in [G5.3] p133.

5 **a)** Look at the questionnaire. Fill in the gaps with *How much* or *How many*.

HOME SWEET HOME

1 *How many* people live in your home?
2 _____ rooms are there?
3 _____ furniture is there in your living room?
4 _____ TVs have you got?
5 _____ time do you spend watching TV every day?
6 _____ phones are there?
7 _____ time do you spend on the phone every day?
8 _____ pictures are there in your living room?

b) Work in pairs. Ask and answer the questions. Are any of your partner's answers surprising?

9 **a)** Alex and Martina now live in the flat. Read their phone conversation. Fill in the gaps with *some*, *any* or *a*.

MARTINA Hi. I'm at the supermarket. Have we got [1] __*any*__ bread?
ALEX Yes, we've got [2] _____ bread, but we haven't got [3] _____ butter.
MARTINA OK. So we need [4] _____ butter. Is there [5] _____ milk?
ALEX No, there isn't. And we need [6] _____ meat and [7] _____ eggs.
MARTINA Right. Have we got [8] _____ fruit?
ALEX We've got [9] _____ big bag of oranges, but we haven't got [10] _____ apples.
MARTINA OK, I'll get [11] _____ more fruit. And [12] _____ cheese.
ALEX And can you get [13] _____ big bottle of water too?
MARTINA Yes, OK. See you later. Bye.

b) [R5.6] Listen and check.

Get ready ... Get it right!

10 Work in two groups. Group A → p106. Group B → p114. Follow the instructions.

5C At the shops

Real World shop language
Vocabulary shops; *one* and *ones*;
things to buy
Help with Listening in a shop
Review *Have you got ...?*;
Can I have ...?; *this/that/these/those*

QUICK REVIEW ●●●
What's your favourite room in your home? Work in pairs. Tell your partner five things about your favourite room using *There is/There are.*

Shopping

1 Work in groups. Discuss these questions.

1 Do you like shopping? Why?/Why not?
2 When do you usually go shopping?

2 Tick the words you know. Then do the exercise in **V5.3** p131.

> a supermarket   a bookshop
> a bank   a dry cleaner's
> a chemist's [US: a pharmacy]
> a kiosk   a newsagent's
> a butcher's   a baker's
> a department store
> a greengrocer's   a post office

3 Look at Alex and Martina's shopping list. Where do people buy these things?

You buy stamps at/in a post office.

> **Shopping list**
>
> stamps
> aspirin
> cigarettes
> dictionary
> sausages
> bread
> apples
> bananas
> pasta
> TV
> new sofa!

4 a) [R5.7] Listen to two conversations. Which shops are Martina and Alex in?

b) Listen again and fill in the gaps. What do they buy?

1

MARTINA	Excuse me, how much is this ¹ _sofa_ ?
SHOP ASSISTANT	This one? Let me see. It's ²£_____ .
MARTINA	OK and what about that one?
SHOP ASSISTANT	That one is ³£_____ .
MARTINA	Thanks. I'll ⁴_____ about it.

2

ALEX	Can I have a kilo of ⁵_____ , please?
SHOP ASSISTANT	Yes, of course. The ⁶_____ ones?
ALEX	Er, no, not those. The ⁷_____ ones.
SHOP ASSISTANT	OK. Anything else?
ALEX	Yes, I'd like some ⁸_____ , please.

Help with Vocabulary *one* and *ones*

5 Look at these examples from the conversations in **4b).** Then complete the rules with *singular* or *plural.*

*How much is this **sofa**? → This **one**?*
*A kilo of **apples**, please. → The green **ones**?*

● We use **one** in place of a _____ noun.
● We use **ones** in place of a _____ noun.

6 a) Read these conversations. Which shops are Martina and Alex in?

1

MARTINA	Excuse me, how much are the TVs?
SHOP ASSISTANT	Well, this **TV** is £329. But the **TVs** over there are in the sale at £279.

2

ALEX	Have you got any sausages?
SHOP ASSISTANT	Yes, these Polish **sausages** are very nice.

3

MARTINA	Excuse me, how much are these dictionaries?
SHOP ASSISTANT	This **dictionary** is £12.95 and that **dictionary** is £14.95.

b) Change the nouns in **bold** to *one* and *ones.*

c) [R5.8] Listen and check.

At the newsagent's

7 a) Tick the words you know. Then do the exercise in **V5.5** p132.

stamps	cigarettes	a map	phone cards	batteries
a film	envelopes	postcards	tissues	a magazine
a lighter	a bottle of water	a newspaper	chocolate	

b) Which of the things in **7a)** are in the photo?

c) Make a list of things you need. Then compare in groups.

> I need some stamps and a phone card.

8 **R5.9** Alex and Martina are in a newsagent's. Listen. Which things in **7a)** do they <u>buy</u>?

Help with Listening In a shop

9 a) **R5.9** Listen again. Put what the shop assistant says in the correct order.

a) That's £22.70, please.
b) Yes, they're there.
c) They're £10 and £20.
d) Hello, can I help you? *1*
e) Here's your change and your receipt.
f) Sure. Here you are. Anything else?
g) No, sorry, we haven't.
h) Do you need any stamps?

b) Look at R5.9, p152. Listen again and check.

Real World Shop language

10 a) Fill in the gaps with these words.

~~I'll~~	Can	much	that	any

SAYING WHAT YOU WANT
....*I'll*.... have these ones, please.
Have you got .... big bottles of water?
.... I have four stamps for Europe, please?

ASKING ABOUT PRICES
How .... are the phone cards?
How much is .... ?

b) Check in **RW5.1** p133.

11 a) **R5.10** **P** Listen and practise the sentences in **10a)**. Copy the stress and intonation.

b) Work in pairs. Look again at R5.9, p152. Practise the conversation. Take turns to be the shop assistant and the customer.

12 Work in pairs. Student A → p107. Student B → p115. Follow the instructions.

VOCABULARY IN CONTEXT

QUICK REVIEW ● ● ●
Work in pairs. Write three things you can buy in: a newsagent's, a greengrocer's, a department store, a supermarket. Which of these things do you buy every week?

1 Tick the words you know. Then do the exercise in **V5.6** p132.

> trousers   shorts   jeans   a dress   shoes
> a suit   a skirt   a jumper   trainers   a jacket
> a hat   a tie   boots   a shirt   socks
> a T-shirt   a top   a coat   a cap

2 a) Write lists for you.
1 clothes/colours I usually wear
2 clothes/colours I sometimes wear
3 clothes/colours I never wear

b) Work in groups. Tell other students about the clothes and colours you wear.

> I usually wear a suit in the week.

> I sometimes wear boots.

> I never wear red.

Help with Vocabulary   Plural nouns

3 a) Some nouns look plural, but can mean *one thing*. Look at these examples.
Your jeans are nice.   (= 1 pair of jeans)
Where are my shoes? (= 2 shoes)

b) Which of these nouns can mean *one thing*? Which can be singular?

> jeans   shoes   socks   shorts
> boots   trousers   trainers

c) Choose the correct words.
1 These trousers *is/are* very big.
2 Where *'s/are* my blue shirt?
3 I want to buy *a/some* new jeans.
4 There's *a/some* shoe under the bed.

TIP! • We can use *a pair of* … with both types of plural noun: *I've got a new pair of shoes/jeans.*

d) Check in **V5.7** p132.

4 a) Fill in the gaps with *some, any* or *a*.
1 I haven't got _____ white shirts.
2 I've got _____ black jeans.
3 I haven't got _____ suit.
4 I want to buy _____ shoes.
5 I need _____ new pair of boots.
6 I haven't got _____ shorts.
7 I've got _____ clothes that I never wear.

b) Which sentences are true for you? Compare with a partner.

5 Read the article. Match paragraphs 1–3 to the people in the photos.

Do you live to shop or

How important are clothes to you? We talk to three people from different countries to see what they think about clothes, shopping – and, of course, shoes!

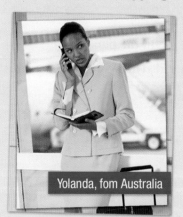
Yolanda, fom Australia

Michael, from the USA

1 I don't buy clothes very often and I don't think what people wear is very important. When I go shopping, I buy the clothes I need and that's all. I usually wear a pair of jeans, a T-shirt and some trainers, and a jumper or a jacket when it's cold. And I hate buying shoes – I've only got three pairs!

2 Oh, I love clothes! I buy fashion magazines every week and watch programmes about clothes on TV. And I really love shoes – I've got more than fifty pairs at home! My friends and I talk about clothes a lot and we go shopping every Saturday afternoon. What do I want to buy today? Some new shoes, of course!

6 Read the article again. Match 1–6 to Yolanda, Michael or Libby.

1 goes shopping every weekend
2 buys clothes to look good at work
3 likes reading about clothes
4 doesn't spend very much on clothes
5 doesn't have many pairs of shoes
6 loves buying shoes

7 Work in groups. Discuss these questions.

1 Do you like shopping for clothes? Why?/Why not?
2 Which person from the article is similar to you? Why?
3 What's your favourite clothes shop? What do you usually buy there?

Libby, from England

3 I like looking good and I spend a lot of money on clothes every year, especially shirts and ties. I'm a lawyer so what I wear at work is important. I go shopping every month, and today I want to get some new trousers and a suit. Yes, what I wear is really important to me – and to my girlfriend!

---

5 Review
Language Summary 5, p131

1
a) Write the words for places. **V5.1**

1	**feac**	c*afé*
2	**terkam**	m_____
3	**nattios**	s_____
4	**partrio**	a_____
5	**virre**	r_____
6	**sumume**	m_____
7	**oelth**	h_____
8	**timoaunns**	m_____

b) Where is the stress on the words in 1a)?

cafe

2 Tick the true sentences. Make the other sentences true. **G5.1**

1 There's a park near here.
   There isn't a park near here.
2 There's a TV in our classroom.
3 There are ten students in our class.
4 There's a café near here.
5 There aren't any men in our class.
6 There isn't a station near here.

3
a) Which word is the odd one out? Why? **V5.2**

1 table chair (balcony)
2 cooker bed fridge
3 bathroom kitchen shower
4 sink desk washbasin
5 bath toilet living room
6 flat apartment bedroom
7 washing machine sofa armchair

b) Work in pairs. Compare your answers.

4
a) Draw a plan of your home. Then draw the furniture in each room.

b) Work in pairs. Take turns to describe your home to your partner. **G5.3**

> This is my living room. There's a sofa and some chairs, but there aren't any ...

5
a) Write questions with *you* about your daily routine. Start each question with *How much* or *How many*. **G5.2**

1 / meals / have?
   How many meals do you have?
2 / coffee / drink?
3 / hours / spend travelling?
4 / TV / watch?
5 / time / spend on a computer?
6 / emails / write?

b) Work in pairs. Take turns to ask and answer the questions.

6
a) Write a list of six things you buy in six different shops. **V5.3**

b) Work in pairs. Take turns to ask your partner where you buy the things on your list.

> Where do you buy sausages?

> In a butcher's.

7 Find the clothes. **V5.6**

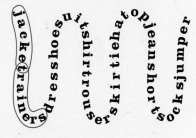

6 Good times, bad times

6A Three generations

Vocabulary adjectives (2); years
Grammar Past Simple (1): *be*
Help with Listening *was* and *were*
Review clothes

QUICK REVIEW ●●●
Write all the clothes you know. Work in pairs and compare lists. Then tell your partner about your favourite clothes: *I've got a beautiful blue shirt ...*

Vocabulary Adjectives (2)

1 Work in pairs. Look at Helen, Margaret and Rebecca in photo A. Discuss these questions.

1 What's their relationship?
2 How old are they, do you think?
3 Whose thirteenth birthday parties are photos A and B?

2 **a)** Match the adjectives to their opposites. Then do the exercise in Language Summary 6 V6.1 p134.

happy	interesting
poor	tall
hot	unhappy
friendly	dirty
noisy	ill
short	cold
boring	empty
well	rich
clean	stupid
intelligent	quiet
crowded	unfriendly

b) Work in pairs. Use the adjectives to talk about photos A and B.

> Margaret looks friendly.

> This party looks noisy.

Helen

Margaret

Rebecca

A

Listening, Reading and Grammar

3 **a)** R6.1 Listen and read. Who is talking?

I live in Perth, Australia, with my parents and my three brothers. Yesterday was my thirteenth birthday and about forty friends were here. There was a lot of food and drink – burgers, chicken, Coke and orange juice. It was a great party, and my Mum and I were really happy because my grandmother's here from England. There were only two things wrong. My grandfather wasn't here for my party and my other two brothers are in the USA, so they weren't here either.

b) Read about the party again. Underline these things in the text.

place	number of people	food
drink	people not at the party	

Help with Grammar *was/were/wasn't/weren't*

4 **a)** Look at the text in **3a)** again. Find all the examples of *was, wasn't, were* and *weren't*.

b) Fill in the gaps with *was, wasn't, were* and *weren't*.

POSITIVE	NEGATIVE
I ...was...	I .... (= was not)
you /we /they	you /we /they .... (= were not)
he /she /it	he /she /it ....

c) Check in G6.1 p135.

(B)

5 Read about Helen's thirteenth birthday party. Choose the correct words.

> HELEN I ¹*was/were* born in England in a village near Liverpool. I ²*was/were* thirteen in 1975 and I remember my party very well. Our house ³*wasn't/weren't* very big, so my party ⁴*was/were* in the village hall. It ⁵*wasn't/weren't* a very nice place and there ⁶*wasn't/weren't* much to eat. Only about twenty people ⁷*was/were* there – and there ⁸*wasn't/weren't* any boys. So the party ⁹*was/were* a bit boring.

6 **a)** R6.2 Listen to Rebecca and her grandmother. Was Margaret's thirteenth birthday party good? Why?/Why not?

b) Listen again and answer the questions.

1 When was Margaret's thirteenth birthday?
2 Where was the party?
3 Was the weather good?
4 What food was there?
5 Were her friends at her party?
6 How many people were at her party?

Help with Listening was and were

7 **a)** R6.3 Listen and notice the strong and weak forms of *was* and *were*.

	strong form	weak form
was	/wɒz/	/wəz/
were	/wɜː/	/wə/

I was /wəz/ in London.
There were /wə/ parties in every street.
Was /wəz/ it good?   Yes, it was /wɒz/.
Were /wə/ they big parties?   Yes, they were /wɜː/.

b) Complete the rules with *strong* or *weak*.

- In statements and questions *was* and *were* are usually ....

- In short answers *was* and *were* are ....

Help with Grammar
Questions and short answers with *was/were*

8 **a)** Look at the word order of questions with *was/were*. Then write questions 2 and 3 from **6b)** in the table.

question word	*was/were*	subject	
When	was	Margaret's 13ᵗʰ birthday?	
	Were	her friends	there?

b) Fill in the gaps in these short answers with *was*, *were*, *wasn't* or *weren't*.

1 Yes, I/he/she/it ....
  No, I/he/she/it ....
2 Yes, you/we/they ....
  No, you/we/they ....

c) Check in G6.2 p135.

9 R6.4 P Listen and practise.
I was /wəz/ in London.

10 **a)** Work in pairs. How do we say these years?

1953	1970	1895	1900	2000	2005

b) Check in V6.2 p134.

c) Write the names of five people in your family. Then work in pairs. Take turns to ask your partner when and where the people were born.

> When/Where was Ana born?   In 1978/Rome.

11 **a)** Make questions with *you*.

1 / at work yesterday? *Were you at work yesterday?*
2 Where / last night?
3 / at home yesterday afternoon?
4 Where / on your last birthday?
5 / in this class last month?
6 Where / last New Year's Eve?

b) Work in pairs. Take turns to ask and answer the questions. Give more information if possible.

Get ready ... Get it right!

12 Work in pairs. Student A → p111. Student B → p119. Follow the instructions.

47

People who changed the world

Vocabulary life events
Grammar Past Simple (2) regular and irregular verbs: positive and *Wh-* questions
Review *was/were*; dates; years

QUICK REVIEW ●●●
Write six times of the day. Work in pairs. Ask your partner where he/she was at these times yesterday: *Where were you at six in the evening?*

Vocabulary Life events

1 Work in pairs. Fill in the gaps in the phrases with these verbs. Check in V6.3 p134.

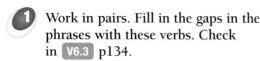

~~start~~	get	meet	finish

1 ....*start*.... school/my first job
2 .... school/university
3 .... my husband/my wife
4 .... married/divorced

~~have~~	write	become	study

5 ....*have*.... a son/three children
6 .... a lawyer/president
7 .... a book/a letter
8 .... languages/law

Reading and Grammar

2 **a)** What do you know about Nelson Mandela?

b) Read about Mandela's life. Fill in the gaps in the text with the correct dates and numbers from the box.

1943	two	1996	four
1957	eighteen	18th July	

c) R6.5 Read, listen and check your answers.

3 Read the text again. Put these events in Mandela's life in order.

a) He went to prison.
b) He got married to Winnie.
c) He and his first wife got divorced.
d) He went to university. *1*
e) He left prison.
f) He got married for the third time.
g) He became President of South Africa.

Help with Grammar
Past Simple regular and irregular verbs: positive

4 **a)** Look again at the text about Mandela's life. Find the Past Simple of these verbs.

Regular verbs							
start	study	finish	live	work	want	stay	marry

Irregular verbs							
become	have	get	meet	go	forget	leave	write

b) Answer these questions.

1 What are the last two letters of regular verbs in the Past Simple?
2 What are the endings of regular verbs that end in *-e*, and in consonant + *y*?
3 Is the Past Simple the same for all subjects (*I, you, he, they*, etc.)?

c) Check in G6.3 p135 and in the Irregular Verb List, p159.

From prison to President

Nelson Mandela was born in South Africa on ¹_____ , 1918.

He started university in 1938 and studied law. After he finished university in ²_____ he lived and worked in Johannesburg. He was very interested in politics and wanted to change the political system. He became President of the ANC (the African National Congress) in the Transvaal in 1952.

He had two children with his first wife, Evelyn. They got divorced in ³_____ and in the same year he met a woman named Winnie Madikizela. Nelson and Winnie got married a year later and they also had ⁴_____ children.

In 1964 he went to prison. He stayed there for 26 years and was in solitary confinement for ⁵_____ years. But the world never forgot Nelson Mandela. And in 1994, only ⁶_____ years after he left prison, he became President of South Africa.

Nelson and Winnie Mandela got divorced in ⁷_____ and two years later he married his third wife, Graça Machel.

When he was President, he wrote a book about his life called *Long Walk to Freedom*.

5 a) R6.6 P Listen and practise the regular Past Simple forms from **4a**. Which end with the sound /ɪd/?

b) R6.7 P Listen and practise the irregular Past Simple forms from **4a**.

6 Fill in the gaps with the Past Simple of these verbs.

> ~~live~~   have   go   study
> win   become   be   leave

1 When Nelson Mandela was a child he _lived_ in a village called Mvezo.
2 He .... law at Witwatersrand University – he .... the first black student there.
3 Evelyn and Nelson .... their first child, Thembi, in 1945.
4 Nelson .... South Africa in 1962 and .... to live in Algeria.
5 He .... President of the ANC in 1991 and he .... the Nobel Prize in 1993.

7 a) Work in groups. Do the quiz.

HISTORY-MAKERS

1 Where did Albert Einstein come from?
 a) Switzerland   b) Germany   c) Austria

2 When did the Wright brothers fly the first plane?
 a) 1903   b) 1918   c) 1933

3 Where did Mother Teresa live for most of her life?
 a) China   b) India   c) Europe

4 When did George Washington become the first President of the USA?
 a) 1789   b) 1839   c) 1889

5 When did the Italian explorer Marco Polo first go to China? When he was …
 a) 17   b) 37   c) 77

b) Check your answers on p158. How many did you get right?

Help with Grammar   Past Simple: *Wh-* questions

8 a) Look at the table. Notice the word order in questions.

question word	auxiliary	subject	infinitive	
Where	did	Albert Einstein	come	from?

b) Write questions 2 and 3 from the quiz in **7a)** in the table.

c) Check in G6.4 p135.

9 a) Make questions with these words.

1 last night / did / you / What / do ?   *What did you do last night?*
2 you / did / your best friend / Where / meet ?
3 Where / your parents / meet / did ?
4 to another country / When / you / first go / did ?
5 What / last weekend / do / you / did ?

b) R6.8 P Listen and check. Then listen again and practise.
What did you do last night?

c) Work in pairs. Take turns to ask and answer the questions in **9a)**.

Get ready … Get it right!

10 Look at p120. Follow the instructions.

Four weekends

> **Real World** showing interest and continuing a conversation
> **Vocabulary** weekend activities
> **Help with Listening** showing interest
> **Review** Past Simple

QUICK REVIEW ●●●
Write ten verbs you know. What is the Past Simple of these verbs? Which are regular/irregular? Work in pairs. Say the Past Simple to your partner. He/She says the infinitive.

Ⓐ
Dear Gianluca and Valeria

It was so good to see you again. We really needed to go away for the weekend and we had a wonderful time with you in Rome.

Thanks again.

Love Sarah

Ⓑ
Mick's things to do

take children swimming ✓
clean the car ✓
do the shopping ✓
drive Sonia to party ✓
write report ✓

Mick

Sarah

How was your weekend?

1 **a)** Look at the picture. Who do you think had:

1 a great weekend?   3 a busy weekend?
2 a quiet weekend?   4 a terrible weekend?

b) Read texts A–D. Were your guesses correct? How do you know?

2 **a)** Look at phrases 1–8. Then fill in the gaps with these words/phrases. Check in **V6.4** p134.

| ~~all day~~ | the house | tired | a bad cold | an email |
| for a couple of days | the shopping | until 11 a.m. |

1 **work**	every evening *all day*	5 **go away**	for the weekend ....
2 **clean**	the car	6 **sleep**	for eight hours ....
3 **write**	a report	7 **be**	ill ....
4 **do**	the washing	8 **have**	a wonderful time ....

b) Work in pairs. Take turns to test your partner on the phrases.

> the washing

> do the washing

c) How many of the phrases in their present or past forms can you find in texts A–D?

d) What is the Past Simple of the verbs in **2a)**?

3 **a)** Think of six things you did last weekend. Use phrases from **2a)** or your own ideas.

b) Work in pairs. Ask your partner what he/she did last weekend. Find three things you both did.

> What did you do last weekend?

> I cleaned the house.

> Me too.

Being a good listener

4 **R6.9** Listen and match the conversations to the people in the picture.

1 Conversation 1 is between .... and ....
2 Conversation 2 is between .... and ....

©

Hi Tom

Just a note to say I'm sorry I wasn't at the party. I was ill all weekend. I think it was because I worked every evening last week! I'll phone you.

Henry

Jane

Henry

Saturday 16 September

Slept until 11 a.m. on Saturday, then did the washing and watched TV.

Sunday 17 September

Went to the cinema with Annie. Bed at 10.

Help with Listening Showing interest

5 **a)** R6.10 Listen to parts of the conversations in **4** again. Match sentences 1–8 to responses a)–h).

1 I was really ill on Saturday.
2 I had a really bad cold.
3 I stayed at home.
4 I went away for the weekend. To Italy!
5 We went to Rome – it was wonderful!
6 We stayed with some old friends.
7 I worked all weekend.
8 It took me ten hours.

a) Oh, right.
b) Wow!
c) Oh, dear.
d) What a shame.
e) Oh, great!
f) You're joking!
g) Oh, nice.
h) Really?

b) Fill in the table with responses a)–h). Check in RW6.1 p135.

I'm happy for you.	I'm sorry for you.	I'm surprised.	I'm not surprised.
			Oh, right.

6 R6.11 P Listen and practise the responses in **5b)**. Copy the intonation.

7 Work in pairs. Student A → p105. Student B → p113. Follow the instructions.

Real World
Continuing a conversation

8 **a)** Look at these follow-up questions from the conversations in **4**. Fill in the gaps with *did*, *was* or *are*.

1 What .... wrong?
2 .... you OK now?
3 What .... you do?
4 What .... you see?
5 What ...*was*... it like?
6 Where .... you go?
7 Who .... you go with?
8 Where .... you stay?

b) Which of the questions in **8a)** can you ask someone who:

a) went to the cinema?
b) stayed at home all weekend?
c) was ill?
d) went away for the weekend?

c) Check in RW6.2 p135.

d) R6.9 Look at R6.9, p152. Listen again and read. Find the follow-up questions in **8a)**.

9 **a)** Make notes on what you did at these times.

1 last week
2 last weekend
3 yesterday
4 before you came to this lesson
5 on Friday evening

b) Work in pairs. Take turns to ask and answer questions about the times. Use the follow-up questions from **8a)**. How long can you continue each conversation?

What did you do last week?

Well, I went to a wedding last Friday.

Oh, nice! What was it like?

It was really good.

VOCABULARY IN CONTEXT

QUICK REVIEW ● ● ●
Work in pairs. Take turns to tell your partner five things you did last week: *I went to the cinema.* Then ask questions to get more information: *What did you see?*

1 Work in groups. Discuss these questions.

1 Do you or your friends enter competitions?
2 What things do people win in competitions?
3 What is your perfect competition prize?

2 Read only the first paragraph of the magazine article. What is the article about?

3 **a)** Work in pairs. Student A, read about Jim. Student B, read about Sandra. Answer these questions.

1 What did he/she win?
2 Who did he/she go with?
3 Where did they stay?
4 What was the weather like?
5 What did they do on Saturday?
6 What did Jim/Logan do on Sunday?

b) Work with your partner and ask the questions. Student A, ask about Sandra. Student B, ask about Jim.

4 **a)** Read your text again. Make a list of the adjectives.

b) Work with your partner. Show your list of adjectives to your partner. How many opposites can you find?

Help with Vocabulary
Adjectives with *very, really, quite, too*

5 **a)** Match the sentences to pictures A–C. Which word is negative and means 'more than you want'?

1 It's **too** big.　2 It's **quite** big.　3 It's **very/really** big.

b) Read both texts and find examples of *very, really, quite, too* + adjective. Then compare with a partner.

c) Complete the rule with *before* and *after.*

- *Very, really, quite* and *too* come _____ the verb *be* and _____ adjectives.

d) Check in V6.5 p134.

COMPETITION WINNERS – AND LOSERS!

Millions of people enter competitions every year and 99% never win anything. But what happens to the winners? We talked to two people who had very different experiences.

Jim I won a weekend for two in Paris. My girlfriend, Naomi, and I went to the airport in a really big limousine. We travelled first class and we had champagne on the plane. Then we stayed in a very expensive hotel near the River Seine. The weather was quite hot all weekend and the food and wine were really good. On Saturday morning we wanted to go up the Eiffel Tower but the queues were too long, so we had coffee by the river. In the afternoon we went to the Louvre Museum. It was quite crowded but we thought it was really interesting. Then on Sunday I asked Naomi to marry me – and she said yes! It was a wonderful weekend in a beautiful city.

Sandra I won a weekend for two in Scotland. I was really happy because I love Scotland. I went with my boyfriend, Logan. The hotel was nearly empty and now I know why! It was a really cheap, ugly place – the restaurant was very dirty and the rooms were too small. On Saturday the weather was really bad and we didn't go out because it was too cold. It was a really boring day and then in the evening Logan and I had a fight. I went to bed quite early and he stayed and talked to the receptionist for hours. She was very young and friendly – too friendly! On Sunday my boyfriend left me and went away with her. Yes, it was a terrible weekend!

6 Choose the correct words.

1 I can't wear these shoes. They're *quite*/*too* small.
2 I want to buy that bag. It's *very*/*too* nice.
3 Let's go to that new restaurant. It's *really*/*too* cheap.
4 Mmm, this food is *very*/*too* good.
5 Sorry sir, you're *very*/*too* late. The plane left at six o'clock.
6 Sam's got a new job and he's *really*/*too* happy.
7 They've got a new flat. It's *quite*/*too* nice.
8 You're only fifteen. You're *quite*/*too* young to drive.

7 a) Write the name of a place in your town/city that is:

1 too expensive or quite cheap
2 really beautiful or really ugly
3 very dirty or very clean
4 really boring or really interesting
5 too noisy or very quiet
6 very friendly or very unfriendly

b) Work in groups and compare places. Do you know any of the places the other students talk about? If yes, do you agree?

> I think the new coffee shop is quite cheap.

> Me too.

> Really? I think it's very expensive!

♫ **R6.12** Look at the song *Da Do Ron Ron* on p102. Follow the instructions.

6 Review Language Summary 6, p134

1 Write the opposites of these adjectives. **V6.1**

1	ill *well*	6	tall
2	happy	7	friendly
3	rich	8	stupid
4	crowded	9	quiet
5	clean	10	boring

2 a) Make these sentences true for you. Fill in the gaps with *was*, *were*, *wasn't* and *weren't*. **G6.1**

1 I _____ at home yesterday.
2 My family _____ all together last New Year's Eve.
3 I _____ with my friends on Saturday evening.
4 Both my parents _____ born in the same country.
5 I _____ born in the place I live in now.

b) Work in pairs. Compare your sentences.

3 a) Write *yes/no* questions for the sentences in 2a). **G6.2**

Were you at home yesterday?

b) Work in new pairs. Take turns to ask and answer your questions.

4 Read about Stan, Rebecca's grandfather. Fill in the gaps with the Past Simple of these verbs. **G6.3**

~~be~~	meet	have	go	be
live	move	meet	get	

I ¹ *was* born in **1940** and my family ² _____ in **London**. In 1959 I ³ _____ my wife, Margaret, at **a party** and we ⁴ _____ married on **April 5ᵗʰ 1960**. We ⁵ _____ our first child, Helen, in **1962**. Helen ⁶ _____ to **Australia** on holiday in 1986 and ⁷ _____ **her husband** there. They ⁸ _____ to **Perth** in 1990 and our granddaughter, Rebecca, ⁹ _____ born **two years later**.

5 a) Make questions for the words/phrases in **bold** in 4. **G6.4**

When was Stan born?
Where did his family live?

b) Work in pairs. Take turns to ask and answer the questions.

6 a) Choose the best response in these conversations. **RW6.1**

1 A I was ill last weekend.
  B *Oh, nice.*/*Oh, dear.*
2 A We went away for the weekend.
  B *What a shame.*/*Oh, great!*
3 A I went to the cinema last night.
  B *Oh, nice.*/*Wow!*
4 A I met the President of the USA last month.
  B *You're joking!*/*Oh, dear.*
5 A I stayed in all weekend.
  B *Oh, right.*/*What a shame.*

b) Work in pairs. Choose one of the conversations 1–5. Write six more lines. **RW6.2**

c) Role-play the conversation for other students.

Progress Portfolio

a) Tick the things you can do in English.

☐ I can describe people and places.
☐ I can talk about things that happened in my life.
☐ I can ask questions about things other people did in the past.
☐ I can say and understand years.
☐ I can talk about what I did last weekend.
☐ I can respond to people's news and ask follow-up questions.

b) What do you need to study again? **● 6A–D**

7 Films, music, news

7A Licence to kill

> **Vocabulary** types of film
> **Grammar** Past Simple (3): negative, *yes/no* questions and short answers
> **Help with Listening** Past Simple questions
> **Review** Past Simple: positive and *Wh-* questions

QUICK REVIEW ● ● ●
Think of three places you went to last year. Work in pairs. Tell your partner about the places. Use *very/really/quite/too* + adjectives: *I went to Venice last year. It was really beautiful.*

Vocabulary Types of film

1 a) Tick the types of film you know. Check in Language Summary 7 **V7.1** p136.

> action films   thrillers   horror films
> science-fiction (sci-fi) films   cartoons
> love stories   comedies   historical dramas

b) Work in groups. Talk about the types of film you like and don't like.

> (I love sci-fi films.)   (Yes, me too. / Really? I don't like them at all.)

Reading and Grammar

2 Work in groups. What do you know about James Bond? Think of five or more things.

3 a) Check these words with your teacher or in a dictionary.

> die   a climbing accident   a secret agent
> the navy   a licence   kill

b) Read the article about James Bond and choose the best title.

1 Around the world with James Bond
2 From schoolboy to spy
3 James Bond – movie star

c) Read the article again and answer these questions about James Bond.

1 Where and when was he born?
2 Why did he live with his aunt?
3 Which schools did he go to?
4 What did he do after he left school?
5 When did he become 007?
6 How many days was he married?

The book **You Only Live Twice** by Ian Fleming tells us that James Bond was born in Scotland in 1924, and he didn't have any brothers or sisters. When he was eleven, his parents died in a climbing accident in Switzerland, so he went to live in England with his aunt. When he was twelve he went to Eton, a famous private school, but he didn't like it there. He left after only one year and went to Fettes, his father's old school. James wasn't a good student and he didn't study very much, but he was very good at sports.

SEAN CONNERY IS JAMES BOND
IAN FLEMING'S "YOU ONLY LIVE TWICE"
...and "TWICE" is the only way to live!

Help with Grammar Past Simple: negative

4 a) Complete the rules with words from this sentence.
James wasn't a good student and he didn't study very much.

- To make the Past Simple negative of *be*, we use .... or *weren't*.
- To make the Past Simple negative of all other verbs, we use .... + infinitive.

b) Check in **G7.1** p137.

c) Find four more Past Simple negatives in the article.

7 R7.2 Listen to the beginning of a radio interview with the writer, Will Forbes. Choose the correct answers.

1 Will Forbes's new book is about *Ian Fleming/James Bond*.
2 He says Fleming and Bond's lives are *very different/quite similar*.

Help with Listening Past Simple questions

8 a) R7.3 Listen to questions from the interview. Fill in the gaps.

1 _____ Ian Fleming _____ for the _____ Secret Service too?
2 _____ Fleming _____ a 'licence to _____'?
3 _____ he _____ for the Secret Service after the _____ ?
4 _____ Fleming and Bond _____ to the same _____ ?
5 When _____ Ian Fleming _____ the first Bond book?
6 _____ he _____ a lot of _____ ?

b) Listen again. Is *did* stressed or unstressed in Past Simple questions?

9 a) R7.4 Listen to the whole interview. Answer the questions in 8a).

b) Listen again. Find four things that are true for Ian Fleming and James Bond.

Help with Grammar
Past Simple: *yes/no* questions and short answers

10 a) Fill in the gaps in these questions and short answers with *did* or *didn't*.

YES/NO QUESTIONS	SHORT ANSWERS
_____ he make a lot of money?	Yes, he _____ . No, he _____ .
_____ they go to the same school?	Yes, they _____ . No, they _____ .

b) Check in G7.2 p137.

11 a) Make questions with these words.

1 last week / go / you / to the cinema / Did ?
2 Did / last year / you / a Bond film / see ?
3 last weekend / a film on TV / you / watch / Did ?
4 an actor / want to be / Did / you / when you were a child ?

b) R7.5 P Listen and practise the questions in 11a) and the short answers.

c) Work in pairs. Take turns to ask and answer the questions. Continue the conversation if possible.

Get ready ... Get it right!

12 Work in two groups. Group A → p108. Group B → p116. Follow the instructions.

He left school in 1941 and worked as a secret agent for the British navy in World War 2. After the war James Bond stayed in the British Secret Service, but he didn't get his famous 'licence to kill' number (007, of course) until 1950. He married Teresa di Vicenzo on New Year's Day 1962, but they weren't married for long – his wife died on their wedding night. And for the rest of James Bond's life ... well, watch the movies!

5 R7.1 P Listen and practise.

He didn't have any brothers or sisters.

6 a) Tick the sentences that are true for you. Make the other sentences negative.

1 I got up early last Sunday.
I didn't get up early last Sunday.
2 I had a big breakfast today.
3 I was at home yesterday afternoon.
4 I went out last Saturday night.
5 I went to bed after midnight last night.
6 I arrived late for class today.

b) Compare sentences with a partner. How many are the same?

Vocabulary types of music; past time phrases with *ago*, *last* and *in*; question words
Grammar question forms
Review Past Simple; Present Simple

QUICK REVIEW ● ● ●
Write five questions with *Did you ...?* about yesterday. Choose a partner and guess his/her answers. Then work in pairs and ask the questions. How many guesses were correct?

Vocabulary
Types of music and past time phrases

1 **a)** R7.6 Listen and put these types of music in the order you hear them.

> rap *1* rock music pop music classical music
> opera jazz dance music reggae rock'n'roll

b) Work in pairs. Talk about the types of music you like and don't like. Who are your favourite bands, singers or composers?

2 **a)** Put these past time phrases in order.

the day before yesterday	last year
about 250 years ago	in February 1964
last month	in 1946
five minutes ago *1*	in the eighties
in the sixteenth century	about 80 years ago

b) Fill in the gaps with one of the past time phrases in **2a)**.

1 Mozart wrote his first symphony ...., when he was only eight.
2 Adolph Rickenbacker, an engineer, and George Beauchamp, a musician from Hawaii, made the first electric guitar ....
3 The Beatles' first concert in the USA was at the Washington Coliseum .... Tickets cost $2 and $4.
4 The first performance of an opera was in Florence, Italy, ...
5 Elvis Presley's mother, Gladys, bought him his first guitar .... It cost $12.95 – but eleven-year-old Elvis wanted a bicycle!

c) Check your answers on p158. How many did you get right?

3 Work in pairs. Student A → p110. Student B → p118. Follow the instructions.

4 **a)** Match the question words to the things they ask about.

1	Who	a)	a reason (*because ...*)
2	Where	b)	a time
3	When	c)	a person
4	Why	d)	possessive (*Susan's*)
5	Whose	e)	a place
6	Which	f)	a thing (from many possible answers)
7	What	g)	a period of time (*for two years*)
8	How many	h)	a number
9	How long	i)	age
10	How old	j)	a thing (from a small number of possible answers)

b) Check in V7.3 p136.

Reading, Listening and Grammar

5 **a)** Work in pairs. Look at the quiz on page 57. Fill in the gaps with question words 1–10 from **4a)**. Then choose the correct answers.

b) R7.7 Listen to two people do the quiz. Check the question words and your answers. How many did you get right?

6 **a)** Look at two questions from the quiz in the table. Which question is in the present? Which is in the past? How do you know?

question word	auxiliary	subject	infinitive	
When	did	Madonna	make	her first record?
Where	do	U2	come	from?

b) Write quiz questions 3 and 4 in the table. Are they in the present or past?

c) Which verb is in quiz questions 5–9? Do we use the auxiliaries *do/does/did* with this verb?

d) Check in G7.4 p137.

Are you a musical genius?

1 .... did Madonna make her first record?

a) In the seventies. **b)** In the eighties. **c)** In the nineties.

2 .... do U2 come from?

a) England **b)** Ireland **c)** the USA

3 .... did Sting do before he became a singer?

a) He was a teacher. **b)** He was a writer. **c)** He was an actor.

4 .... instrument does Elton John play?

a) the trumpet **b)** the piano **c)** the guitar

5 .... were the Beatles together?

a) For five years. **b)** For ten years. **c)** For fifteen years.

6 .... was Colombian singer Shakira when she released her first album, *Magic*?

a) thirteen **b)** seventeen **c)** twenty-two

7 .... was the first singer to have a number one album and film in the USA at the same time?

a) Eminem **b)** Jennifer Lopez **c)** David Bowie

8 .... people were in the Swedish group, Abba?

a) three **b)** four **c)** five

9 .... real name is or was Faroukh Bulsara?

a) George Michael **b)** Bob Dylan **c)** Freddie Mercury

10 .... didn't Elvis Presley make any records between 1958 and 1960?

a) He got married. **b)** He was in hospital. **c)** He was in the army.

Get ready ... Get it right!

7 **a)** Look at column A. Decide if the question is in the present or past. Make *yes/no* questions with *you.*

b) Make follow-up questions with the words in column C.

A	B	C
1 / go to any concerts last year? *Did you go to any concerts last year?*	....	Who / see ? *Who did you see?*
2 / listen to lots of different types of music?	....	What kind of music / listen to ?
3 / be / musical when you / be / a child?	....	Which instrument / play ?
4 / go to a club last month?	....	Where / go ?
5 / like classical music?	....	Which composers / like ?
6 / watch music videos on TV?	....	What / be / your favourite video ?
7 / buy any CDs last week?	....	What / buy ?
8 / listen to a personal stereo on the train/bus?	....	What / usually listen to ?

8 **a)** Ask other students the questions from column A. If the answer is *yes*, write his/her name in column B. Then ask your follow-up question from column C.

b) Work in pairs. Tell your partner five things about the students you talked to.

7C What's in the news?

Real World talking about the news
Vocabulary irregular Past Simple forms; verbs and nouns from news stories
Help with Listening stressed words
Review Past Simple

QUICK REVIEW ●●●
Write all the types of film and music you know (*horror films*, *jazz*, etc.). Compare your lists with a partner. Which do you both like?

The one o'clock news

1 Work in groups. Discuss these questions.

1 Where do you usually get your news – the TV, the radio, newspapers or the Internet?
2 Do you watch or listen to the news every day? If yes, at what time of day?
3 What was in the news yesterday?

2 **a)** Check these words with your teacher or in a dictionary.

> a plane crash   missing (on Mount Everest)
> rain   the lottery   choose (past: chose)
> climb   a flood   a helicopter   lucky

b) Look at photos A–D of some TV news stories. Which words in **2a)** are in each story, do you think?

3 **a)** R7.8 Listen to the news and put the photos in order.

b) Listen again and choose the correct answers.

1 **a)** Over *100/200* people died in the plane crash.
  b) The plane crashed in *China/Thailand*.
2 **a)** Terry and Carla Ellis are *brother and sister/married*.
  b) They are now *in a helicopter/missing*.
3 **a)** There are floods in *one place/lots of places* in India.
  b) *20/32* people died yesterday near Calcutta.
4 **a)** Joe Hall won over *£3/£13* million last night.
  b) *Joe/His dog* chose the lottery numbers.

Help with Listening Stressed words

4 **a)** R7.8 In English we stress the important words. Listen again to the first two sentences from the news. Notice the stressed words.

It's one o'clock and here's Teresa Ross with the news.
Over a hundred people died in a plane crash in China last night.

b) Look at R7.8, p153. Listen again and notice the stressed words.

Read all about it!

5 **a)** Look at the headlines on page 59 of news reports 1 and 2 from the next day. Which TV news stories are they about, do you think?

b) Match each infinitive to its irregular Past Simple form. Then check in V7.4 p136.

Infinitive	Past Simple
lose find take say	chose lost told
fall break choose	won found broke
win put tell	put said fell took

c) R7.9 P Listen and practise the infinitives and Past Simple forms in **5b)**.

A   B   C   D

Joe Hall   BANK

EVEREST CLIMBERS FOUND

Terry and Carla Ellis, the British couple who wanted to be the first husband-and-wife team to climb Everest, are now safe. An army helicopter found them on the side of the mountain yesterday afternoon and took them to a hospital in Kathmandu.

"The weather was terrible and climbing was very difficult," said Carla. "Two days ago Terry fell a hundred metres down the mountain and broke his leg. He lost the radio when he fell and so we stayed on the mountain and waited for help. We were really happy to see the helicopter. We're lucky to be alive."

Do they want to try and climb Everest again in the future? "Maybe," said Terry from his hospital bed. "Carla really wants to come back next year. I'm not so sure."

2 NEWS 365 - ALL the news ALL the time.

http://www.news365.net/dogwin.html

NEWS 365
···· dog wins lottery! ····

Europe | Americas | Oceana
Asia | Middle East | Africa

Dog wins lottery!

Wednesday night's lottery winner Joe Hall received a cheque for over £13 million yesterday at the supermarket where he works. His dog, Max, who chose the winning numbers, was with him.

"I usually choose the numbers," said 28-year-old Joe from Liverpool. "But I never win anything. So this time I asked Max to choose the numbers for me – and I won over £13 million!"

But how did the dog choose the numbers? "I wrote the numbers 1 to 49 on envelopes and put a dog biscuit in each envelope," Joe explained. "I put the envelopes in different places in my house and told Max to find the biscuits. Then I wrote down the numbers from the first six envelopes he found – and now I'm a millionaire!"

Now Joe wants Max to find him a girlfriend!

link: http://www.news365.net/dogwin.html

Talking about the news

7 a) R7.10 Listen to four conversations about the news. Which news story is each conversation about?

b) Listen again and match sentences 1–6 to responses a)–f).

1 Over thirteen million pounds.
2 His dog chose the numbers for him!
3 Did you hear about the floods?
4 Over a hundred people died.
5 One of them fell and they lost their radio.
6 Yes, a helicopter found them yesterday.

a) Yes, isn't it awful?
b) Really?
c) Oh, that's good.
d) Oh, dear. Are they OK?
e) Oh no, that's terrible.
f) You're joking!

Real World Talking about the news

8 a) Fill in the gaps in the questions and responses with these words.

was   happened   about   hear

1 A Did you .... about that plane crash?   B No, where .... it?
2 A Did you read .... the couple on Everest?   B No, what .... ?

b) Fill the table with responses a)–f) in **7b)**.

good news	bad news	suprising news
		b) Really?

c) Check in **RW7.1** p137.

9 R7.11 P Listen and practise the questions and responses in **8a)** and **8b)**.

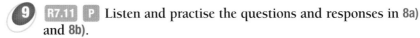

Did you hear about that plane crash?   No, where was it?

10 Work in pairs. Student A → p110. Student B → p118. Follow the instructions.

6 a) Work in two groups. Group A, read report 1 and answer questions 1–5. Group B, read report 2. Answer questions a)–e).

1 Where are Terry and Carla now?
2 When did Terry fall?
3 What did he break when he fell?
4 Why didn't they call for help?
5 Do they want to come back next year?

a) Where did Joe receive the cheque?
b) What did Joe write on the envelopes?
c) Where did Joe put them?
d) Why did the dog want to find the envelopes?
e) What does Joe want his dog to do now?

b) Work in pairs. Student A, ask your partner questions a)–e). Student B, ask your partner questions 1–5.

7D Do you know any jokes?

QUICK REVIEW ●●●
Work in pairs. What can you remember about the four news stories from 7C? Compare ideas with another pair. Then check on p58 and p59.

1 Work in groups. Discuss these questions.

1 What's your favourite comedy programme or film?
2 Do you like listening to or telling jokes?

2 a) Tick the verbs you know. Check new verbs with your teacher or in a dictionary.

love	hate	come	laugh	cry	say
buy	sit	wait	start	see	happen

b) What is the Past Simple of each verb? Which verbs are irregular? Check in the Irregular Verb List, p159.

3 a) **R7.12** Read and listen to the joke. Fill in the gaps in the last line.

b) Read the joke again. Match paragraphs 1–4 to pictures A–D.

Help with Vocabulary *a*, *an* and *the*

4 a) Look at these sentences. Then complete the rules with *a/an* or *the*.

An *old man in **a** long coat came and sat near him.*
The *old man had **a** big black dog.*
*He sat in **the** front row.*

● We use .... to talk about things or people for the first time.
● We use .... when we know which thing or person.
● We use .... when there is only one thing or person in a particular place.

TIP! ● We also use *the* in some fixed phrases: *go to the cinema*, *in the evening*, etc.

b) Check in **V7.5** p136.

5 Read the joke again and find all the examples of *a*, *an* and *the*. Work in pairs and decide why they are used.

(A)

(B)

1 One day Mike went to the cinema to see a film. He bought a drink and an ice-cream. Then he sat in the front row of the cinema and waited for the film to start.

2 A few minutes later, an old man in a long coat came and sat near him. The old man had a big black dog, and the dog sat on the floor by the man's feet.

3 When the film started, Mike saw that the dog was very interested in the film. When something funny happened, the dog laughed and laughed. When a person in the film died or something bad happened, the dog cried and cried. This happened all the way through the film.

4 At the end of the film, Mike went to talk to the old man. "That was amazing," said Mike. "Your dog really loved the film." The old man looked at him and said, "Yes, it *was* amazing. He .... the ...."

(C)

(D)

6 **a)** Check these words with your teacher or in a dictionary.

> cut down   a tree   an axe
> a noise   a chainsaw

b) Read another joke. Fill in the gaps with *a*, *an* or *the*.

One morning ¹............ man wanted to cut down ²............ tree in his garden. He went to ³............ shop to buy ⁴............ axe. ⁵............ manager of ⁶............ shop said, "Why don't you buy ⁷............ chainsaw? It will save you a lot of time."

⁸............ man agreed and bought ⁹............ very expensive chainsaw. He took it home and started cutting down ¹⁰............ tree. He worked very hard for six hours, but ¹¹............ tree didn't fall down. ¹²............ man was very angry and went back to ¹³............ shop.

"This chainsaw is no good," he said.

"Hmm, it looks OK to me," said ¹⁴............ manager. He looked at it for a minute, then started ¹⁵............ chainsaw.

"What's that noise?" asked ¹⁶............ man.

7 **a)** Choose the correct words.

1 Did you have *a/the* big breakfast this morning?
2 Is there *a/the* park near your home?
3 Did you go to *a/the* capital city of another country last year?
4 Do you often go to *a/the* theatre at *a/the* weekend?
5 Do you watch *a/the* TV programme *The Simpsons*?
6 Who was *a/the* main actor in *a/the* film *The Terminator*?

b) Work in pairs. Take turns to ask and answer the questions. Ask follow-up questions if possible.

7 Review   Language Summary 7, p136

1 **a)** Write the missing letters in these types of film. **V7.1**

1 h o r r o r   f i l m s
2 s _ i e _ c e - f _ c t _ _ n   f _ _ m s
3 c _ r t _ _ n s
4 l _ v _   s _ _ r _ e s
5 t h _ i _ _ e r s
6 a _ t _ _ n   f _ l _ s
7 c _ m _ _ i e s
8 h _ s t _ r _ c _ l   d r _ m _ s

b) Tick three types of film you like. Find two students who like the same types of film.

2 **a)** Tick the correct sentences. Don't look at p54.

1 James Bond was born in England.
2 He had two sisters.
3 His parents died in an accident.
4 He lived with his grandparents.
5 He liked studying.
6 He worked as a doctor in World War 2.
7 He got married in 1962.

b) Check your answers on p54.

c) Make the incorrect sentences in **2a)** negative. Then write correct sentences. **G7.1**

James Bond wasn't born in England. He was born in Scotland.

3 **a)** Fill in the gaps in these questions about yesterday with *Did*, *Was* or *Were*. **G7.2**

1 .... you get up early?
2 .... you at work/school all day?
3 .... your manager/teacher nice to you?
4 .... you listen to any music?
5 .... you at home in the evening?
6 .... you go to bed late?

b) Work in pairs. Take turns to ask the questions about yesterday.

4 **a)** Match questions 1–7 with answers a)–g). **V7.3**

1 When did you last go to a birthday party?
2 Whose birthday party was it?
3 Who did you go with?
4 Where was the party?
5 How many people were there?
6 What music did they play?
7 How long did you stay?

a) Until 2 a.m.
b) About fifty.
c) My cousin, Tim's.
d) Dance music.
e) Two months ago.
f) My boyfriend, Leo.
g) In Tim's flat.

b) Work in pairs. Take turns to ask questions 1–7. Answer for you.

5 **a)** Find fifteen verbs.

W	A	C	H	O	O	S	E	D
Y	M	O	T	S	L	T	L	E
E	C	M	H	G	S	A	O	Q
B	R	E	A	K	L	R	V	W
U	Y	I	P	K	A	T	A	A
Y	X	F	P	P	U	T	M	I
T	S	E	E	W	G	D	L	T
W	I	N	N	F	H	A	T	E
S	T	O	L	I	S	T	E	N

b) Work in pairs. What is the Past Simple of the verbs? Which are irregular?

Progress Portfolio

a) Tick the things you can do in English.

☐ I can talk about types of film and music.
☐ I can say when things happened in the past.
☐ I can ask and answer questions about the past and the present.
☐ I can understand simple news stories.
☐ I can start a conversation about the news.
☐ I can respond to news stories.

b) What do you need to study again? ● **7A–D**

8 Let's go away

8A Holiday USA

Vocabulary holiday activities
Grammar *can/can't* for possibility
Help with Listening *can/can't*
Review Past Simple

QUICK REVIEW ●●●
Work in pairs. How many different things do you both do in your free time? Make a list. How many of these things did you do last week?

Vocabulary Holiday activities

1 Think of three places tourists go to in your country. What do they do there? Compare your places with a partner.

2 **a)** Tick the words/phrases you know. Then do the exercise in Language Summary 8 **V8.1** p138.

> go for walks   go fishing
> go sightseeing   go shopping
> go to the beach   go skiing
> go swimming   go cycling
> go on boat trips   sunbathe
> have picnics   stay in a hotel
> stay with friends/family   camp
> rent a car   rent a bike
> travel by public transport
> go on holiday [US: go on vacation]

b) Work in pairs. Which of the things in **2a)** do you usually do on holiday?

3 **a)** Make questions with these words.

1 last / holiday / your / was / When ?
  When was your last holiday?
2 did / go / Where / you ?
3 Who / with / did / go / you ?
4 stay / you / did / Where ?
5 did / What / in the day / do / you ?
6 around / How / you / did / travel ?
7 have / you / a good time / Did ?

b) Work in pairs. Take turns to ask and answer the questions about your last holiday.

Nob Hill

Fisherman's Wharf

WELCOME TO SAN FRANCISCO!

Listening and Grammar

4 **a)** What do you know about San Francisco?

b) Work in pairs. Find these things in the photos.

> a prison   a cable car   a bridge   a park   an island   tourists   boats

5 **a)** **R8.1** James is asking his friend, Rachel, about San Francisco. Listen and put photos A–D in order.

b) Work in pairs. Match activities 1–8 that Rachel talks about to these places – Golden Gate Park (G), Nob Hill (N) and Fisherman's Wharf (F).

1 go for long walks *G*
2 go there by cable car
3 see street musicians
4 see the whole city
5 eat good seafood
6 walk from there to Chinatown
7 relax in the Japanese Tea Garden
8 go from there to Alcatraz

c) Listen again and check your answers.

Alcatraz

Golden Gate Bridge and Park

Help with Grammar
can/can't for possibility

6 **a)** Look at these sentences. Then complete the rules with *can* or *can't*.

You can go on a boat trip.
You can't stay on the island.

- We use .... to say that something is possible.
- We use .... to say that something isn't possible.

b) Look at the sentences in **6a)** again. Complete the rules with *can* and *can't*.

- For positive sentences, we use: subject + ... + infinitive.
- For negative sentences, we use: subject + ... + infinitive.
- .... and .... are the same for all subjects (*I, you, he, they,* etc.).

c) Make questions with the words in 1 and 2 and fill in the gaps in short answers 3 and 4.

QUESTIONS
1 do / What / there / you / can ?
2 stay / Can / on the island / you ?

SHORT ANSWERS
3 Yes, you ....
4 No, you ....

d) Check in **G8.1** p139.

Help with Listening *can/can't*

7 **a)** **R8.2** Listen to these sentences. Notice how we say *can* and *can't*. Which is stressed?

You can /kən/ go by cable car.
You can't /kɑːnt/ stay on the island.

b) **R8.3** Listen and tick the sentence you hear first.

1 a) You can go for walks. b) You can't go for walks.
2 a) You can go shopping. b) You can't go shopping.
3 a) You can go swimming. b) You can't go swimming.
4 a) You can stay there. b) You can't stay there.
5 a) You can rent a car. b) You can't rent a car.

c) **R8.1** Look at R8.1, p153. Listen again and read. Notice the difference between *can* and *can't*.

8 **R8.4** **P** Listen and practise. Copy the strong and weak forms of *can*.

Can /kən/ you go swimming there?
Yes, you can /kæn/.
No, you can't /kɑːnt/.

9 James also wants to visit Yellowstone Park in Wyoming, in the USA. Work in pairs. Student A → p108. Student B → p116. Follow the instructions.

Get ready ... Get it right!

10 **a)** Work in pairs. Choose a holiday place that you know, but your partner doesn't know. It can be in your country or another country.

b) Work on your own. Which of these activities can/can't you do in the place you chose?

- go dancing late at night
- go to the cinema after 11 p.m.
- watch films in English
- go shopping on Sundays
- go to football matches
- go out to eat at 2 a.m.
- travel by public transport after midnight
- go to museums

11 Work in pairs. Take turns to ask and answer questions about your holiday places. Use the phrases from **10b)** and **2a)**. Give more information if possible.

Can you go dancing late at night?

Yes, you can. There's a really good club called *The Bronze*.

Vocabulary adjectives to describe places
Grammar comparatives
Review *can* for possibility; holiday activitie

QUICK REVIEW ● ● ●
Imagine a friend is on holiday in your town/city/region. Think of five things he/she can do there. Work in pairs. Tell your partner your ideas.

Vocabulary

Adjectives to describe places

1 Find the opposites. Check new words in **V8.2** p138.

> noisy   clean   boring
> old   friendly   dangerous
> crowded   unfriendly
> empty   safe   modern
> quiet   dirty   interesting

2 **a)** Choose eight adjectives from **1**. For each adjective write the name of a place you know.

b) Work in pairs. Take turns to tell your partner about the places. Use *very/really/quite* with the adjectives.

> Oxford Street in London is always very crowded.

Reading and Grammar

3 **a)** Look at the photos. What do you know about Thailand?

b) Read about two holiday places in Thailand. Choose one for a holiday. Tell another student why you chose it.

c) Read the texts again. Find three things you can do in each place.

4 Read these sentences comparing Phuket and Bangkok. Which sentence is false?

a) The Kata Hotel is smaller than the Sawadee Hotel.
b) Phuket is hotter than Bangkok.
c) Bangkok is probably noisier.
d) Bangkok is more crowded than Phuket.
e) The holiday in Bangkok is more expensive.

Phuket

The beautiful island of Phuket is famous for its fantastic beaches, delicious food and friendly people. It's the perfect place for a week's break. You can relax and sunbathe all day on one of the island's wonderful beaches, or rent a motorbike and travel round the whole island. In the evening you can eat fresh fish in one of Phuket's excellent restaurants, then enjoy a quiet walk along the beach under the stars. Whatever you want from your holiday, it's here in Phuket!

Accommodation:
Kata Hotel ★★★★
(23 rooms)

Cost per week
(including flight): €1570

Average temperature
(April–May): 32°C

Help with Grammar   Comparatives

5 **a)** Look at the sentences in **4** and find the comparatives (*smaller*, etc.). Then complete the rules.

● With most 1-syllable adjectives (*small, old*), add _____ .
● With 1-syllable adjectives ending in consonant + vowel + consonant (*hot, big*), double the last consonant and add _____ .
● With 2-syllable adjectives ending in -*y* (*noisy, happy*), change the -*y* to _____ and add _____ .
● With most other 2-syllable and 3-syllable adjectives (*crowded, expensive*), put _____ before the adjective.
● The comparatives for *good* and *bad* are irregular: *good* → *better, bad* → *worse*.

b) Look at sentences a), b) and d) in **4**. Which word do we use after the comparative?

c) Check in **G8.2** p139.

6 Write the comparatives.

1 boring 3 beautiful 5 safe 7 big
2 dirty 4 good 6 bad 8 dangerous

7 **a)** R8.5 Listen to Luke and Monica planning a holiday in Thailand. Where does each person want to go? Find one reason why they want to go there.

b) Fill in the gaps with the comparative form of the adjectives in brackets. Use *than* if necessary.

1 Phuket's ...*more beautiful than*... Bangkok. (beautiful)
2 Bangkok's _____ . (interesting)
3 Phuket looks _____ Bangkok. (good)
4 But Bangkok's _____ . (crowded)
5 And the people in Phuket are probably _____ . (friendly)
6 But Phuket's _____ . (expensive)
7 I still think Bangkok's _____ Phuket. (interesting)
8 Phuket's probably _____ too. (safe)
9 And it's _____ . (quiet)

c) Work in pairs. Who says the sentences in 7b), do you think – Luke or Monica?

d) Listen again and check.

8 R8.6 P Listen and practise the sentences in 7b).

Phuket's more beautiful than /ðən/ Bangkok.

9 R8.7 Where do you think Luke and Monica went on holiday? Listen and check.

10 **a)** Choose one of the adjectives in brackets. Then fill in the gaps with its comparative form and *than*.

MY TOWN/CITY
1 Food is _____ it was last year. (expensive/cheap)
2 It's _____ it was five years ago. (dangerous/safe)
3 Public transport is _____ it was ten years ago. (good/bad)

MY LIFE
4 My English is _____ it was last month. (good/bad)
5 My hair is _____ it was last year. (long/short)
6 My life is _____ it was five years ago. (interesting/boring)

b) Write two more sentences about your town/city or your life.

c) Work in pairs. Compare your sentences from 10a) and 10b) with your partner. How many are the same?

Get ready ... Get it right!

11 Work in two groups. Group A → p109. Group B → p117. Follow the instructions.

Bangkok

The capital of Thailand is always a wonderful place to visit. You can go sightseeing in the city and visit beautiful Buddhist temples, and the amazing Royal Palace. Or why not take a boat trip on the river and go shopping in the colourful markets?

You can enjoy traditional Thai food in restaurants all over the city and then go dancing in the evening in one of Bangkok's many exciting nightclubs.

Come to Bangkok – it's the holiday of a lifetime!

Accommodation:
Sawadee Hotel ★★★
(162 rooms)

Cost per week
(including flight): €1240

Average temperature
(April–May): 29°C

8C Planning a day out

Real World planning a day out:
I'd rather … / I'd like … / I want …
Help with Listening *I'd* and the
schwa /ə/
Review *can/can't*; free time activities

QUICK REVIEW ● ● ●
Think of two holiday places in your country. Write five sentences comparing them. Work in pairs. Tell your partner your sentences. Which place does he/she think is nicer to visit? Why?

A day out

1 Work in pairs. Think about places near where you live. Where can people go for: an exciting, an interesting, a relaxing day out?

2 **a)** Read the articles and answer the questions.

CHESSINGTON

1 Can you go to Chessington on Sundays?
2 Which animals can you see there?
3 How long is Chessington open every day?
4 What are the names of two rides?

REGENT'S PARK

5 Is the theatre in Regent's Park open in October?
6 Can you go on a bird walk in the evenings?
7 How long is the Royal London Bike Ride?
8 What kind of music can you hear in the park?

b) Read the articles again. How many things can you do in each place?

c) Work in pairs and check your answers.

3 **a)** R8.8 Listen to the Stevens family. Put the places they talk about in order. Where do they decide to go?

a) Chessington
b) Regent's Park
c) the station
d) the beach
e) an open air theatre

b) Listen again. Are these sentences true (T) or false (F)?

1 The Stevens family went to the beach last weekend.
2 Mrs Stevens thinks Regent's Park is boring.
3 Her son wants to go to Chessington.
4 His friends went to Chessington two weeks ago.
5 He can bring a friend with him.

CHESSINGTON WORLD OF ADVENTURES

Chessington is a really fun day out for all the family. There are lots of exciting rides to go on, including the frightening Vampire ride in *Transylvania* – but don't have lunch first!

You can also visit *Mexicana* and go on the amazing Runaway Train ride – it's really scary! Then why not have lunch in the excellent Mexican restaurant nearby? And in *Animal Land* you can meet a family of gorillas and see some beautiful big cats, including a pair of Sumatran tigers (there are only 400 left in the wild).

Chessington World of Adventures is open every day from April to October from 10.00 a.m.–7.00 p.m.

Ticket office: **0870 444 7777**

Help with Listening *I'd* **and the schwa** /ə/

4 **a)** R8.8 Listen again to the first two sentences of the conversation. Notice how we say *I'd* (= *I would*) and the schwa /ə/.

What do you want to do tomorrow?
　　/dʒə/　　/tə/　/ə/
Well, I'd like to go to the beach.
　　/aɪd/　/tə/　/tə ðə/

b) Look at R8.8, p154. Listen again. Notice how we say *I'd* and /ə/ in the sentences in bold.

WHAT'S ON
in Regent's Park

Most people who visit Regent's Park go to the world-famous London Zoo, but there are many other things happening in the park this summer – and a lot of them are free!

MUSIC: June–September. Everything from rock and jazz to classical.

OPEN AIR THEATRE: June–September. This season includes *Romeo and Juliet* and *High Society*.

ROYAL LONDON BIKE RIDE: A 12-mile ride through Regent's Park and other Royal Parks in central London.

GUIDED BIRD WALKS: 8.30–11.30 a.m. every Sunday in August.

INFORMATION LINE: TEL. 020 7486 7905

Real World Planning a day out

5 **a)** Look at how we ask and answer about a day out.

asking people what they want to do	saying what you want to do
What do you want to do tomorrow?	**I'd like** to go to the beach.
Where would you like to go?	**I want** to go to Chessington.
Do you want to go to Regent's Park?	**I'd rather** stay at home.

TIP! • *would like* is more polite than *want*.

b) Complete the rule with *I want to do this* or *I want to do this more than something else*.

● We use *I'd rather* to say ....

c) Complete the rules with *would rather, would like* and *want*.

● After .... we use the infinitive (*go, do,* etc.).
● After .... and .... we use the infinitive with *to* (*to go, to do,* etc.).

d) Check in RW8.1 p139.

6 R8.9 P Listen and practise. Copy the stress and intonation.

Would you /wʊdʒə/ *like to go to the beach?*

I'd /aɪd/ *rather stay at home.*

7 **a)** Work in pairs, A and B. Take turns to suggest plans for Friday.

> Would you like to go to the cinema?
> I'd rather watch a video.
> Do you want to go for a walk?
> Yes, that's a good idea.

1	A go to the cinema?	B	watch a video
2	B go for a walk?	A	✓
3	A go to a club?	B	✓
4	B watch TV?	A	go out
5	A play tennis?	B	go swimming
6	B go out for a meal?	A	go for a drink

b) Take turns to make three more suggestions of your own.

8 **a)** Choose Regent's Park or Chessington for a day out. Read the article about this place again. Find three reasons why you want to go there.

b) Work in threes. Plan a day out to Regent's Park or Chessington. Decide on these things.

> which place   when to go   how to get there
> where/when to meet   things to do there

> Where shall we go?
> Let's go to …

c) Tell the class where your group wants to go for a day out. Which place is more popular?

VOCABULARY IN CONTEXT

QUICK REVIEW ● ● ●
Write the alphabet from A to Z. Work in pairs.
Try to think of one verb for each letter: *A = ask*,
B = buy, etc. Compare with another pair.

1 **a)** Answer these questions.

1 When did you last go to a wedding?
2 Where was it?
3 Whose wedding was it?
4 How many people were there?
5 What did you wear?
6 What did/didn't you like about the wedding?

b) Work in pairs. Take turns to ask and answer the questions.

2 **a)** Read email 1 and tick the correct sentences.

1 Phil can go to the wedding.
2 The wedding is in England.
3 He can only stay for three days.
4 He wants to travel around by motorbike.

b) Work in pairs. Check your answers. Correct the false sentences.

3 **a)** Read email 2 and answer the questions.

1 How many weeks can Phil stay with Ellen?
2 Did Ellen rent a motorbike for Phil?
3 Is it easy to get to Ellen's home?
4 Does Uncle Jeff always work in Canada?

b) Work in pairs. Check your answers.

Help with Vocabulary **Verb collocations**

4 **a)** Read the emails again. Find two more words or phrases that go with these verbs. Fill in the gaps. Then check in V8.3 p138.

book	rent	get	stay
a flight	*a motorbike*	*to your/our place*	
			with you/us

b) Work in pairs. Think of two words or phrases that go with these verbs: *play, have, write, go, study*.

①

From: philipbanks@global.co.uk
To: ellenjbanks@aol.com.ca
Subject: Oliver's wedding
Date: 14 February

Dear Aunt Ellen and Uncle Jeff

Thanks very much for the invitation to cousin Oliver and Becky's wedding. Of course I'd love to come. I'm on holiday then, so I can stay in Canada for three weeks. Actually, I booked my flight yesterday and I arrive the day before the wedding. Can I stay with you when I arrive? If that's not possible, don't worry. I can stay in a hotel. Also, do you know where I can rent a motorbike after the wedding? If not, I can rent a car. See you soon.

Love

Phil

PS How do I get to your place from the airport?

②

From: ellenjbanks@aol.com.ca
To: philipbanks@global.co.uk
Subject: Great news!
Date: 16 February

Dear Phil

We're really pleased you can come to the wedding. I'm afraid you can't stay with us for the first week, because Becky's parents are with us then. If you want, I can book a hotel room for you nearby and then you can stay with us for the rest of your holiday after they leave. And yes, you can rent motorbikes. Shall I send you a list of companies and then you can email them?

It's easy to get to our place. You can get a taxi from the airport or you can get a bus to Yonge and Spadina. Our apartment is 2 minutes from the bus stop. Let me know the time of your flight. We can book a table at our favourite restaurant that evening with Becky and her family. See you in June!

Lots of love

Aunt Ellen

PS Uncle Jeff has some work in England soon and we want to rent an apartment in north London. Can you check prices for us? Thanks.

5 Work in pairs. Take turns to test your partner on the verb collocations in **4a)**.

> a flight

> book a flight

6 a) Fill in the gaps with the correct form of *book*, *rent*, *get* or *stay*.

1 When was the last time you *stayed* with a friend?
2 Do you .... your home or did you buy it?
3 How do you .... to your English class?
4 Do you ever .... a taxi home after class?
5 Where was the last hotel you .... in?
6 Do you ever .... flights on the Internet?
7 How much is it to .... a car in your town/city?
8 Do you need to .... a table at your favourite restaurant?

b) Work in pairs. Take turns to ask and answer the questions.

7 Two friends from another country want to visit you. Write them an email and answer their questions.

1 Where can we stay?
2 How can we get there from the airport?
3 Can we rent a car?
4 What can we see and do?

♪ **R8.10** Look at the song *Holiday* on p102. Follow the instructions.

8 Review
Language Summary 8, p138

1 a) Fill in the gaps with these prepositions or –. **V8.1**

> by to with in on for

1 travel __by__ public transport
2 go .... sightseeing
3 go .... the beach
4 go .... a boat trip
5 go .... walks
6 rent .... a car
7 stay .... a hotel
8 stay .... friends

b) Think about the last time you went away for the weekend. What did you do?

c) Work in groups. Tell the other students about your last weekend away.

2 a) Make questions with these words. **G8.1**

1 to / a bus / can / get / I / the airport / Where ?
   Where can I get a bus to the airport?
2 Can / for under $30 / I / a hotel room / find ?
3 museums / can / Which / visit / I / for free ?
4 buy / some nice presents / can / Where / I ?
5 a really good / get / Where / pizza / I / can ?

b) Work in pairs. Take turns to ask and answer the questions about your home town, or the town/city you are in now.

3 a) Fill in the gaps with the comparatives. **G8.2**

1 Which country is .... (small)?
2 Which capital city is .... (big)?
3 Which country is .... (expensive)?
4 Which capital city is .... (modern)?
5 Which country's football team is .... (good)?

b) Work in groups. Answer the questions about England and your country.

England's smaller than my country.

4 Fill in the gaps with the infinitive or the infinitive with *to*. **RW8.1**

A What do you want [1] *to do* (do) tomorrow?
B I'd like [2] .... (go) shopping in town.
A We did that last weekend. I'd rather [3] .... (go) to the beach.
B OK, let's [4] .... (do) that. Where would you like [5] .... (go)?
A Can we [6] .... (go) to Angel Beach? It's really nice.
B Yes, good idea. Let's [7] .... (go) there.

5 a) Think of three things you would like to do tomorrow evening.

b) Work in groups. Tell the other students your ideas. Then choose one place to go tomorrow evening. **RW8.1**

Progress Portfolio

a) Tick the things you can do in English.

☐ I can talk about things I do on holiday.
☐ I can say what you can and can't do where I live.
☐ I can describe and compare places I know.
☐ I can find important facts in tourist information articles.
☐ I can discuss and plan a day out.
☐ I can understand a simple email or personal letter.

b) What do you need to study again? **8A–D**

9 All in a day's work

9A The meeting

Vocabulary work
Grammar Present Continuous for 'now'
Review jobs; common verbs

Work in pairs. Write all the jobs you know. Do you know any people with these jobs? Tell your partner about them.

Frank

Liz

Janet

Vocabulary Work

1 **a)** Tick the words you know. Then do the exercise in Language Summary 9 **V9.1** p140.

> a customer   a report   notes   a letter
> a message   a contract   a company
> a meeting   a conference

b) Which word does <u>not</u> go with the verb?

1 write ~~customers~~/reports/letters
2 answer the phone/notes/emails
3 take contracts/messages/notes
4 sign contracts/letters/meetings
5 work for a company/in an office/a report
6 go to meetings/contracts/conferences
7 write to a contract/customer/company

2 Work in groups. Talk about what you (and/or people you know) do at work.

Listening and Grammar

3 **a)** Look at pictures 1 and 2. It's 9.50 a.m. Where are the people?

b) **R9.1** Listen. What is Frank's problem?

c) Listen again and choose the correct answers.

1 Frank isn't at work because the *bus/train* was late.
2 The meeting with the Tamada brothers is at *ten/eleven* o'clock.
3 Frank wants Janet to *start the meeting/wait for him*.
4 The contract is *Frank's/Janet's*.
5 Adriana is *in the office/at home*.
6 Janet wants Liz to *take notes in the meeting/finish some reports*.

①    ②

4 **a)** Who says these sentences – Frank, Janet or Liz?

1 I'm waiting for a taxi.
2 They're sitting in your office.
3 They aren't looking very happy.
4 She's working at home today.
5 I'm not doing anything important at the moment.
6 Danny isn't doing anything.

b) **R9.1** Listen again and check your answers.

Help with Grammar
Present Continuous: positive and negative

5 **a)** Are the sentences in 4a) about now or every day?

b) We use *be* + verb+*ing* to make the Present Continuous. Fill in the gaps in the tables.

POSITIVE			NEGATIVE		
I'*m*			I'_____ not		
you/we/they'_____	verb+*ing*		you/we/they _____	verb+*ing*	
he/she/it'_____			he/she/it _____		

c) Write the -*ing* form of these verbs.

> play *playing*   smoke   study   sit
> look   go   run   write   live   stop

d) Check in **G9.1** p141.

Bob

Liz

Danny

③

Help with Grammar Present Continuous: questions and short answers

10 **a)** Write questions 3 and 4 from **9** in the table.

question word	auxiliary	subject	verb+*ing*	
Where	is	Frank	calling	from?
	Is	the taxi	moving?	

b) Write positive and negative short answers for these questions.

1 Am I working here today?
Yes, you are. / No, ...
2 Is Janet answering her phone?
3 Are they having the meeting now?

c) Check in **G9.2** p141.

6 **R9.2** **P** Listen and practise.
I'm waiting for a taxi.

7 **a)** Look at picture 3. Liz is talking to Danny. It's 9.55 a.m. Put the verbs in the Present Continuous.

LIZ Danny, are you busy?
DANNY Well, er, I ¹.......... (write) a letter.
LIZ Can you take notes at the meeting, please?
DANNY Why me? Look, Bob ².......... (read) the newspaper. Ask him.
LIZ He ³.......... (not read) the newspaper. He ⁴.......... (study) the business pages.
DANNY Well, I ⁵.......... (wait) for a phone call from New York.
LIZ They ⁶.......... (not work) in New York now, Danny. It's 5.00 a.m. there!
DANNY OK, OK, I ⁷.......... (go) now. Which room?

b) **R9.3** Listen and check your answers.

8 Work in pairs. It's 10.05 a.m. What are these people doing now, do you think?

1 Janet   3 The Tamada brothers   5 Frank
2 Bob   4 Danny   6 Liz

I think Janet's having a meeting.

9 **R9.4** It's now 10.15 a.m. Frank is phoning Liz. Listen and answer the questions.

1 Where is Frank calling from?
2 Is the taxi moving?
3 What are Janet and Danny doing?
4 Where are they having the meeting?
5 What is Frank doing at the end of the phone call?

11 **R9.5** Who signs the contract, do you think – Janet or Frank? Listen and check.

12 **a)** It's now 6.30 p.m. Frank is talking to his wife, Karen, on the phone. Make questions in the Present Continuous.

FRANK Hi! It's me.
KAREN Hello, darling. ¹*you / still / work ?*
Are you still working?
FRANK No, I'm having a drink with Liz. I signed the contract today.
KAREN Oh, that's wonderful! ²*you / have / a nice time ?*
FRANK Yes, thanks. ³*What / you / do ?*
KAREN I'm making dinner.
FRANK ⁴*the kids / do / their homework ?*
KAREN Er ... no, they're not.
FRANK ⁵*What / they / do ?*
KAREN They're watching TV.

b) **R9.6** Listen and check.

c) **R9.7** **P** Listen and practise the questions in 12a).

Are you still working?

Get ready ... Get it right!

13 Work in two groups. Group A → p110. Group B → p118. Follow the instructions.

9B Strike!

Vocabulary transport
Grammar Present Simple or Present Continuous?
Help with Listening linking (2)
Review question forms

QUICK REVIEW ●●●
Write six actions (*get up*, *watch TV*,
etc.). Work in pairs. Take turns to
mime the actions to your partner.
He/She guesses what you are doing.

Vocabulary Transport

1 **a)** Draw pictures of six of these
types of transport. You have
three minutes!

> a car   a plane   a train
> a taxi [US: a cab]   a bus
> a tram   a bike   a scooter
> a boat   a motorbike

b) Work in pairs. Take turns
to show your pictures and say
what the pictures are.

> That's a scooter.

> That's right.

> No, it isn't. It's a bike!

2 **a)** Match phrases 1–6 to a)–f).
Check in **V9.3** p140.

1 go by bike   a) sail
2 go on foot   b) fly
3 go by plane   c) walk
4 go by car   d) drive
5 go by boat   e) cycle
6 go by train/   f) take the train/
  tube/bus   tube/bus

b) Work in groups. Talk about
how you travel:

1 to work/school/university
2 to parties
3 to the centre of your town/city
4 to other places in your country
5 when you're on holiday

> I usually go to work by bus.

> I always drive to work.

The Daily News   50p

TRANSPORT STRIKE TODAY

No buses, trains or tubes for 24 hours

Listening and Grammar

3 **a)** Look at the newspaper headline. What is happening today?

b) **R9.8** Listen to a news report about the strike. Fill in the table.

	how he/she usually gets to work	how he/she is getting to work today
first man		
woman		
second man		

c) Listen again and answer these questions.

1 When did the first man leave home?
2 How long is his journey on a normal day?
3 Why does the woman usually cycle to work?
4 How long is her journey to work on a normal day?
5 Why is the second man walking to work?

Help with Listening Linking (2)

4 **a)** Find the consonant-vowel linking in these sentences.

1 What do you think of the strike?
2 It's about forty minutes, that's all.
3 And it's taking a very long time.
4 Here's someone on a bike.
5 I'm in the centre of the city.
6 The traffic isn't moving at all.

b) **R9.9** Listen to the sentences. Notice the linking.

c) **R9.8** Look at R9.8, p155. Listen again and notice the consonant-vowel linking.

5 **R9.10** **P** Listen and practise the sentences in **4a)**.

*think of → think of the strike →
What do you think of the strike?*

Help with Grammar Present Simple or Present Continuous?

6 **a)** Look at this sentence. Then complete the rules with *Present Simple (PS)* or *Present Continuous (PC)*.

I usually go to work by train, but I'm driving today.

● We use the .... to talk about things that happen every day/week/month, etc.
● We use the .... to talk about things happening now.
● We use *am*, *are* and *is* in .... questions.
● We use *do* and *does* in .... questions.

b) Do we usually use the Present Simple (PS) or the Present Continuous (PC) with these words?

usually *PS*	now	today
sometimes	always	often
normally	at the moment	
never	hardly ever	every day

c) Check in **G9.3** p141.

7 **a)** Read what some other people are doing on the day of the strike. Put the verbs in the Present Simple or Present Continuous.

ELLA I'm a journalist and I ¹ *write* (write) for a national newspaper. I usually ² .... (work) in the city, but today I ³ .... (work) at home because of the strike. At the moment I ⁴ .... (sit) in the garden and writing an article on my laptop. I ⁵ .... (not work) at home very often – but it's much nicer than the office!

ROSE On Thursdays we usually ⁶ .... (drive) into town and ⁷ .... (visit) some friends. But we ⁸ .... (stay) at home today because there are too many cars on the roads. At the moment my husband, Albert, ⁹ .... (answer) his emails and I ¹⁰ .... (watch) tennis on TV. Normally I ¹¹ .... (not watch) TV in the day, but I ¹² .... (enjoy) this match very much.

b) **R9.11** Listen and check your answers.

8 **a)** Make questions about the people in **7a)**.

1 What *does* Ella *do* ? (do)
2 .... she .... in the office today? (work)
3 What .... she .... at the moment? (do)
4 .... she .... at home very often? (work)
5 What .... Albert and Rose usually .... on Thursdays? (do)
6 What .... they .... today? (do)
7 .... Rose normally .... TV in the day? (watch)
8 .... she .... the tennis match? (enjoy)

b) Work in pairs. Take turns to ask and answer the questions.

(What does Ella do?) (She's a journalist.)

Get ready ... Get it right!

9 **a)** Write the names of four people in your family and four friends on a piece of paper.

b) Think what these people are doing at the moment and what they usually do in their free time. Don't write anything.

10 Work in pairs. Swap papers. Ask about your partner's people.

(Who's Alexis?) (What's he doing now, do you think?)

(What does he do in his free time?)

9C On the phone

Real World phone messages; talking on the phone
Help with Listening phone messages
Review *can* for requests and possibility; suggestions

QUICK REVIEW ● ● ●

Write four phone numbers you know. Work in pairs. Take turns to say them to your partner once only. Write your partner's numbers. Check the numbers.

I'll get back to you

1 Emily is at work. Look at 1–3 and answer the questions.

a) What is Chris Morris's job?
b) What type of play is *Say Cheese!*?
c) What is the postcode of Morris Computers?
d) In which month is the conference?
e) How many phone calls does Emily want to make?
f) What is Chris Morris's email address?
g) Who are the actors in *Say Cheese!*?
h) Is Katrina a friend or a customer, do you think?

Help with Listening Phone messages

2 **a)** R9.12 Listen to these phone messages. Fill in the gaps with these words.

~~voicemail~~	person	choose
back	message	press	try

1 Hello, this is Alan Wick's _voicemail_ .
2 If you leave a message, I'll get _____ to you.
3 I'm sorry, but the _____ you called is not available.
4 Please leave your _____ after the tone.
5 Please _____ one of the following three options.
6 For any other enquiries, _____ three.
7 Please _____ later.

b) R9.13 Listen to four messages. For each message, do you:

a) hang up?
b) leave a message?
c) press a number on the phone?

3 **a)** R9.14 Listen and answer these questions.

1 When does Emily want to:
a) meet Alan Wick?
b) meet Katrina?
c) go to the theatre?
2 How much are the theatre tickets?

b) Look at R9.14, p155. Listen again and check your answers.

① 3DUK

Things to do – Mon 16th
phone Chris Morris
check contract
call Alan Wick
check date of Sept conference
call theatre – prices?
phone Katrina – coffee later?

② **Morris Computers Ltd**

Chris Morris
Business Manager

103 Dean St
Manchester
M1 7FT

Tel: 0161 788 4553
email: cmorris@mc.co.uk

Say Cheese!
by Michael Hutton
starring
Jenny Ross and Brian Winter

"This year's best comedy!"
The Manchester News

The King's Theatre, Manchester
Box office: **0800 411 411**

③

(A)

(B)

Can I call you back?

4 **a)** Read conversations 1 and 2. Match them to photos A and B.

b) R9.15 Listen and choose the words/phrases the people say.

1

TIM   Hello, 3DUK. Can I help you?
KATRINA   Hello. ¹*I want to/*(Can I) speak to Emily, please?
TIM   ²*Hold on/Stop* a moment, I'll get her.
EMILY   Hello. Emily Wise.
KATRINA   Hi. ³*It's/I'm* Katrina. I ⁴*got/had* your message.
EMILY   Good. Shall we go for a coffee after work?
KATRINA   Sure. Is six o'clock OK?
EMILY   Yes. Let's meet at Café Uno.
KATRINA   OK. See you there at six. Bye.

2

EMILY   Hello, ⁵*is that/are you* Chris Morris?
CHRIS   ⁶*Speaking./I am.*
EMILY   ⁷*This is/I'm* Emily Wise, from 3DUK.
CHRIS   Hello, Emily. Look, I'm in a meeting now. Can I call you ⁸*back/again*?
EMILY   Of course. If it's after five, call me ⁹*on/by* my mobile.
CHRIS   Right. ¹⁰*I'll call/I'm calling* you later.
EMILY   Thanks a lot. Bye.

c) Listen again and check.

d) Work in pairs. Answer these questions.

1 Which conversation is a:
   a) business call?   b) call between friends?
2 In which conversation do they plan to:
   a) meet?   b) talk later?
3 Who:
   a) is in a meeting? b) works with Emily at 3DUK?

Real World Talking on the phone

5 **a)** Write these headings in the correct places a)–d) in the table.

~~other useful phrases~~   calling people back
saying who you are   asking to speak to people

a)	b)
Hello, can I speak to (Emily), please? Hello, is that (Chris Morris)?	This is (Emily Wise), from (3DUK). It's (Katrina). Speaking.
c)	**d) other useful phrases**
Can I call you back? I'll call you later. Can you call me back?	I got your message. Call me on my mobile. Hold on a moment, I'll get him/her.

b) Check in RW9.1 p141.

6 R9.16 P Listen and practise the sentences in 5a).
Hello, can I speak to Emily, please?

7 **a)** Katrina is making some phone calls. Fill in the gaps with parts of the phrases from 5a).

1

KATRINA   Hello, ¹ *is that* Simon Dale?
SIMON   Speaking.
KATRINA   Hi, Simon. ² _____ Katrina Clark.
SIMON   Oh, hello, Katrina. Look, I can't talk right now. ³ _____ you back?
KATRINA   Yes, of course. ⁴ _____ my mobile.
SIMON   Right. I'll ⁵ _____ later. Bye.

2

KATRINA   Hi, Veronica. ⁶ _____ Katrina.
VERONICA   Hi, Katrina. How are you?
KATRINA   I'm fine, thanks. ⁷ _____ to Rob, please?
VERONICA   ⁸ _____ a moment, I'll get him.
ROB   Hello, Katrina. I ⁹ _____ your message. Let's meet at 8.30 outside the cinema.
KATRINA   OK, see you then. Bye.

b) R9.17 Listen and check.

8 **a)** Work in pairs. Write a phone conversation.

b) Swap conversations with another pair. Practise the new conversation in your pairs. Then role-play it for the pair who wrote it.

9 Work in pairs. Student A → p111. Student B → p119. Follow the instructions.

Vocabulary indoor and outdoor activities; adverbs and adjectives
Review *can/can't*

VOCABULARY IN CONTEXT

QUICK REVIEW ●●●
Work in pairs. Write all the telephone phrases you can remember. Compare with another pair. Which pair has more phrases?

1 a) Tick the words/phrases you know. Then do the exercise in **V9.4** p140.

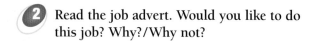

> swim   ski   type   surf   windsurf   sail
> sing   cook   drive   speak another language
> use a computer   ride a horse
> ride a motorbike   play tennis   play chess
> play a musical instrument

b) Work in pairs. Find four things that you can do, but your partner can't do. Use the words/phrases in **1a)** or your own ideas.

(Can you play chess?)   (Yes, I can./No, I can't.)

2 Read the job advert. Would you like to do this job? Why?/Why not?

Group Leaders – The Mayo Adventure Centre

We are looking for people to work as group leaders at our outdoor centre in County Mayo, Ireland. We offer holidays and weekend breaks for adults and teenagers (including school groups from Europe).

We want people who:
● like working with young people
● enjoy doing outdoor activities
● are good at water sports
● can ride and like working with horses
● are good at languages
● have a driving licence
● are friendly and helpful

For an application form
email us at: mayoadventure@iol.ie
Experience and references required.

3 a) Read Melanie's reference. Do you think she's a good person for the job?

b) Read the reference and advert again. Find six reasons why she can do the job.

The Highland Outdoor Centre
**Galloway   DG7 3NQ
Scotland**

Tel: 01644 457899   Fax: 01644 457898
email: h.outdoor@scotweb.com

23rd March 2005

Dear Sir or Madam

Reference: Ms Melanie Simms

I am writing to recommend Melanie for the position of group leader with your company. She worked for our outdoor centre last summer and was a very **hard** worker. She made friends **easily** and was a **popular** group leader with everyone at the centre.

Melanie loves all sports, particularly climbing and mountain biking. She can sail very **well** and is a **good** windsurfer and a **fast** swimmer. She can also play the guitar **beautifully** – the children loved listening to her around the campfire in the evening! She speaks French **fluently** and is an **excellent** driver.

Please contact me by phone or email if you would like any further information.

Yours faithfully

Andrew McCaffrey
Centre Manager

Help with Vocabulary Adverbs and adjectives

4 a) Look at this sentence. Then complete the rules with *adverbs* or *adjectives*.

adverb   adjective
*She speaks French **fluently** and is an **excellent** driver.*

● We use .... to describe nouns. They usually come **before** the noun.
● We use .... to describe verbs. They usually come **after** the verb.

b) Look at the adverbs and adjectives in **bold** in the letter. Which nouns or verbs do they describe?

c) Write the adverbs for these adjectives. What are the spelling rules? Which adverb is irregular?

1 beautiful   2 fluent   3 easy   4 good

d) Check in **V9.5** p140 and look at the other irregular adverbs.

Melanie

5 Write the adverbs.

1 quick *quickly*   5 careful
2 happy   6 hard
3 fast   7 quiet
4 slow   8 bad

6 **a)** Choose the correct words.

1 I'm a (good)/ well tennis player.
2 I usually sleep quite *bad/badly*.
3 I work very *hard/hardly*.
4 I always do my English homework very *careful/carefully*.
5 I'm a *bad/badly* driver.
6 I speak more than one language *fluent/fluently*.
7 I'm a very *well/good* cook.

b) Change the sentences to make them true for you.

I'm not a very good tennis player.
I usually sleep very well.

c) Compare sentences with a partner. How many are the same?

7 **a)** Choose three adjectives or adverbs from **4c)** or **5**. Write a sentence about you for each word. Give the sentences to your teacher.

b) Listen to your teacher read sentences about different students. Can you guess who he/she is talking about?

♫ **R9.18** Look at the song *Dancing in the Street* on p103. Follow the instructions.

---

9 Review   Language Summary 9, p140

1 **a)** Write two words/phrases that go with these verbs. **V9.1**

1 sign   4 answer
   a contract 5 take
2 write   6 work for/in
3 write to   7 go to

b) Work in pairs. Compare your answers.

2 **a)** Draw six pictures of people doing different activities.

b) Work in pairs. Swap pictures. Guess what the people in the pictures are doing. **G9.1**

I think he's dancing.
No, he isn't. He's running!

3 Put the verbs in the correct form of the Present Continuous. **G9.1** **G9.2**

MUM Jim, can you help me?
JIM Sorry, Mum, I'¹ _m_ _doing_ my homework. (do)
MUM What'² ____ your sister _____ ? (do)
JIM She'³ ____ _____ a shower. (have)
MUM And what ⁴_____ Gary and Sam _____ ? (do)
JIM They'⁵____ _____ football. (play). But Dad ⁶_____ _____ anything. (not do)
DAD Yes, I am. I'⁷____ _____ the paper. (read)
MUM Not any more!

4 **a)** Write these travelling verbs/phrases. **V9.3**

1 ylf   _fly_
2 leccy   _____
3 vired   _____
4 lisa   _____
5 kawl   _____
6 kate het ratin _____

b) What is another way to say these verbs/phrases?

fly   go by plane

---

5 **a)** Put the verbs in the Present Simple or Present Continuous. **G9.3**

1 Where _does_ your best friend _work_ or study? (work)
2 What _____ your best friend _____ at the moment? (do)
3 Which TV programmes _____ you _____ every week? (watch)
4 What _____ your parents _____ today, do you think? (do)
5 Where _____ you usually _____ on Friday evenings? (go)
6 What _____ the teacher _____ now? (do)

b) Work in pairs. Take turns to ask and answer the questions.

6 **a)** Write three things you can do quite well and three things you can't do. **V9.4**

b) Compare ideas in groups. Can the other students do the things you can't do?

Progress Portfolio

a) Tick the things you can do in English.

☐ I can talk about things people do at work.
☐ I can describe things that are happening now.
☐ I can talk about types of transport.
☐ I can understand simple phone messages.
☐ I can have a conversation on the phone.
☐ I can talk about things I can and can't do.
☐ I can understand a simple letter.

b) What do you need to study again? ● **9A–D**

77

10 Mind and body

10A A healthy heart

Vocabulary health; *How often …?* and frequency expressions
Grammar imperatives; *should/shouldn't*
Review Present Simple questions

QUICK REVIEW ●●●
Work in groups. Tell other students one thing you: always, usually, often, sometimes, don't often, hardly ever, never do at home.

Vocabulary Health

1 a) Tick the phrases you know. Then do the exercise in Language Summary 10 **V10.1** p142.

do exercise	lose weight	stop smoking
get stressed	get fit	go to the gym
have a heart attack	eat fried food	
drink alcohol	high/low in fat	

b) Which of these phrases match a healthy or unhealthy lifestyle?

c) Work in groups. Do you think you have a healthy or an unheathy lifestyle? Why?

Reading and Grammar

2 a) Work in pairs. Guess the answers to these questions. Don't read the article.

1 Which disease kills more people in Britain: cancer or heart disease?
2 How many adults die of heart disease in Britain every hour?
3 Do women have more heart attacks than men?
4 Where do people have more heart attacks – the UK or Japan?
5 How many grams of salt is it good to eat every day?
6 How many portions of fruit and vegetables is it good to eat every day?
7 Is alcohol always bad for your heart?

b) Read the article and check your answers.

c) Read the article again and find four things that are good for your heart and four that are bad. Does anything in the article surprise you?

TOP TIPS FOR A HEALTHY HEART!

Heart disease kills more people in Britain than any other disease, including cancer. One adult dies every three minutes from heart disease and it's more common in men than women. Age is also important. 80% of people who die of heart attacks are 65 or older. And it's an amazing fact that five times more men die of heart disease in the UK than in Japan. But there are many things you can do to help your heart stay healthy. Here are our top tips for a healthy heart!

- Stop smoking. Everyone knows that cigarettes give you cancer, but they're also very bad for your heart. If you only do one thing to help your heart, do this!

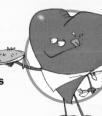

- Do more exercise. Regular exercise (**four times a week** for 30 minutes) is very good for your heart.

- Don't eat a lot of fried food and only eat red meat **once a week**. This type of food is bad for your heart because it's high in fat.

- Eat fish **twice or three times a week**. It's good for your heart because it's low in fat and high in Omega-3 oils.

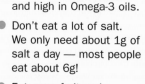
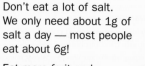

- Don't eat a lot of salt. We only need about 1g of salt a day — most people eat about 6g!

- Eat more fruit and vegetables (at least five portions a day).

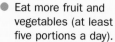

- Lose some weight. Overweight people have more heart attacks!

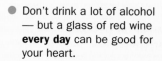
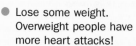

- Don't drink a lot of alcohol — but a glass of red wine **every day** can be good for your heart.

Help with Grammar Imperatives

3 **a)** We often use imperatives to give very strong advice. Look at these sentences and answer the questions.

Stop smoking.   Don't eat a lot of salt.

1 Is the positive imperative the same as the infinitive?
2 How do we make the negative imperative?

b) Check in G10.1 p143.

4 **a)** Write five tips on how to get fit. Use positive and negative imperatives.

Walk to work/school.
Don't sit and watch TV every night.

b) Work in groups of three. Compare sentences and choose your top five tips. Tell the class what they are.

Help with Vocabulary *How often …?* and frequency expressions

5 **a)** Look at the frequency expressions in **bold** in the article. Then fill in the gaps.

once	a day		....
....	a	every	week
three times	a month		month
four times	a year		year

b) We use *How often …?* to ask about frequency. Make questions with these words.

1 do / How often / go / you / to the theatre ?
2 your brother / does / How often / phone you ?
3 did / visit / you / your grandfather / How often ?

c) Check in V10.2 p142.

6 **a)** Work in pairs. Ask your partner how often he/she does these things.

How often do you eat red meat?   About twice a week.

1 eat red meat
2 do some exercise
3 get very stressed
4 go on holiday
5 eat fish
6 drink more than one glass of alcohol
7 have less than six hours' sleep

b) Who has a healthier lifestyle – you or your partner? Why?

Listening and Grammar

7 **a)** R10.1 Listen to Mr Taylor at the doctor's. Is he healthy, do you think? Why?/ Why not?

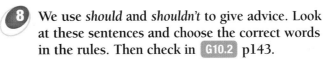

b) Listen again and answer the questions.

1 How much does he weigh?
2 How often does he do exercise?
3 How often does he eat red meat?
4 When did he stop smoking?
5 How often does he drink alcohol?
6 What advice does the doctor give him?

Help with Grammar *should/shouldn't*

8 We use *should* and *shouldn't* to give advice. Look at these sentences and choose the correct words in the rules. Then check in G10.2 p143.

You shouldn't eat so much red meat.
And you should do more exercise.

- We use *should* to say something is a *good/bad* thing to do.
- We use *shouldn't* to say something is a *good/bad* thing to do.
- After *should* and *shouldn't* we use the *infinitive/infinitive with to*.

9 **a)** The doctor gave Mr Taylor more advice. Fill in the gaps with *should* or *shouldn't*.

1 You .... eat salad more often.
2 You .... eat so many pizzas.
3 You .... go to a gym twice a week.
4 You .... get too stressed at work.
5 You .... try to lose some weight.
6 You .... walk to work every day.

b) R10.2 P Listen and practise.

You should eat salad more often.

c) Write three more pieces of advice for Mr Taylor. Compare sentences in pairs.

Get ready … Get it right!

10 Work in groups of three. Student A → p106. Student B → p114. Student C → p120. Follow the instructions.

What's he like?

Vocabulary describing people's appearance and character
Grammar questions with *like*
Help with Listening sentence stress (3)
Review clothes; free time activities

QUICK REVIEW ●●●
Work in pairs. Write all the words for clothes you know. What clothes are you wearing today?

Vocabulary Appearance

1 a) Look at photos 1–4 for two minutes. Remember the people and their clothes!

b) Work in pairs. Close your book. Say what the people are wearing.

2 a) Work in pairs. Tick the words you know. Check new words in V10.3 p142.

A

young   middle-aged   old
tall   short
fat   overweight   thin   slim
beautiful   good-looking   attractive
white   black   Asian
bald

B

blue/brown/green eyes
long/short hair
dark/fair/blonde/grey hair
a beard   a moustache

---

b) Which group of words do you use with *have got*? Which do you use with *be*?

3 a) Write a description of one person in photos 1–4. Don't write his/her name.

b) Work in pairs. Read your partner's description. Who is it? Are there any mistakes?

4 a) R10.3 Tina and Leo want someone for a poster to advertise *Break*, a new chocolate bar. Listen and put the people they talk about in order.

b) Listen again. Make notes on the people's good points and bad points.

c) Work in pairs. Compare your answers. Who do Tina and Leo choose, do you think? Why?

d) R10.4 Listen to the end of the conversation. Who did they choose? Why?

Help with Listening Sentence stress (3)

5 a) Look at the beginning of the conversation. Remember: we stress the important words.

OK, Leo. I've got four people for the Break poster. See what you think.

b) R10.3 Look at R10.3, p156. Listen again and notice the sentence stress.

① Jake
② Lily
③ Pete
④ Zoë

Vocabulary Character

6 **a)** Tick the sentences that are true for you.

1 I like giving people money and presents.
2 It's difficult for me to talk to new people.
3 I don't like working and I watch TV all day.
4 I like doing things to help other people.
5 I make people laugh a lot.
6 I usually think about myself, not other people.
7 I'm friendly and I like meeting new people.
8 When I promise to do something, I always do it.

b) Work in pairs. Compare your answers. How many are the same?

7 Match these words to one of the sentences in **6a)**. Check in V10.4 p142.

> generous *1*   kind   funny   selfish
> outgoing   shy   lazy   reliable

8 Work in groups. Use the adjectives in **7** to describe members of your family.

> My brother is quite shy.

> My father is very kind and generous.

Listening and Grammar

9 R10.5 Tina asks Leo about his new girlfriend. Listen and match questions 1–3 to answers a)–c). Who is Leo's girlfriend?

1 What's she like?
2 What does she like doing?
3 What does she look like?

a) She's tall and slim, and she's got long dark hair.
b) She likes dancing and going to restaurants.
c) She's really friendly and outgoing. And she's very beautiful.

Help with Grammar Questions with *like*

10 **a)** Complete the rules with questions 1–3 in **9**.

● We use .... to ask for a general description. The answer can include character and physical appearance.
● We use .... to ask about physical appearance only.
● We use .... to ask about people's likes and free time interests.

TIP! ● *How is he/she?* asks about health, not personality. Example answer: *She's fine, thanks.*

b) Check in G10.3 p143.

---

11 **a)** Write the questions for these answers.

1 She's tall, attractive and very friendly. *What's she like?*
2 She's quite short and has got dark hair.
3 He's selfish and lazy, but really good-looking!
4 She likes gardening and cycling.
5 He's not very tall and he's bald.
6 They're both quite shy.

b) R10.6 P Listen and check. Then listen again and practise.

What's she like?

Get ready ... Get it right!

12 Write the names of four friends on a piece of paper. Think how you can describe their character, appearance and the things they like doing. Don't write this information.

13 **a)** Work in pairs and swap papers. Take turns to ask and answer the questions in **9** about your partner's friends.

b) Choose one of your partner's friends that you would like to meet. Tell the class why you chose that person.

Real World talking about health; giving advice with *Why don't you ...?*
Vocabulary health problems and treatment
Help with Listening being sympathetic
Review *have got*; imperatives; *should/shouldn't*

QUICK REVIEW ●●●
Think of three famous people. Work in pairs. Take turns to describe the people but don't say their names. You can talk about their appearance, character, job, age, nationality, etc. Guess your partner's people.

What's the matter?

1 **a)** Match the sentences to the people.

1 I've got a stomach ache. *B*
2 I've got a cold.
3 My back hurts.
4 I feel sick.
5 I've got a cough.
6 My arm hurts.

b) R10.7 Listen and check.

2 **a)** Work in pairs. Fill in the table with these words. Check in V10.5 p142.

~~back~~	~~ill~~	~~a stomach ache~~	terrible	arm	foot
a temperature	a headache	leg	a toothache
a sore throat	a cold	sick	better	a cough

I've got	*a stomach ache*		
I feel	*ill*		
My ... hurts.	*back*		

b) R10.8 P Listen and practise.

c) Work in pairs. Take turns to test your partner.

(a cough) (I've got a cough.) (sick) (I feel sick.)

Get better soon!

3 **a)** Match these phrases to the verbs. Check in V10.6 p143.

~~to bed~~	~~at home~~	~~the day off~~	some painkillers
home	to the doctor	some cough medicine
in bed	to the dentist	some antibiotics

go *to bed*   stay *at home*   take *the day off*

b) Work in groups. Look at the words in **2a)** again. What do you usually do when you are ill?

(When I've got a cold I normally stay in bed.)

 (I usually take some aspirin.)

4 **a)** Read the conversations and match them to photos A and B. Then fill in the gaps with the words in the boxes.

1

can't	stomach	wrong	dear	how

A Hi, Diana, ¹_____ are you?
B I'm not very well.
A Oh, what's ²_____ ?
B I've got a bad ³_____ ache.
A That's a shame. **Why don't you go home?**
B I ⁴_____ . I've got a meeting this afternoon.
A Oh, ⁵_____ . **I hope you get better soon.**
B Thanks. See you later.

2

headache	terrible	throat	drink	should

A Hello, Gerry. Are you OK?
B No, I feel ⁶_____ .
A Oh, dear. **What's the matter?**
B I've got a ⁷_____ and a sore ⁸_____ .
A You ⁹_____ take the day off and go to bed.
B Yes, good idea.
A And ¹⁰_____ lots of water.
B OK. See you tomorrow, maybe.

b) R10.9 Listen and check.

Real World Talking about health

5 **a)** Fill in the gaps in the table with the sentences in **bold** in **4a)**.

asking about someone's health	expressing sympathy	giving advice
How are you?	Oh, dear.	_____
Are you OK?	That's a shame.	You should take the day off.
What's wrong?	_____	Drink lots of water.
_____		

b) Check in RW10.1 p143.

Help with Listening Being sympathetic

6 R10.10 Listen. Which sounds sympathetic, a) or b)?

1 What's wrong?   (a)   b)
2 What's the matter?   a)   b)
3 Oh, dear.   a)   b)
4 That's a shame.   a)   b)
5 Why don't you go home?   a)   b)
6 You should take the day off. a)   b)

7 R10.11 P Listen and practise the sentences in **5a)**. Copy the intonation.
How are you?

8 **a)** Work in pairs. Choose conversation 1 or 2 from **4a)**. Practise the conversation until you can remember it.

b) Close your book. Practise the conversation again.

9 **a)** Choose an illness from **2a)**. Have conversations with other students. Be sympathetic and give advice.

Hi, how are you?

I'm not very well.

Oh, dear. What's wrong?

I've got ... /I feel ... /My ... hurts.

Why don't you ...?/You should ...

b) Tell the class your illness. What advice did students give you? Was it good advice, do you think?

10D Are you SAD in winter?

QUICK REVIEW ●●●
Work in pairs. Take turns to mime illnesses to your partner.
Don't speak! He/She guesses what's wrong and gives advice.

a) Put the seasons in order. Then check in V10.7 p143.

> winter   summer
> autumn [US: fall]   spring *1*

b) Look at photos 1 and 2. Which seasons are they, do you think?

a) Read the first paragraph of the article. Why does the woman in photo 1 have a light on her desk?

b) Read the whole article. Answer these questions.

1 How did Herb Kern feel in summer/winter?
2 What did the scientists make for him?
3 In which countries is SAD quite common?
4 Why do people get SAD?
5 Do men get SAD more often than women?
6 How do you know if people have SAD?
7 How long should you use a light box a day?

c) Work in pairs. Check your answers.

Work in groups. Discuss these questions.

1 Do you feel depressed in winter? Why?/Why not?
2 What activities do you usually do in winter?
3 Which is your favourite season? Why?

If you're SAD, see the light!

Many people feel depressed in winter – and now scientists think they know why.

In the 1970s, an American engineer called Herb Kern noticed that in spring and summer he was happy and had a lot of energy, but every winter he became depressed and lazy. He thought it was because there wasn't much daylight in the winter and asked some scientists to make a 'light box'. He put the box on his desk and after a few days he felt a lot better. In 1982 the scientists gave his illness a name – Seasonal Affective Disorder, or SAD.

In the USA about 6–20% of people have SAD and it is common in other countries like the UK and Sweden. People get SAD in autumn and winter, when the days are shorter and there is less daylight. It is more common in women than in men. People with SAD usually sleep a lot and feel tired all the time. They also eat a lot of sweet food and feel depressed. The answer is bright light. People with SAD should use a light box for half an hour a day. Or you can go on holiday to a sunny country, of course!

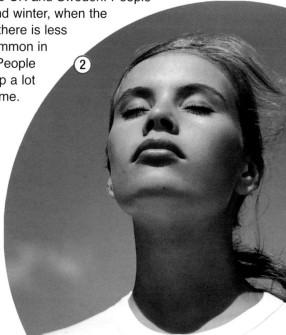

4 a) Tick the words you know. Then do the exercise in **V10.8** p143.

> What's the weather like?

> It's ...

hot	warm	cold	wet	dry
raining	snowing	windy		
cloudy	sunny	34° (degrees)		

b) What's the weather like today?

5 Work in pairs. Student A → p109. Student B → p117. Follow the instructions.

Help with Vocabulary
Word building

6 a) Look at the table. How do we make the adjectives from the nouns? Then fill in the gaps.

noun	adjective	verb
rain	rainy	
	snowy	snow
wind		–
	cloudy	–
sun		–

b) Check in **V10.9** p143.

7 a) Choose the correct words.

1 It *rainy/rained* a lot last night.
2 It's a beautiful *sun/sunny* day.
3 There's usually a lot of *snow/snowy* in January.
4 It was very *wind/windy* last weekend.
5 It's *cloud/cloudy* today.
6 Look – it's *rainy/raining* again!

b) Make the sentences true for where you are living now. Compare sentences with a partner.

It was really cold last night.

10 Review

Language Summary 10, p142

1 a) Match the verbs in A to the words/phrases in B. **V10.1**

A	B
do	stressed
eat	exercise
drink	fried food
get	alcohol
lose	smoking
stop	to the gym
get	fit
go	weight

b) Choose four phrases that you do now, or did in the past.

c) Work in groups. Discuss why you chose your phrases.

2 Work in pairs. Take turns to ask your partner how often he/she does these things. **V10.2**

1 eat out
2 get up late
3 go to the theatre
4 check your email
5 watch sport on TV
6 go to parties

3 a) Write two pieces of advice for these people. **G10.2**

1 Ana can't get up in the morning.
Ana should go to bed earlier.
2 Gail is tired all the time.
3 Rob can't remember people's names.

b) Work in groups. Compare your advice. Which is the best advice for each person?

4 a) Do these words describe appearance (A) or character (C)? **V10.3** **V10.4**

beautiful *A*	generous *C*	
overweight	good-looking	
attractive	funny	selfish
lazy	reliable	slim
outgoing	bald	short

b) Work in pairs. Where is the stress on these words?

beautiful

5 a) Make questions with these words. **G10.3**

1 Who / Joe / is ? *Who is Joe?*
2 like / What / look / he / does ?
3 doing / he / like / does / What ?
4 he / 's / like / What ?

b) Match questions 1–4 with answers a)–d).

a) He likes travelling.
b) He's very kind and quite shy.
c) He's my brother.
d) He's tall and he's got fair hair.

c) Write the names of three of your friends.

d) Work in pairs. Take turns to ask the questions in 5a) about your partner's friends.

6 a) Cover the words in **1** p84 and **4** p85. Then add words to these groups. **V10.5** **V10.7** **V10.8**

1 health problems *a cold*
2 parts of the body *leg*
3 seasons *summer*
4 weather adjectives *hot*

b) Work in groups and compare lists. Who has got the most words?

Progress Portfolio

a) Tick the things you can do in English.

☐ I can say how often I do things.
☐ I can ask for and give advice.
☐ I can talk about people's appearance and character.
☐ I can say what's wrong when I'm ill.
☐ I can express sympathy.
☐ I can talk about the weather.

b) What do you need to study again? **● 10A–D**

11 Future plans

11A New Year's resolutions

Vocabulary
verb collocations
Grammar *be going to* (1):
positive, negative and
Wh- questions
Review weather

QUICK REVIEW ●●●
Work in groups. Talk about a country you know (not your own). What's the weather like in January/April/July/October? When is the best time to visit? Why?

Jack   Meg

Vocabulary Verb collocations

1 Work in pairs. Discuss these questions.

1 How do people in your country celebrate New Year?
2 What did you do last New Year?
3 Do people in your country make New Year's resolutions? If yes, what kind?

2 Tick the phrases you know in box A. Then match the words/phrases in box B with the verbs in **bold**. There is one word/phrase for each verb. Check in Language Summary 11 V11.1 p144.

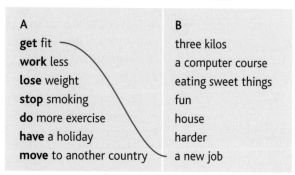

A	B
get fit	three kilos
work less	a computer course
lose weight	eating sweet things
stop smoking	fun
do more exercise	house
have a holiday	harder
move to another country	a new job

Listening and Grammar

3 R11.1 Look at the picture of a New Year's Eve party. Listen to two conversations and match the people to their New Year's resolutions A–E.

4 a) Look at the people's New Year's resolutions. Fill in the gaps with words from 2.

1 I'm going to work __less__ and have more __fun__ .
2 And I'm going to have a _____ this year.
3 I'm going to _____ to Australia.
4 I'm going to do a _____ .
5 We're going to get _____ and Val's going to stop _____ .
6 And David's going to _____ weight.
7 I'm going to do more _____ .
8 I'm not going to eat _____ any more.

b) R11.1 Listen again and check.

Help with Grammar
be going to: positive and negative

5 a) Look at the sentences in 4a). Then choose the correct words in the rules.

● These sentences talk about the *present/future/past*.
● The people decided to do these things *before/when* they said them.
● We use *be going to* + infinitive for *future plans/things we do every day*.

b) Look at the sentences in the table. Then write sentences 7 and 8 from 4a) in the table.

subject	auxiliary (+ *not*)	*going to*	infinitive	
We	're (are)	going to	get	fit.
Val	's (is)	going to	stop	smoking.

c) Check in G11.1 p145.

6 R11.2 P Listen and practise.

I'm going to /ɡəʊɪŋtə/ *work less and have more fun.*

HAPPY NEW YEAR!

Val   David   Ed

Help with Grammar *be going to*: *Wh-* questions

9

a) Look at the question in the table. Then write the other two questions from email 2 in the table.

question word	auxiliary	subject	*going to*	infinitive	
What	are	you	going to	do	all day?

b) Check in **G11.2** p145.

10

a) Make questions with *you* and *going to*.

1 What / do after class ?
   What are you going to do after class?
2 How / get home today ?
3 What / do next weekend ?
4 What / have for dinner tonight ?
5 Where / have lunch tomorrow ?
6 When / do your English homework ?

b) **R11.3** **P** Listen and practise the questions in **10a**).

c) Work in groups. Take turns to ask and answer the questions in **10a**).

Get ready ... Get it right!

11
What are you going to do in the future? Write at least three things about: next week, next month and next year. Use the phrases in **2** or your own ideas.

12
a) Work in groups of four. Take turns to ask and answer questions about your plans. Are your plans the same or different?

What are you going to do next week?

b) Tell the class about people with the same plans as you.

7

a) Fill in the gaps with the correct form of *be going to* and the verb in brackets.

1 I *'m going to look for* a new job soon. (look for)
2 He _____ any fried food. (not/eat)
3 She _____ her house. (sell)
4 They _____ to a gym. (go)
5 I _____ any cigarettes. (not/buy)
6 He _____ a lot. (study)

b) Work in pairs. Match the sentences to the people at the party.

I think Ed's going to look for a new job soon.

8

a) Read email 1 from Jack to Meg after the party. Why is Jack sending this photo to her?

b) Read email 2. Find three questions.

c) Read email 3. Find Jack's answers.

1

Meg, have a look at this picture! This is where I'm going on holiday. What do you think?

Jack

2

Hi Jack

It looks amazing! But what are you going to do all day? There's nothing there! And where are you going to stay? I can't see any hotels. And what are you going to eat?!

Meg

3

Hi Meg

Don't worry about me. I'm going to stay in a small house by the beach and there's one restaurant on the island. They say it only has fish, but that's OK. I love fish. And I'm not going to do any work – I'm going to sit on the beach and read lots of books.
See you when I get back!

Jack

 **No more exams!**

Vocabulary studying
Grammar *might*; *be going to* (2):
yes/no questions and short answers
Help with Listening *going to*
Review *be going to*: positive,
negative and *Wh-* questions

QUICK REVIEW ● ● ●
Work in pairs. Take turns to say three things you're going to do tomorrow evening, and three things you aren't going to do. Are you going to do the same things?

Tim　　　Debbie　　Sid　　Clare

Vocabulary Studying

1 Fill in the gaps with these words/phrases. Then check in **V11.2** p144.

start	revise for	take	go to	a qualification
pass	fail	leave	a degree	a job

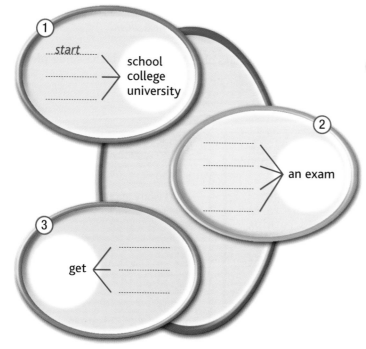

① ....start.....
→ school
college
university

② ------
-----→ an exam
------

③ get ←------
------

2 Work in groups. Discuss these questions.
1 Which things in **1** do people usually celebrate?
2 What was the last exam you took? Was it difficult?
3 Did you celebrate when you finished? If yes, what did you do?

Listening and Grammar

3 a) **R11.4** Listen to Tim, Debbie and Sid talking after their final university exam. Tick the things they talk about.

a job	a drink	a concert
a party	a club	a video	a film

b) Listen again and tick the true sentences.
1 The exam was quite easy.
2 Tim is sure that he's going to Jane's party.
3 Debbie wants to go home and sleep.
4 Debbie's going to meet her boyfriend, Tony, in town later.
5 Debbie and Tony are sure that they're going to a club.
6 Sid and Clare are sure they're going to the cinema.

Help with Grammar *might or be going to*

4 **a)** Look at these sentences. Then choose the correct words in the rules.

I might go for a drink with Peter, or I might go to Jane's party.
I'm going to meet Tony in town.

- We use *might/be going to* to say a future plan is **decided**.
- We use *might/be going to* to say something in the future is **possible**, but **not decided**.
- After *might* we use the *infinitive/infinitive with to*.

b) Check in G11.3 p145.

5 R11.5 P Listen and practise.

I might gŏ for a drink with Pĕter.

6 Fill in the gaps with the correct form of *be going to* or *might* and the verb in brackets.
(✓) = decided, (✓✗) = not decided.

TIM

1 (✓) I .... (not do) another course next year.
2 (✓✗) My brother and I .... (go) to France for a couple of weeks.
3 (✓) I .... (not work) in the family business.

DEBBIE

4 (✓✗) I .... (get) a job in Italy.
5 (✓) I .... (do) a Spanish course.
6 (✓✗) Tony and I .... (get) married next year.

7 **a)** Write three things you might do and two things you're going to do next year.

b) Work in pairs. Take turns to say your sentences. Are any of your sentences the same?

Help with Listening *going to*

8 **a)** R11.6 Listen and notice the two different ways we say *going to*. Both are correct.

I'm going to /gəʊɪŋtə/ meet Tony in town.
What are you going to /gənə/ do this evening?

b) R11.7 Listen to these sentences. Which way do these people say *going to*, a) or b)?

	/gəʊɪŋtə/	/gənə/
1 Are you going to get a job?	a)	(b)
2 I'm going to study law.	a)	b)
3 We're going to talk to the bank.	a)	b)
4 Are you going to stay here?	a)	b)
5 I'm going to get a job.	a)	b)
6 I'm going to sell my car.	a)	b)

9 R11.8 Listen to Tim talking to Sid and Clare about their plans. Answer the questions.

1 Are Sid and Clare going to study in the UK?
2 Are they going to study the same thing?
3 Is Tim going to stay in the UK?
4 Is he going to do another course?
5 Is Sid going to sell his car?

Help with Grammar *be going to*: *yes/no* questions and short answers

10 **a)** Fill in the gaps with part of the verb *be*.

1 A .... you going to get a job?
  B Yes, I ..../No, I .... not.

2 A .... he going to sell his car?
  B Yes, he ..../No, he ....

3 A .... they going to study in the UK?
  B Yes, they ..../No, they ....

b) Check in G11.4 p145.

11 Work in pairs. Student A → p107.
Student B → p115. Follow the instructions.

Get ready ... Get it right!

12 Look at these possible plans. Make *yes/no* questions with *you*.

Find someone who is going to:
- meet a friend after class
  Are you going to meet a friend after class?
- work next weekend
- study tonight
- stay at home tomorrow
- go away next weekend
- have a holiday in the next three months
- watch a video or DVD this evening
- buy some clothes next weekend
- take an exam this year

13 **a)** Ask other students your questions. Find one person who is going to do each thing. Then ask two follow-up questions.

b) Tell the class about another student's plans.

Real World asking for and giving directions
Vocabulary prepositions of place and movement
Review rooms in a house; places in a town; imperatives

QUICK REVIEW ● ● ●
Write a list of places you can find in a town or city (*museum*, *station*, etc.). Work in pairs and compare lists. How many of these places are near where you are now?

Choosing a holiday home

1 a) Read the adverts for holiday homes in Seaton. Which place is better for Sue's family, do you think? Why?

Sue Daniels and her family

Craven Holiday Homes

Hill Place
SEATON
- Three bedrooms. Sleeps up to 5 people.
- Living room with TV and DVD player.
- Fully equipped kitchen with dining area.
- Shower room and separate toilet.
- Small garden.
- 5 minute walk to town centre.
- 10 minute walk to beach.
- From £280 per week.

Benton House
SEATON
- Three bedrooms. Sleeps up to 6 people.
- Small living room with TV.
- Large fully equipped kitchen with dining area.
- Bathroom and separate shower.
- 10 minute walk to town centre.
- 1 minute from the beach.
- From £360 per week.

For more details call
01834 654389

b) Work in groups. Say which holiday home you chose and why. Do you agree?

2 R11.9 Listen to Sue phone Craven Holiday Homes. When is the family's holiday? Which place does she choose? Why?

Directions

3 Tick the phrases you know. Then do the exercise in RW11.1 p145.

turn right   turn left   go over the bridge
go past the pub   go along this street
it's on the/your left   it's on the/your right
it's opposite   it's next to

4 a) Look at the map on page 91 and read the email. Draw the route from *You are here* to the holiday home.

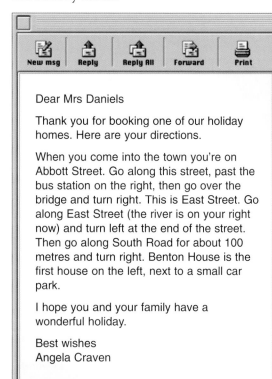

New msg   Reply   Reply All   Forward   Print

Dear Mrs Daniels

Thank you for booking one of our holiday homes. Here are your directions.

When you come into the town you're on Abbott Street. Go along this street, past the bus station on the right, then go over the bridge and turn right. This is East Street. Go along East Street (the river is on your right now) and turn left at the end of the street. Then go along South Road for about 100 metres and turn right. Benton House is the first house on the left, next to a small car park.

I hope you and your family have a wonderful holiday.

Best wishes
Angela Craven

b) Work in pairs. Check your route. Which number is the holiday home on the map?

5 R11.10 Look at the map and listen. Start at *You are here*. Which four places do the directions take you to?

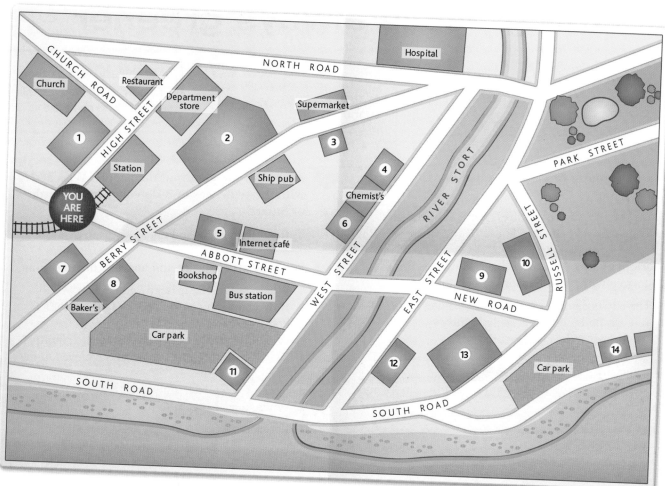

6 **a)** Sue is now at the bus station. She is asking for directions. Put each conversation in order.

1

SUE ☐ Where's that?

MAN ☐ Yes, there's one in Berry Street.

SUE ☐ Thanks very much.

SUE [1] Excuse me. Is there a newsagent's near here?

MAN ☐ Go along this road and turn right. That's Berry Street. Go past the pub and the newsagent's is on the right, opposite the supermarket.

2

SUE ☐ Oh yes, I can see it. Thanks.

SUE ☐ Excuse me. Where's the police station?

GIRL ☐ No problem.

GIRL ☐ It's over there, next to the Internet café.

3

MAN ☐ Yes. You go along this street, over the bridge and it's on your left, in New Road. You can't miss it.

SUE ☐ Great. Thanks a lot.

SUE ☐ How far is it?

MAN ☐ Oh, it's not far. Only about five minutes' walk.

SUE ☐ Excuse me. Do you know the Park Hotel?

b) R11.11 Listen and check. Find the places on the map. What numbers are they?

Real World Asking for and giving directions

7 **a)** Read conversations 1–3 in **6a)**. Fill in the gaps.

ASKING FOR DIRECTIONS

Excuse me. Is .... (a newsagent's) near here?

............'s (the police station)?

Do you .... (the Park Hotel)?

GIVING DIRECTIONS

There's .... in (Berry Street).

Go .... this road and turn right/left.

Go .... the pub.

Go .... the bridge.

(The newsagent's) is .... the/your right/left.

It's .... (the supermarket).

It's .... to (the Internet café).

It's .... there.

You can't .... it.

b) Check in RW11.2 p145.

8 R11.12 **P** Listen and practise the sentences in **7a)**.

Excuse me. Is there a newsagent's near here?

9 Work in pairs. Student A → p104.
Student B → p112. Follow the instructions.

VOCABULARY IN CONTEXT

QUICK REVIEW ● ● ●

Work in pairs. Write five places near where you are now that you both know. Take turns to give directions to two of the places. Your partner guesses the place. Start with: *Go out of the building and …*

Vocabulary verb patterns
Review comparatives; things you like and don't like

1 Work in groups. Discuss these questions.

1 Do you live in a city or in the country?
2 Do you like where you live? Why?/Why not?
3 Would you like to move house? If yes, where to? Why?

2 Work in groups. Which of these sentences do you agree with? Give reasons if possible.

1 The city is dangerous for young people.
2 You can find jobs more easily in the city.
3 It's cheaper to live in the country.
4 Life in the country is easier.
5 Transport is better in the city.
6 The cost of living in the country and the city is the same.

3 **a)** Look at the photos of the people. Who agrees with the sentences in **2**, do you think – Matthew or Stuart?

b) Read the article and check your answers.

4 Read the article again and answer the questions.

1 Where are the Lane family going to move to?
2 How many days a week does Matthew see his children?
3 Do all the family want to move to the country?
4 Did Stuart find a job easily when he moved to the city?
5 Has he got a car?
6 Does he sleep well, do you think?
7 Where does he want to live in the future?

Time for a change!

THEY SAY that the grass is always greener on the other side of the fence. But can moving house really solve your problems?

We asked two people from different parts of the UK why they decided to try a new way of life.

Stuart Reed

Matthew Lane and his family

Matthew Lane

We're going to sell our house in the city and move to a beautiful village in the mountains – I've got a job as a National Park manager there. We want an easier life and I want to spend more time with my family. I really enjoy spending time with my children, but I only see them on Sundays at the moment. I work six days a week because you need a lot of money to live in a city – everything's very expensive here. But the kids aren't very happy about moving. They love living in the city, but my wife and I think the country is safer for them. Of course, teenagers like going out on their own, but it can be quite dangerous around here, especially at night.

Stuart Reed

I moved to the city because I needed to get a job. There were no jobs for me in the country, but when I moved here I found one in the first week. People say it's more expensive in the city, but you don't need a car here and cars are very expensive. I live in an old part of the city and I can walk to work or go by tube. So I think generally the cost of living is about the same. But I'd like to go back to the country one day. Sometimes I hate living here – it's dirty, crowded and really noisy at night. When I'm old, I'd love to have a little place somewhere by the sea where it's really quiet.

Help with Vocabulary
Verb patterns

5 **a)** Look at these sentences. What comes after *want*? What comes after *love*?

*I **want** to spend more time with my family.*
*They **love** living in the city.*

b) Find these verbs in the article. What comes after them? Write the verbs in the correct column in the table.

need	would like	hate
would love	enjoy	like

+ infinitive with *to*	+ verb+*ing*
want	love

c) Check in **V11.3** p144.

6 **a)** Fill in the gaps with the correct form of these verbs.

buy	be	study	read
watch	find	go	

1 I need *to buy* some new clothes.
2 I like _____ newspapers.
3 I hate _____ football on TV.
4 I want _____ a new job.
5 I enjoy _____ languages.
6 I love _____ to the cinema.
7 I'd like _____ famous!

b) Make questions with *you* from the sentences in **6a)**. Then make two more questions of your own.

Do you need to buy some new clothes?

c) Work in pairs. Take turns to ask and answer the questions.

♫ **R11.13** Look at the song *Chapel of Love* on p103. Follow the instructions.

11 Review   Language Summary 11, p144

1 **a)** Fill in the gaps with the verbs in the box. **V11.1**

~~do~~	lose	stop	work
move	have	get	

1 __*do*__ more exercise/ a language course
2 _____ fit/a new job
3 _____ house/ to another country
4 _____ more fun/a holiday
5 _____ less/harder
6 _____ smoking/ eating chocolate
7 _____ weight/five kilos

b) Tick three things that you want to do in the future.

c) Work in groups. Compare your ideas. How many people want to do the same thing as you?

2 **a)** Make questions with these words. **G11.2**

1 going to / you / tomorrow evening / are / do / What ?
What are you going to do tomorrow evening?
2 next year / a holiday / have / you / Are / going to ?
3 you / tomorrow afternoon / be / are / going to / Where ?
4 do / after class / going to / What / you / are ?
5 Are / study / going to / you / next year / English ?

b) Work in pairs. Take turns to ask and answer the questions in **2a)**.

3 **a)** Write three things you're going to do and three things you might do next weekend. **G11.3**

I'm going to visit friends.
I might rent a DVD.

b) Work in groups. Compare your sentences.

4 **a)** Draw pictures of five of these phrases on a piece of paper. Don't write the phrase. **RW11.1**

turn right	turn left
go over	go past	go along
on the left	on the right
opposite	next to

b) Work in pairs. Swap papers. Guess your partner's phrases.

5 **a)** Put the verbs in brackets in the correct form: infinitive with *to* or verb+*ing*. **V11.3**

1 I want *to buy* (buy) a car.
2 I love _____ (eat) out.
3 I hate _____ (take) exams.
4 I'd love _____ (live) in the USA.
5 I don't like _____ (drive).
6 I need _____ (get up) early tomorrow.
7 I'd like _____ (be) a teacher.
8 I enjoy _____ (study) English!

b) Tick the sentences that are true for you.

c) Work in groups. How many of your sentences are the same?

Progress Portfolio

a) Tick the things you can do in English.

☐ I can talk about future plans that are decided or possible.

☐ I can ask other people about their plans.

☐ I can talk about exams and studying.

☐ I can find information in holiday adverts.

☐ I can ask for, give and understand directions in the street.

☐ I can understand a simple magazine article.

b) What do you need to study again? ⊙ **11A–D**

12 Life experiences

12A World records

QUICK REVIEW ●●●
Write something you: love doing, want to do tomorrow, need to do when you get home, enjoy doing, hate doing, are going to do tonight. Work in pairs and compare answers. How many are the same?

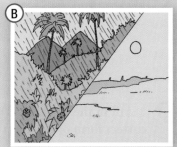

Vocabulary
Big and small numbers

1 Match the numbers to the words. Then check in Language Summary 12 **V12.1** p146.

0.6	1,000,000	3.25
2,300	45,270	156
650,000	70,000,000	

1 nought point six   *0.6*
2 three point two five
3 a hundred and fifty-six
4 two thousand, three hundred
5 forty-five thousand, two hundred and seventy
6 six hundred and fifty thousand
7 a million
8 seventy million

2 **R12.1** Listen and write the numbers. Check your answers in pairs.

Reading and Grammar

3 Read the article. Match the world records 1–5 to pictures A–E.

4 a) Read the article again. Fill in the gaps a)–h) with these prices and numbers.

£12,300	$120,000	335
85	£44,007	11.68
82	0.01	

b) **R12.2** Listen and check.

c) Which record is the most interesting or surprising, do you think?

Record breakers

1 A Mexican couple, Octavio Guillén and Adriana Martínez, had the longest engagement in the world. They got engaged in 1902 – and got married in 1969. They were both a)_____ years old on their wedding day.

2 The wettest place in the world is probably Mount Wai'ale'ale, in Hawaii. It rains b)_____ days a year, with an average rainfall of c)_____ m a year. And the world's driest place is the Atacama Desert in Chile. It only gets d)_____ cm of rain a year.

3 The earliest computer game was called *Spacewar*. A group of American students wrote it in 1960 for a computer called PDP-1. This computer cost e)_____ – and there were only fifty in the world.

4 The most boring film in the world is probably *A Cure for Insomnia*, directed by John Henry Timmis IV of Chicago. It's f)_____ hours long and is also the world's longest film.

5 In July 2001, six businessmen spent g)_____ at the Petrus Restaurant in London, making this the world's most expensive meal per person. Most of the bill was for the five bottles of wine they drank – the best bottle cost h)_____ . The restaurant didn't ask them to pay for the food!

Help with Grammar
Superlatives

5 **a)** Fill in the table with superlatives from the article.

adjective	comparative	superlative
long	longer	*longest*
wet	wetter	
early	earlier	
boring	more boring	
expensive	more expensive	
good	better	
bad	worse	*worst*

b) Complete the rules with *comparatives* or *superlatives*.

● We use .... to compare three or more things.
● We use .... to compare two things.

c) Work in pairs. Look at the words in **5a)** again. What are the rules for making superlatives? (Think about spelling and the number of syllables.)

d) Check in **G12.1** p146 and read the **TIPS!**.

6 **a)** Write the superlatives.

1	rich *richest*	7	safe
2	difficult	8	crowded
3	thin	9	friendly
4	happy	10	beautiful
5	hot	11	bad
6	modern	12	good

b) **R12.3** **P** Listen and practise the superlative adjectives in **6a)**.

richest
　/ɪst/

7 **a)** Work in teams. Read the quiz. Fill in the gaps with the superlative form of the adjectives in brackets. Then do the quiz.

b) Check your answers on p158. How many points did your team get?

The BEST quiz in the world!

1 Which of these cities has the .... population? (large)
　a) Istanbul　**b)** Buenos Aires　**c)** New York

2 Which of these film stars is the .... ? (old)
　a) Mel Gibson　**b)** Julia Roberts　**c)** Brad Pitt

3 Which is the world's .... country? (crowded)
　a) Bangladesh　**b)** Singapore　**c)** Monaco

4 Which of these countries is the .... ? (big)
　a) The USA　**b)** Brazil　**c)** Australia

5 What's the world's .... city to live in? (expensive)
　a) Moscow　**b)** Tokyo　**c)** New York

6 Who was the .... person to score a goal in a football World Cup final? (young)
　a) Maradona　**b)** Pelé　**c)** Ronaldo

7 Which is the .... first language in the world? (common)
　a) English　**b)** Chinese　**c)** Spanish

8 Which of these cities is the .... to the Equator? (near)
　a) Mexico City　**b)** Rio de Janeiro　**c)** Madrid

Get ready … Get it right!

8 Write six of these things on a piece of paper. Write one or two words, not complete sentences. Don't write the answers in order.

● the name of the oldest or youngest person in your family
● your oldest or most important possession
● the most interesting or boring thing you did last weekend
● the latest or earliest you went to bed last month
● the best or worst present you got last birthday
● the best or worst film you saw last year

9 **a)** Work in pairs. Swap papers. Take turns to ask questions about your partner's words. Ask follow-up questions.

Is Stefan the oldest person in your family?

Yes, he is. He's my grandfather.

How old is he?

He's 79.

b) Tell the class two things about your partner.

Have you ever...?

Vocabulary past participles
Grammar Present Perfect for life experiences: positive and negative, *Have you ever ... ?* questions and short answers
Review Past Simple

QUICK REVIEW ● ● ●
Write ten adjectives. Work in pairs. Say the adjectives to your partner. He/She says the comparative and superlative form.

Listening, Reading and Grammar

1 **Work in groups. Discuss these questions.**

1 Do you know anyone who is self-employed? What do they do?
2 What are the good and bad things about being self-employed?
3 Would you like to be self-employed? Why?/Why not?

2 **a)** R12.4 **Listen and read about three friends, Steve, Lucy and Guy. Do they like being self-employed?**

b) Tick the true sentences. Correct the false ones.

1 Steve went to Mexico two weeks ago.
2 He was in Barbados two months ago.
3 He wants to go to Australia on holiday.
4 Guy and Lucy were self-employed three years ago.
5 The Prime Minister came to their restaurant last month.
6 Guy and Lucy want to go to the USA next year.

Help with Grammar Present Perfect: positive and negative

3 **a) Look at sentences 1 and 2. Then answer questions a) and b).**

1 I've **been** to about forty countries. (Present Perfect)
2 Two weeks ago I **went** to Mexico. (Past Simple)

a) In sentence 1, do we know when Steve went to these countries?
b) In sentence 2, do we know when he went to Mexico?

b) Complete the rules with *Present Perfect* (PP) or *Past Simple* (PS).

● We use the .... to talk about experiences in life until now. We don't say when they happened.
● We use the .... if we say when something happened.

c) Find seven more examples of the Present Perfect in the texts. Fill in the gaps in the table with *have, has, haven't* and *hasn't*.

POSITIVE	NEGATIVE
I/you/we/they + ... + past participle	I/you/we/they + ... + past participle
he/she/it + ... + past participle	he/she/it + ... + past participle

d) Check in G12.2 **p147. Read the rules for making past participles and the** TIPS!**.**

I love being self-employed. I've been to about forty countries and I've stayed in some of the world's best hotels. I've written travel articles about lots of amazing places – two weeks ago I went to Mexico and last month I spent five days in Barbados, in the Caribbean. But I've never been to Australia. I'd love to go there one day, when I have time – but for a holiday, not for work!

Steve White – travel writer

4 **a) What are the past participles of these verbs? Check new past participles in the Irregular Verb List, p159. Which three verbs are regular?**

1	write *written*	6	lose
2	stay	7	meet
3	be	8	study
4	have	9	see
5	work	10	go

b) R12.5 P **Listen and practise the infinitive, Past Simple and past participle of the verbs in 4a).**

write, wrote, written

> We've had lots of other jobs. Three years ago Guy was a teacher and I worked in an office. But we'd rather be self-employed and we love having our own restaurant. We've met some really interesting people – last year the Prime Minister had dinner here! But it's very hard work and Guy and I have never had a holiday together. We might go to Miami next year – Guy hasn't been to the USA before.

Guy and Lucy Rogers – restaurant owners

5 **a)** Look at these phrases and write six sentences about your experiences. They can be positive or negative.

- work in a restaurant
  I've worked in a restaurant.
- go to the UK
  I haven't been to the UK.
- meet someone from Ireland
- see a Japanese film
- stay in a five-star hotel
- be on television/the radio
- work in an office
- study another foreign language

b) Work in groups. Tell other students your sentences. How many are the same?

6 **a)** R12.6 Listen to a conversation between Steve and Lucy. Where are they? What do they talk about?

b) Listen again. Are these sentences true (T) or false (F)?

1 Steve has been to Rio de Janeiro.
2 He went there three years ago.
3 Lucy wants to go to Brazil on holiday.
4 She's been to Australia.
5 She travelled around Australia by bus.
6 Guy hasn't been to Australia.

Help with Grammar Present Perfect: *Have you ever ... ?* questions and short answers

7 **a)** Fill in the gaps in the questions and short answers with *have* or *did*.

.... *you ever been to Australia?*   Yes, I ....
.... *you have a good time?*   Yes, I ....

b) Complete the rule with *Present Perfect (PP)* or *Past Simple (PS)*.

- We use the .... to ask about people's experiences. If the answer is *yes*, we use the .... to ask for (or give) more information.

TIP! • *ever* + Present Perfect = any time in your life until now. We often use it in questions.

c) Check in G12.3 p147.

8 R12.7 P Listen and practise.

Have you ever worked in a restaurant?   *Yes, I have.*

9 **a)** Fill in the gaps. Put the verbs in brackets in the Present Perfect or Past Simple and complete the short answers.

1
A ¹........... you ever .... to France? (go)
B Yes, I ²........... . I ³........... there six years ago. (go)
A Where ⁴........... you .... ? (stay)
B I ⁵........... a flat near Bordeaux. (rent)

2
A ⁶........... you ever .... a diary? (write)
B Yes, I ⁷........... . I ⁸........... one when I was a teenager. (write)
A ⁹........... you .... it every day? (write)
B No, I ¹⁰........... . Only when I ¹¹........... on holiday. (be)

b) R12.8 Listen and check.

Get ready ... Get it right!

10 Work in two groups. Group A → p111. Group B → p119. Follow the instructions.

Have a good trip!

Real World at the airport; saying goodbye
Vocabulary things and places at an airport
Help with Listening questions on the phone
Review prices; times; requests

QUICK REVIEW ● ● ●

Work in pairs. Ask your partner questions and find three things you have both done in your life: *Have you ever been to / met / worked / seen / studied / had … ? Yes, I have. / No, I haven't.*

Buying a plane ticket

1 Discuss these questions in pairs or groups.

1 What are you going to do at the end of this course?
2 Are you going on holiday soon? If yes, how are you going to get there?
3 How do people usually buy plane tickets in your country?

2 a) Look at the adverts for two travel companies and answer these questions.

1 Which company is open longer on Sundays?
2 Which is more expensive – a return flight to Istanbul or Rome?
3 How many nights is the city break to Miami?
4 How much is the cheapest flight to the USA?
5 Which is cheaper – a return to Prague or Lisbon?
6 What's the most expensive ticket?
7 Does the special offer to California include car hire?
8 Do both companies fly to Boston? If yes, which is cheaper?

b) Imagine you have £500. Which flight or holiday would you like to buy? Why?

Call-a-Flight

call us now

For the cheapest flights – try us first!

	RETURN FROM
SYDNEY	£759
BOSTON	£240
NEW YORK	£199
LOS ANGELES	£276
ROME	£119
LISBON	£130

0870 777 6565

★ **SPECIAL OFFERS!** ★

Hong Kong	California
4nts from **£685** incl flights and 2★ hotel	7nts from **£473** incl flights and car hire

Book online at:
www.call-a-flight.co.uk

Open 08.00–21.00
seven days a week

Good Trips Ltd

0207 899 6532

CITY BREAKS!

New York
flights + 3nts
3★ hotel: £479

Miami, Florida
flights + 7nts
2★ hotel: £349

	rtn from
New York	£219
San Francisco	£271
Boston	£269
Istanbul	£158
Prague	£139
Round the world	£829

Mon–Fri 9.00–19.00 │ Sat–Sun 10.00–17.00 │ www.goodtrips.co.uk

Help with Listening Questions on the phone

3 a) Joe Hunter wants a ticket to Boston. Match the travel agent's questions a)–g) to the things she asks about 1–7.

a) How many people are travelling?
b) How can I help you?
c) When would you like to go?
d) And what's your name, please?
e) How would you like to pay?
f) When do you want to come back?
g) And from which airport?

1 by credit card, cheque
2 the date you leave
3 the date you return
4 the reason you're calling
5 the name of an airport or city
6 number of passengers
7 a name

b) **R12.9** Listen and put questions a)–g) in order.

4 **R12.10** Listen to Joe's phone call to Call-a-Flight. Fill in gaps 1–7 in his notes.

Boston trip

Leaving Saturday 1 .... February
depart London Heathrow 2 ....
arrive Boston 3 ....

Return flight Sunday 4 .... March
depart Boston 5 ....
arrive London 6 ....

Price 7 £ ....

At the airport

5 Work in pairs. Tick the words/phrases you know. Then do the exercise in `V12.2` p146.

> a passport   a boarding card   hand luggage
> a ticket   sharp items   pack your bags
> passengers   a flight number   a gate
> a check-in desk   a window/a middle/an aisle seat

6 **a)** Joe is at the airport. Work in pairs. What does the woman at the check-in desk say to him?

WOMAN   Can I have your  and your

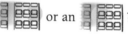 , please?

JOE   *Yes. Here you are.* ....

WOMAN   How many [bag] have you got?

JOE   ....

WOMAN   Did you [hand] yourself?

JOE   ....

WOMAN   Have you got any [scissors] in your

[bag] ?

JOE   ....

WOMAN   And would you like a [seat] or an [seat] ?

JOE   ....

WOMAN   OK. Here's your [BOARDING CARD 16A] . You're in seat 16A.

JOE   ....

WOMAN   [gate 12] .

JOE   ....

WOMAN   Yes, it is. It leaves at [13:20] Enjoy your [plane] .

JOE   ....

b) Fill in Joe's part of the conversation in **6a)** with these phrases.

> ~~Yes. Here you are.~~   Is the flight on time?   Thanks. Bye.
> Two.   Which gate is it?   No, I haven't.   Yes, I did.
> A window seat, please.

c) `R12.11` Listen and check.

7 **a)** Work in pairs. Practise the conversation in **6a)**. Take turns to be Joe.

b) Work in new pairs. Practise again. When you're Joe, close your book.

Real World Saying goodbye

8 **a)** Fill in the gaps with these words.

> holiday   See   Have   postcard   Send

.... a	nice weekend! nice .... ! good trip!	You too. Thanks, I will.
.... you	in two weeks. next year. on the next course.	Yes, see you.
.... me/us	an email. a	Yes, of course.

b) Check in `RW12.2` p147.

9 `R12.12` `P` Listen and practise the sentences in **8a)**.

Have a nice weekend!

10 **a)** `R12.13` Joe is saying goodbye to his friends. Listen and tick the sentences in **8a)** that you hear.

b) Imagine you're at an airport. Say goodbye to other students in the class!

1 a) Write the superlatives with *the*. `G12.1`

1 Who's *the tallest*? (tall)
2 Who's got _____ cousin? (young)
3 Whose home is _____ ? (near)
4 Who's got _____ job? (interesting)
5 Who's _____ today? (happy)
6 Whose watch is _____ ? (big)
7 Who's _____ at English? (good)

b) Work in groups. Find answers to these questions.

2 a) Put the verbs in the Present Perfect or Past Simple. `G12.2`

1 I *'ve seen*. the film *Titanic*. (see)
2 I *watched* TV last night. (watch)
3 I _____ to Australia. (not go)
4 I _____ to the UK last year. (go)
5 I _____ last night. (stay in)
6 I _____ in a shop. (never work)
7 I _____ skiing twice. (go)

b) Make these sentences true for you.

c) Work in pairs. Compare sentences with a partner. Are any the same?

3 a) Write four *Have you ever … ?* questions. Use the past participles of these verbs. `G12.3`

go	meet	stay	have
work	lose	study	
see	write	play	

Have you ever been to the USA?

b) Work in pairs. Take turns to ask and answer your questions. Ask follow-up questions if possible.

4 Do the airport word puzzle. Find the message. `V12.2`

1 Did you have a good _____ ?
2 14C is an _____ seat.
3 The opposite of *depart*.
4 On a plane you're a _____ .
5 Pack your _____ .
6 Have you got any hand _____ ?
7 You can _____ tickets online.
8 14A is a _____ seat.
9 Here's your _____ card.
10 My plane leaves from _____ 7.
11 You can't take any _____ items.
12 Go to the _____ desk.
13 You do this before you travel.

① F L I G H T
② S L
③ A E
④ S S G R
⑤ B S
⑥ L G G
⑦ B
⑧ W W
⑨ B R G
⑩ G
⑪ S
⑫ C C N
⑬ A K

Progress Portfolio

a) Tick the things you can do in English.

☐ I can compare three or more things.
☐ I can talk about my past experiences.
☐ I can ask other people about their experiences.
☐ I can find information in adverts for travel companies.
☐ I can buy a plane ticket on the phone.
☐ I can check in my luggage at the airport.

b) What do you need to study again? ● **12A–C**

Work in groups of four. Read the rules. Then play the game!

Rules

You need: One counter for each student; one dice for each group.

How to play: Put your counters on *START HERE*. Take turns to throw the dice, move your counter and follow the instructions on the square. The first student to get to *FINISH* is the winner.

Grammar and Vocabulary squares: The first student to land on a Grammar or Vocabulary square answers question 1. The second student to land on the same square answers question 2. If the other students think your answer is correct, you can stay on the square. If the answer is wrong, move back to the last square you were on. You can check your answers with your teacher. If a third or fourth student lands on the same square, he/she can stay on the square without answering a question.

Keep Talking squares: If you land on a Keep Talking square, talk about the topic for 20 seconds. Another student can check the time. If you can't talk for 20 seconds, move back to the last square you were on. If a second or third student lands on the same square, he/she also talks about the same topic for 20 seconds.

End of Course Review

START HERE

1 Do we use *a/an* or *some* with each of these words?
1 cheese, book, money, toast
2 water, rice, sandwich, apple

2 Say eight:
1 jobs
2 free time activities

3 Talk about what you did last weekend.

4 MOVE FORWARD TWO SQUARES

9 Say five:
1 types of film
2 types of music

8 What is the Past Simple of each of these verbs?
1 become, find, choose, meet
2 leave, take, write, put

7 HAVE A REST!

6 Talk about your last holiday.

5 Say five:
1 illnesses
2 weather words

10 Describe a person in your family.

11 Make a question with *Where* for this answer.
1 Her mother was born in Rome.
2 Tom's sister lives in the USA.

12 How do we say these prices and numbers?
1 239, 4,500, 0.3, $750,000
2 £250,000, 3.4, 760, 22,650

13 MOVE BACK THREE SQUARES

14 Make a sentence with these words.
1 get up / usually / I / at / nine / about
2 bought / our / ago / a year / We / house

19 Make a question with these words.
1 What / you / last / weekend / do / did ?
2 tonight / you / going to / Who / meet / are ?

18 Do we use the Present Simple or Present Continuous with each of these words?
1 sometimes, at the moment, now
2 never, often, today

17 What is the infinitive of these Past Simple forms?
1 fell, won, lost
2 broke, forgot, told

16 Compare two people you know.

15 Say the nationalities.
1 Spain, China, the USA, Poland
2 France, Turkey, Italy, Brazil

20 Talk about what you do in your free time.

21 HAVE A REST!

22 What are the comparatives?
1 boring, good, long, easy
2 expensive, bad, happy, wet

23 Describe your house or flat.

24 MOVE BACK FOUR SQUARES

29 What is the opposite?
1 cheap, unfriendly, fast, clean
2 boring, poor, happy, noisy

28 Say six:
1 types of shop
2 things you can wear

27 MOVE FORWARD THREE SQUARES

26 Make adverbs from these adjectives.
1 beautiful, fast, bad
2 happy, hard, good

25 Say eight types of:
1 food
2 drink

30 Talk about your daily routine in the week.

31 Make a sentence with these words.
1 going to / I'm / tonight / my sister / not / meet
2 the theatre / might / next / go to / We / weekend

32 Talk about what you're going to do next weekend.

33 Say eight:
1 family members
2 things in the house

34 What are the superlatives?
1 beautiful, short, bad, dirty
2 good, fast, friendly, modern

FINISH

38 Make the sentence negative.
1 We went on holiday last year.
2 They've got a car.

37 HAVE A REST!

36 Talk about things you can/can't do in your town/city.

35 MOVE BACK THREE SQUARES

Da Do Ron Ron 6D p53

 1 What are the Past Simple forms of these verbs? Which verbs are irregular?

1	meet *met*	5	walk
2	stand	6	know
3	tell	7	catch
4	be	8	look

2 a) [R6.12] Listen to the song. Fill in the gaps with the Past Simple forms of the verbs in **1**.

I ¹ *met* him on a Monday
And my heart ² .... still
Da do ron ron ron, da do ron ron
Somebody ³ .... me that his name ⁴ .... Bill
Da do ron ron ron, da do ron ron

Yes, my heart ⁵ .... still
Yes, his name ⁶ .... Bill
And when he ⁷ .... me home
Da do ron ron ron, da do ron ron

I ⁸ .... what he was doing
When he ⁹ .... my eye
Da do ron ron ron, da do ron ron
He ¹⁰ .... so quiet but my oh my
Da do ron ron ron, da do ron ron

Yes, he ¹¹ .... my eye
Yes, my oh my
And when he ¹² .... me home
Da do ron ron ron, da do ron ron

He picked me up at seven
And he ¹³ .... so fine
Da do ron ron ron, da do ron ron
Some day soon I'm going to make him mine
Da do ron ron ron, da do ron ron

Yes, he ¹⁴ .... so fine
Yes, I'll make him mine
And when he ¹⁵ .... me home
Da do ron ron ron, da do ron ron

b) Work in pairs. Compare answers.

3 a) Read the song again. Find two more pairs of words that rhyme.

still   Bill

b) Find words in the song that rhyme with these words.

1	get *met*	3	same	5	take	7	eleven
2	start	4	ten	6	not	8	play

Holiday 8D p69

 1 a) Think of three places you would like to go to on holiday.

b) Work in pairs. Compare places and say why you want to go there.

 2 a) [R8.10] Listen to the song. Choose the correct words/phrases.

Holiday! Celebrate!
Holiday! Celebrate!

CHORUS
If we ¹*took/had* a holiday
Took some time to ²*celebrate/have fun*
Just one ³*week/day* out of life
It would be, it would be so ⁴*great/nice*

If we finally spread the ⁵*word/news*
We're going to have a ⁶*party/celebration*
All across the world
In every ⁷*nation/country*
It's time for the ⁸*happy/good* times
Forget about the ⁹*old/bad* times, oh yeah
One day to ¹⁰*live/come* together
To release the pressure
We ¹¹*need/want* a holiday

CHORUS

We can turn this ¹²*place/world* around
And bring back all of those happy ¹³*days/times*
Put your troubles down
It's time to ¹⁴*celebrate/have fun*
Let love shine
And we will ¹⁵*find/get*
A way to ¹⁶*live/come* together
Can make ¹⁷*life/things* better
We ¹⁸*need/want* a holiday

CHORUS

Holiday! Celebrate!
Holiday! Celebrate!

CHORUS

Holiday! Celebrate!
Holiday! Celebrate!

b) Work in pairs. Compare answers.

 3 a) Read the song again. Find all the adjectives.

great

b) Work in pairs. What are the comparative forms of these adjectives?

Dancing in the Street 9D p77

1 Work in groups. Discuss these questions.

1 What kind of music do you like dancing to?
2 How often do you go dancing?
3 When was the last time you went dancing?
4 Where did you go?

2 **a)** R9.18 Listen to the song. Put the sentences in order.

a) For dancing in the **street**
b) Are you ready for a brand new beat?
c) They're dancing in Chicago
d) Calling out around the world *1*
e) Down in New Orleans
f) Summer's here and the time is right
g) In New York City

CHORUS

h) They'll be dancing, they're dancing in the street
i) There'll be music everywhere
j) All we need is music, sweet music *8*
k) So come on, every guy, grab a girl, everywhere, around the **world**
l) Dancing in the street, oh
m) It doesn't matter what you wear, just as long as you are **there**
n) They'll be swinging, swaying and records **playing**

o) There'll be laughing, **singing** and music swinging
p) A chance for folks to **meet**
q) Philadelphia, PA, Baltimore and DC now
r) This is an invitation across the **nation** *15*
s) Dancing in the street
t) Can't forget the motor city

CHORUS

Way down in LA, every day
They're dancing in the street …

b) Work in pairs. Compare answers.

3 Look at the words in **bold**. Find another word in the song that rhymes with these words.

street   beat

Chapel of Love 11D p93

1 Work in pairs. Match these words/phrases.

1	get married	a)	is blue
2	people can be	b)	in a chapel
3	birds	c)	shines
4	the sky	d)	ring
5	the sun	e)	lonely
6	bells	f)	sing

2 **a)** R11.13 Listen to the song. Match 1–8 to a)–h).

CHORUS
Going to the chapel
And we're going to get married
Going to the chapel
And we're going to get married
Gee, I really love you
And we're going to get married
Going to the chapel of love

1	Spring is here,	a)	as if they knew
2	Birds all sing,	b)	be lonely any more
3	Today's the day	c)	the sky is blue
4	And we'll never	d)	we'll say "I do"

Because we're …
CHORUS

5	Bells will ring,	e)	and he'll be mine
6	I'll be his	f)	be lonely any more
7	We'll love until	g)	the sun will shine
8	And we'll never	h)	the end of time

Because we're …
CHORUS

b) Work in pairs. Compare answers.

3 Work in groups. Discuss these questions.

1 When is the best time of the year to get married? Why?
2 What is the best age to get married? Why?

103

Pair and Group Work: Student/Group A

1A **13** p7

a) Take turns to ask and answer questions. Fill in the gaps in name cards A, C and D. Don't look at your partner's cards.

Card A. Where's he from?
Cards C and D. What are their names?
How do you spell that?

A Name:
Country:

B Name:
Alicia Ballario
Country:
Argentina

C Name:
Country:

D Name:
Country:

E Name:
Alessandra Angeletti
Country:
Italy

F Name:
Adriana Angeletti
Country:
Italy

b) Check your answers with your partner.

11C **9** p91

a) Work on your own. Find these places on the map on p91. Don't show your partner.

2 the cinema   10 the market
6 The Pizza Place   12 the petrol station
7 the bank

b) Work with your partner. Ask for directions to places a)–e) from *You are here*. When you find the place, check the number on the map with your partner. Don't look at your partner's map. You start.

a) the museum   d) The Moon nightclub
b) The Burger Bar   e) the school
c) the post office

4B **9** a) p33

Jo ● ● ● ● ● ● ● ● ● ● ● ● ● ●

Jo is 29 and she's a journalist. In her free time she watches TV, goes shopping and reads a lot. On Saturday evenings she usually goes to the cinema or eats out – she loves Chinese food. She doesn't like sport and she hates football. Her favourite music is rock and she also likes jazz. She likes animals but hasn't got any pets.

1B **12** p9

a) Work on your own. Look at the list of people at the conference. Make *yes/no* questions to check the information in the circles. (Mr =    Mrs =)

Is Mr Popov a doctor?
Are Mr and Mrs Soprano in room 320?
Is Mr Akdeniz from Turkey?

b) Work with your partner. Take turns to ask and answer your questions. There are five mistakes on the list. Correct the wrong information.

Is Mr ... ?   Yes, he is./No, he isn't.
Is Mrs ... ?   Yes, she is./No, she isn't
Are Mr and Mrs ... ?   Yes, they are./No, they aren't.

c) Check your answers with another student in group A.

Mr Popov isn't a doctor. He's a police officer.

CONFERENCE GUEST LIST			
NAME	**COUNTRY**	**JOB**	**ROOM**
MR POPOV	RUSSIA	DOCTOR	116
MR SOPRANO	THE USA	ACCOUNTANT	320
MRS SOPRANO		LAWYER	
MR AKDENIZ	TURKEY	ENGINEER	115
MR TERRY	THE UK	BUILDER	219
MRS TERRY		HOUSEWIFE	
MRS BANAS	GERMANY	MANAGER	102
MR LEE	AUSTRALIA	WAITER	303
MRS LEE		SHOP ASSISTANT	
MRS BARROS	BRAZIL	DOCTOR	412
MR PÉREZ	SPAIN	ACTOR	210
MRS PÉREZ		TEACHER	

2A ⑬ p15

a) Guess the things your partner has got, but don't talk to him/her. Put a tick (✓) or a cross (✗) in the *your guess* column.

	your guess	your partner's answer

b) Look at the pictures. Write questions with *you*.

Have you got a mobile phone?

c) Work with your partner. Take turns to ask and answer your questions. Put a tick or a cross in the *your partner's answer* column. Are your guesses correct?

d) Work with a new partner. Tell him/her five things your first partner has/hasn't got.

2C ⑪ p19

a) You are a customer. Choose one of these films. Buy two tickets from your partner. Fill in the times and the prices for your film. You start.

48 Hours   Time: .... £ ....

Three Long Years   Time: .... £ ....

Two Weeks from Sunday   Time: .... £ ....

Two tickets for .... , please.

How much is that?

What time is the film?

b) You are a ticket seller. Look at the times and prices of the films at your cinema. Sell tickets to your partner. Your partner starts.

today's **films**

60 Seconds	8.10
Nine Months	8.25
A Day in the Life	8.35

Adults: £7.50   Children: £5.00

c) Do **a)** and **b)** again. Buy tickets for different films. Change the tickets you buy.

6C ⑦ p51

Take turns to say sentences 1–6. When your partner says a sentence, respond with one of these words/phrases. You start.

Oh, dear.   What a shame.   Oh, right.   Wow!
Oh, great!   Oh, nice.   Really?   You're joking!

1 I met Tom Cruise on Saturday.
2 I went to an expensive restaurant last night.
3 My sister was very ill last week.
4 I did my washing yesterday.
5 I went to New York last week.
6 I worked all weekend.

3B 10 p25

a) Work on your own. Choose the correct words in the phrases.

	name	name
1 watch TV (every)/in evening		
2 do sport *in/on* Saturdays		
3 go to bed after midnight *in/at* the week		
4 eat out *at/every* week		
5 go to concerts *in/at* the weekends		

b) Make questions with *you* with phrases 1–5 in **a)**.

1 Do you watch TV every evening?

c) Ask other students in the class your questions. Find two people who answer *yes* for each question. Write their names in the table.

d) Tell the class about the people in your table.

Paola and Jurgen both watch TV every evening.

10A 10 p79

a) You have these problems. Check you understand them. Then write one more problem.

1 I can't sleep at night.
2 I forgot my best friend's birthday.
3 I hate my job, but I need the money.
4 _____

b) Work with students B and C. Take turns to ask for and give advice. Whose advice is the best, do you think?

> I can't sleep at night. What should I do?

> (I think) you should …

> (Don't) go …

> Well, you shouldn't …

5B 10 p41

a) Work with a student from group A. Describe the picture.

> **There's a** cat in the picture.
> **There's some** fruit on the table.
> **There are** nine eggs in the fridge.
> **There are some** pizzas on the table.

b) Make questions to ask a student from group B about his/her picture.

> **Is there a** CD player in the room?
> **Are there any** eggs in the fridge?
> **How many** bananas **are there**?
> **How much** milk **is there**?

c) Work with a student from group B. Don't look at your partner's picture. Take turns to ask and answer questions. Find twelve differences.

d) Work with your partner from group A. Compare answers.

5C **12** p43

a) You are a customer. Your partner is a shop assistant. Ask for the things on your shopping list and tick the things you buy. How much do you spend? The shop assistant speaks first.

> Can I have ... please?
>
> Have you got a/any ... ?
>
> I'll have ...
>
> How much is/are ... ?

b) You are a shop assistant. Your partner is a customer. Look at the picture of things in your shop. Then have a conversation with your partner. How much does he/she spend? You start.

> Hello, can I help you?
>
> Sure.
>
> Here you are.
>
> Anything else?
>
> I'm sorry, we haven't got any ...
>
> That's £... , please.

11B **11** p89

a) Look at what Tim, Debbie, and Sid and Clare are going to do next weekend. Take turns to ask and answer *yes/no* questions and fill in the gaps in the table.

> Is Tim going to visit his parents next weekend?

> ✓ Yes, he is.

> ✗ No, he isn't.

> ✓✗ He might.

	Tim	Debbie	Sid and Clare
visit parents		✓	
go running	✓		✗
move house		✗	
watch lots of TV	✓✗		✗
go to a party		✗	
play tennis	✓		✓✗
stay in bed on Sunday		✓	

b) Who is going to have: a lazy weekend, a busy weekend, an active weekend?

7A 12 p55

a) Work on your own. Read about Pierce Brosnan. All the information in black is correct. Some of the information in blue is wrong.

b) Work with a student from group A. Make *yes/no* questions to check the information in blue.

1 Was Pierce Brosnan born in Ireland?

2 Did his father leave after his first birthday?

c) Work with a student from group B. Take turns to ask and answer your questions. You start. Correct the mistakes in the blue information.

d) Check your answers with your partner from group A. Then find three reasons why Pierce Brosnan was 'born to be Bond'.

Pierce Brosnan

Born to be Bond

[1]Pierce Brosnan was born in Ireland in 1952, but [2]his father left after his first birthday. His mother went to England and became a nurse, and [3]Pierce lived with his aunt. He went to live with his mother in 1964, on the same day that Ian Fleming died. A week later he went to see *Goldfinger* – a James Bond film. It was the first film he saw in his life.

[4]Pierce left school when he was fifteen and then he went to drama school. In 1978 [5]he met actress Cassandra Harris at a party. Cassandra was a Bond Girl in the film *For Your Eyes Only*. [6]They got married in 1979 and they had a son. Sadly, [7]Cassandra died in 1993.

Brosnan became James Bond in 1994 and [8]his first Bond film was *Goldeneye*. It made $350 million. Pierce Brosnan was definitely born to be Bond.

8A 9 p63

a) Work on your own. Look at the information about Yellowstone Park. Write questions with *can* for pictures a)–f).

Can you take your dog?

b) Work with your partner. Ask your questions. Put a tick or a cross next to pictures a)–f).

c) Answer your partner's questions.

d) Would you and your partner like to go to Yellowstone Park? Why?/Why not?

Things you can and can't do in Yellowstone Park

8B 11 p65

a) Work with a student from group A. Make sentences about 1–6 with the comparative form of the adjectives in brackets. Don't tell group B your sentences.

São Paolo is bigger than Rio de Janeiro.

1 Rio de Janeiro: 11 million people. / São Paolo: 16 million people. (big)
2 A Big Mac in Australia: $2. / A Big Mac in Switzerland: $5. (expensive)
3 Bill Gates: $39.8 billion. / John Paul Getty: $1.6 billion. (rich)
4 Jennifer Lopez: born 1970. / Leonardo DiCaprio: born 1974. (old)
5 Cuba: 115,000 km². / Ireland: 83,000 km². (small)
6 Elton John: born 25th March 1947. / David Bowie: born 8th January 1947. (young)

b) Work with the same partner. Use the adjectives in brackets to compare the places, people and things a)–f). Then circle the one you think is smaller, more crowded, etc.

a) Spain / Peru (small)
b) Tokyo / Hong Kong (crowded)
c) Tiger Woods / Venus Williams (young)
d) A Rolls Royce Corniche / A Lamborghini (expensive)
e) The Atlantic Ocean / The Pacific Ocean (big)
f) Julia Roberts / Tom Cruise (short)

> Do you think Spain is smaller than Peru?

> Yes, I think so.

> I'm not sure. I think Peru is smaller.

c) Work in a group of four with a pair from group B. Say your sentences from b). The students from group B say if you are right or wrong.

d) Listen to group B's sentences. Say if the sentences are right or wrong.

e) Which pair got more sentences right?

10D 5 p85

a) Take turns to ask and answer questions. Fill in the gaps in the table. You start.

> What's the weather like in ... today?

> It's ... and it's ... degrees.

	weather	°C
Athens		
Buenos Aires		19
Bangkok		
Chicago		21
Helsinki		
Moscow		2
Munich		
Paris		24
Rome		
Stockholm		6

b) Which places are: hot, warm, cold, wet, dry?

c) Where's the best place to go today? Why?

4B 10 c) p33

MARK   I like Kim very much and we like a lot of the same things. We both go to the cinema a lot and we both really like animals. But she doesn't like the same music as me and she hasn't got a TV – I don't believe that! Yes, I'd like to see her again. She's very beautiful.

KIM   Sorry, I don't like Mark very much. He talks about football and TV programmes *all* the time and I don't like watching TV. Also, we don't like the same music – and music's very important to me. I don't want a second date with him. Sorry.

9A ⓭ p71

a) Work with a student from group A. Describe the picture.

> Kevin's talking on the phone.

> He's wearing a jacket, shirt and tie.

b) Work with a student from group B. Don't look at his/her picture. Take turns to ask and answer questions. Find eleven differences in the pictures.

> What's Kevin doing?

> What's he wearing?

c) Work with your partner from group A. Did you find the same differences?

> In picture A Kevin's ... , but in picture B he's ... .

7C ⓾ p59

a) Work on your own. Read about the news stories. Check you understand all the words.

Big flood
USA
about 20 people died

Man who found 1 million dollars
under kitchen floor
gave money to his family

Tourists lost in Africa
Sahara desert
lost for 2 weeks
other tourists found them – OK now

Man, tries post

A woman ...
tioned abo...
bery that t...
on Monday...
in the sleep...
Sandy Ridg...
witness sav...
incident, th...
very conce...
a baseball ...
carried a b...
man was in...
twenties an...
noticeable ...
forehead, ...
police will ...
this further...
today

b) Work with your partner. Take turns to tell your partner about the news stories. Respond with phrases from the box.

> Did you hear/read about ... ?
> No, what happened? No, where was it?
> Oh, dear. Are they OK?   Oh, that's good.
> Oh no, that's terrible.   You're joking!   Really?

7B ❸ p56

a) Ask your partner the last time he/she did these things. Ask follow-up questions if possible.

> When did you last cook a meal?

> What did you cook?

- cook a meal
- go to the theatre
- stay up very late
- play tennis
- watch a good film on TV
- go out with friends

b) Answer your partner's questions. Use phrases with *in*, *last* or *ago*.

> In 2002.   Last weekend.   About three years ago.

6A ⑫ p47

a) Work on your own. Write questions with *you* or *your* about **when you were thirteen**.

	you	your partner
1 / happy at school? *Were you happy at school?*		
2 Who / best friend?		
3 / good at languages?		
4 What / favourite food?		
5 What / favourite TV programme?		

b) Write your answers in the *you* column.

c) Work with your partner. Take turns to ask and answer your questions. Write your partner's answers in the table.

d) Tell another student about you and your partner when you were thirteen.

> I was happy at school when I was thirteen, but Vanessa wasn't.

12B ⑩ p97

a) Work with a student from group A. Write questions with *you* in the Present Perfect and follow-up questions in the Past Simple.

1 / go / on a boat trip?
Have you ever been on a boat trip?
Where / go?
Where did you go?
2 / visit / the capital city of another country?
Which city / visit?
3 / go / to a really fantastic party?
Whose party / be / it?
4 / meet / someone from the USA?
Where / meet them?
5 / rent / a car or a bike?
Where / be / you?

b) Work with a student from group B. Take turns to ask and answer your questions. If the answer is *yes*, ask your follow-up question. Then ask two more questions if possible.

c) Work with your partner from group A. Tell him/her about student B's life experiences.

9C ⑨ p75

a) Work on your own. Read the information for phone conversations 1–4.

1 You work for Morris Computers. Phone Alex Roberts about his new computer. Your mobile number is 07694 35567. You start this conversation.

2 You are Sam Watson. You are a sales manager. You aren't in the office tomorrow afternoon from 2.30 to 3.30.

3 Phone a friend at home. Ask him/her what he/she is doing now. There's a party near your house on Saturday evening. Does he/she want to come? If yes, decide on a time and place to meet. You start this conversation.

4 You are at home. Decide what you are doing at the moment.

b) Decide what you want to say in each conversation. Use language from the box or your own ideas.

> Hello, can I speak to … , please?
> Hello, is that … ?
> Speaking.
> This is … from … .
> It's … .
>
> Can I talk to you about … ?
> Call me on my mobile.
>
> Would you like to … ?
> Yes, good idea.
> Shall we meet at … ?
> Let's meet at … .
> See you then. Bye.

c) Work with your partner. Take turns to phone each other.

Pair and Group Work: Student/Group B

1A ⑬ p7

a) Take turns to ask and answer questions. Fill in the gaps in name cards B, E and F. Don't look at your partner's cards.

Card B. Where's she from?
Cards E and F. What are their names?
How do you spell that?

A Name: Kenji Azuma
Country: Japan

B Name:
Country:

C Name: Nikolai Petrov
Country: Russia

D Name: Olga Petrova
Country: Russia

E Name:
Country:

F Name:
Country:

b) Check your answers with your partner.

11C ⑨ p91

a) Work on your own. Find these places on the map on p91. Don't show your partner.

1 the museum	11 The Moon nightclub
4 The Burger Bar	13 the school
8 the post office	

b) Work with your partner. Ask for directions to places f)–j) from *You are here*. When you find the place, check the number on the map with your partner. Don't look at your partner's map. Your partner starts.

f) the cinema	i) the market
g) The Pizza Place	j) the petrol station
h) the bank	

4B ⑨ a) p33

Susie ·············

Susie's 23 and she's a waitress. She really loves dance music but she doesn't like rock music. She doesn't go to restaurants very often but she loves fast food. On Saturday evenings she goes dancing with friends or stays in and watches TV all night. She doesn't like watching sport on TV but she goes swimming a lot. And she has seven cats!

1B ⑫ p9

a) Work on your own. Look at the list of people at the conference. Make *yes/no* questions to check the information in the circles. (Mr = ♂ Mrs = ♀)

Is Mr Popov in room 116?
Are Mr and Mrs Soprano from Italy?
Is Mr Akdeniz an engineer?

b) Work with your partner. Take turns to ask and answer your questions. There are five mistakes on the list. Correct the wrong information.

Is Mr ... ?   Yes, he is./No, he isn't.
Is Mrs ... ?   Yes, she is./No, she isn't.
Are Mr and Mrs ... ?   Yes, they are./No, they aren't.

c) Check your answers with another student in group B.

Mr and Mrs Sporano aren't from Italy. They're from the USA.

CONFERENCE GUEST LIST

NAME	COUNTRY	JOB	ROOM
MR POPOV	RUSSIA	POLICE OFFICER	116
MR SOPRANO	ITALY	ACCOUNTANT	312
MRS SOPRANO		LAWYER	
MR AKDENIZ	TURKEY	ENGINEER	115
MR TERRY	THE UK	BUILDER	319
MRS TERRY		HOUSEWIFE	
MRS BANAS	POLAND	MANAGER	111
MR LEE	AUSTRALIA	CLEANER	303
MRS LEE		SHOP ASSISTANT	
MRS BARROS	ARGENTINA	DOCTOR	412
MR PÉREZ	SPAIN	MUSICIAN	206
MRS PÉREZ		TEACHER	

2A ⑬ p15

a) Guess the things your partner has got, but don't talk to him/her. Put a tick (✓) or a cross (✗) in the *your guess* column.

	your guess	your partner's answer

b) Look at the pictures. Write questions with *you*.
Have you got a computer?

c) Work with your partner. Take turns to ask and answer your questions. Put a tick or a cross in the *your partner's answer* column. Are your guesses correct?

d) Work with a new partner. Tell him/her five things your first partner has/hasn't got.

2C ⑪ p19

a) You are a ticket seller. Look at the times and prices of the films at your cinema. Sell tickets to your partner. Your partner starts.

today's films

48 Hours	7.20
Three Long Years	7.45
Two Weeks from Sunday	8.10

Adults: £6.90   **Children:** £4.70

b) You are a customer. Choose one of these films. Buy two tickets from your partner. Fill in the times and the prices for your film. You start.

60 Seconds	Time: .... £ ....
Nine Months	Time: .... £ ....
A Day in the Life	Time: .... £ ....

Two tickets for .... , please.

How much is that?

What time is the film?

c) Do **a)** and **b)** again. Buy tickets for different films. Change the tickets you buy.

6C ⑦ p51

Take turns to say sentences 1–6. When your partner says a sentence, respond with one of these words/phrases. Your partner starts.

> Oh, dear.   What a shame.   Oh, right.   Wow!
> Oh, great!   Oh, nice.   Really?   You're joking!

1 Sorry I wasn't at your party – I was ill.
2 I stayed in and watched TV last night.
3 I met Madonna last weekend.
4 I worked from 7 a.m. to 12 p.m. yesterday.
5 I had dinner with my mother on Sunday.
6 I've got a new job. I get $90,000 a year!

3B ⑩ p25

a) Work on your own. Choose the correct words in the phrases.

	name	name
1 watch TV *in*/*on* the morning		
2 go shopping *every*/*in* Saturday		
3 go for a drink *at*/*on* Friday evenings		
4 work *at*/*in* the weekends		
5 phone your friends *at*/*every* day		

b) Make questions with *you* with phrases 1–5 in **a)**.

1 Do you watch TV in the morning?

c) Ask other students in the class your questions. Find two people who answer *yes* for each question. Write their names in the table.

d) Tell the class about the people in your table.

Marco and Kumi both watch TV in the morning.

10A ⑩ p79

a) You have these problems. Check you understand them. Then write one more problem.

1 I want to practise my English more.
2 A friend bought me a picture but I hate it.
3 I need a holiday, but I haven't got any money.
4 _____

b) Work with students A and C. Take turns to ask for and give advice. Whose advice is the best, do you think?

> I want to practise my English more. What should I do?

> (I think) you should ...

> (Don't) go ...

> Well, you shouldn't ...

5B ⑩ p41

a) Work with a student from group B. Describe the picture.

> **There's a** TV in the picture.
> **There's some** fruit on the table.
> **There are** six eggs in the fridge.
> **There are some** chairs in the room.

b) Make questions to ask a student from group A about his/her picture.

> **Is there a** TV in the room?
> **Are there any** eggs in the fridge?
> **How many** apples **are there**?
> **How much** water **is there**?

c) Work with a student from group A. Don't look at your partner's picture. Take turns to ask and answer questions. Find twelve differences.

d) Work with your partner from group B. Compare answers.

5C ⑫ p43

a) You are a shop assistant. Your partner is a customer. Look at the picture of things in your shop. Then have a conversation with your partner. How much does he/she spend? You start.

> Hello, can I help you?
>
> Sure.
>
> Here you are.
>
> Anything else?
>
> I'm sorry, we haven't got any ...
>
> That's £... , please.

b) You are a customer. Your partner is a shop assistant. Ask for the things on your shopping list and tick the things you buy. How much do you spend? The shop assistant speaks first.

> Can I have ... please?
>
> Have you got a/any ... ?
>
> I'll have ...
>
> How much is/are ... ?

11B ⑪ p89

a) Look at what Tim, Debbie, and Sid and Clare are going to do next weekend. Take turns to ask and answer *yes/no* questions and fill in the gaps in the table.

> Is Debbie going to visit her parents next weekend?
>
> ✓ Yes, she is.
>
> ✗ No, she isn't.
>
> ✓✗ She might.

	Tim	Debbie	Sid and Clare
visit parents	✗		✓✗
go running		✗	
move house	✗		✓
watch lots of TV		✓	
go to a party	✓		✓✗
play tennis		✗	
stay in bed on Sunday	✗		✗

b) Who is going to have: a lazy weekend, a busy weekend, an active weekend?

7A 12 p55

a) Work on your own. Read about Pierce Brosnan. All the information in black is correct. Some of the information in blue is wrong.

b) Work with a student from group B. Make *yes/no* questions to check the information in blue.

1 Was Pierce Brosnan born in 1954?

2 Did his mother go to England?

c) Work with a student from group A. Take turns to ask and answer your questions. Your partner starts. Correct the mistakes in the blue information.

d) Check your answers with your partner from group B. Then find three reasons why Pierce Brosnan was 'born to be Bond'.

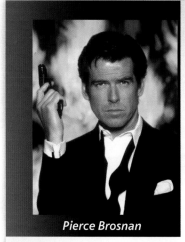

Pierce Brosnan

Born to be Bond

¹Pierce Brosnan was born in 1954 in Ireland, but his father left after his first birthday. ²His mother went to England and became a nurse, and Pierce lived with his grandparents. ³He went to live with his mother in 1966, on the same day that Ian Fleming died. A week later he went to see *Goldfinger* – a James Bond film. It was the first film he saw in his life.

Pierce left school when he was fifteen and then ⁴he went to university. In 1978 he met actress Cassandra Harris at a party. ⁵Cassandra was a Bond Girl in the film *For Your Eyes Only*. They got married in 1980 and ⁶they had a son. Sadly, Cassandra died in 1991.

⁷Brosnan became James Bond in 1994 and his first Bond film was *Goldeneye*. ⁸It made $350 million. Pierce Brosnan was definitely born to be Bond.

8A 9 p63

a) Work on your own. Look at the information about Yellowstone Park. Write questions with *can* for pictures g)–l).

Can you go cycling?

b) Work with your partner. Answer your partner's questions.

c) Ask your questions. Put a tick or a cross next to pictures g)–l).

d) Would you and your partner like to go to Yellowstone Park? Why?/Why not?

Things you can and can't do in Yellowstone Park

8B 11 p65

a) Work with a student from group B. Make sentences about a)–f) with the comparative form of the adjectives in brackets. Don't tell group A your sentences.

Spain is smaller than Peru.

a) Spain: 505,000 km². / Peru: 1,300,000 km². (small)
b) Tokyo: 7,000 people per km². / Hong Kong: 32,000 people per km². (crowded)
c) Tiger Woods: born 1975. / Venus Williams: born 1980. (young)
d) A Rolls Royce Corniche: $360,000. / A Lamborghini: $270,000. (expensive)
e) The Atlantic Ocean: 82 million km². / The Pacific Ocean: 165 million km². (big)
f) Julia Roberts: 1.75m. / Tom Cruise: 1.70m. (short)

b) Work with the same partner. Use the adjectives in brackets to compare the places, people and things 1–6. Then circle the one you think is bigger, more expensive, etc.

1 Rio de Janeiro / São Paolo (big)
2 A Big Mac in Australia / A Big Mac in Switzerland (expensive)
3 Bill Gates / John Paul Getty (rich)
4 Jennifer Lopez / Leonardo DiCaprio (old)
5 Cuba / Ireland (small)
6 Elton John / David Bowie (young)

> Do you think Rio de Janeiro is bigger than São Paolo?

> Yes, I think so.

> I'm not sure. I think São Paolo is bigger.

c) Work in a group of four with a pair from group A. Listen to group A's sentences. Say if the sentences are right or wrong.

d) Say your sentences from b). The students from group A say if you are right or wrong.

e) Which pair got more sentences right?

10D 5 p85

a) Take turns to ask and answer questions. Fill in the gaps in the table. Your partner starts.

> What's the weather like in … today?

> It's … and it's … degrees.

	weather	°C
Athens		21
Buenos Aires		
Bangkok		35
Chicago		
Helsinki		0
Moscow		
Munich		16
Paris		
Rome		20
Stockholm		

b) Which places are: hot, warm, cold, wet, dry?

c) Where's the best place to go today? Why?

4B 10 c) p33

MARK Jo and I like some of the same things – we both like going to the cinema and going to Chinese restaurants. But she talks about books and shopping *all* the time. We both like rock music but she hates sport and I love it! No, I don't want to see her again. Sorry!

JO I *really* like Mark. He's very different from me but that's a good thing, I think. I hate football but he loves it. And he plays computer games all the time and he never reads books. But yes, I'd like a second date with him. Definitely. He's very nice.

9A ⓭ p71

a) Work with a student from group B. Describe the picture.

> Kevin's sleeping.

> He's wearing a shirt and tie.

b) Work with a student from group A. Don't look at his/her picture. Take turns to ask and answer questions. Find eleven differences in the pictures.

> What's Kevin doing?

> What's he wearing?

c) Work with your partner from group B. Did you find the same differences?

> In picture B Kevin's ... , but in picture A he's ... .

7C ⓾ p59

a) Work on your own. Read about the news stories. Check you understand all the words.

3 students lost in Brazil
Amazon jungle
lost for six days
helicopter found them –
OK now

Train crash
in Africa
over 60 people died

Man who won the lottery
dog ate ticket
gave dog to friend

FATHER
THE BR
CHARG
BREAC
PEACE

Party-goe
astonishe
Mike Far
son of M
"We cann
has happ
nor can l
There wa
from the
Meanwhi
It is agair
Reverend
John Mcl
everyone
the pews
laughing
while the
bridesma
aftermath

b) Work with your partner. Take turns to tell your partner about the news stories. Respond with phrases from the box.

> Did you hear/read about ...?
>
> No, what happened? No, where was it?
>
> Oh, dear. Are they OK?   Oh, that's good.
> Oh no, that's terrible.   You're joking!   Really?

7B ❸ p56

a) Answer your partner's questions. Use phrases with *in*, *last* or *ago*.

> In 2002.   Last weekend.   About three years ago.

b) Ask your partner the last time he/she did these things. Ask follow-up questions if possible.

> When did you last go dancing?

> Where did you go?

- go dancing
- go to the cinema
- watch sport on TV
- read a good book
- go shopping for clothes
- eat out

6A ⓬ p47

a) Work on your own. Write questions with *you* or *your* about **when you were thirteen**.

	you	your partner
1 / tall for your age? *Were you tall for your age?*		
2 Who / favourite teacher?		
3 / good at sport?		
4 What / favourite drink?		
5 Where / thirteenth birthday party?		

b) Write your answers in the *you* column.

c) Work with your partner. Take turns to ask and answer your questions. Write your partner's answers in the table.

d) Tell another student about you and your partner when you were thirteen.

> I was tall for my age when I was thirteen, but Federico wasn't.

12B ❿ p97

a) Work with a student from group B. Write questions with *you* in the Present Perfect and follow-up questions in the Past Simple.

1 / go / on holiday to a cold country?
  Have you ever been on holiday to a cold country?
  Where / go?
  Where did you go?
2 / lose / anything important?
  What / lose?
3 / study / music?
  What instrument / learn?
4 / have / a really bad holiday?
  What problems / have?
5 / cook / a meal for more than eight people?
  What / cook?

b) Work with a student from group A. Take turns to ask and answer your questions. If the answer is *yes*, ask your follow-up question. Then ask two more questions if possible.

c) Work with your partner from group B. Tell him/her about student A's life experiences.

9C ❾ p75

a) Work on your own. Read the information for phone conversations 1–4.

1 You are Alex Roberts. You're talking to a customer at the moment. If someone calls, get his/her phone number. Say you'll call him/her back later.

2 Phone Sam Watson, the sales manager in your company. You want to meet him tomorrow afternoon. You start this conversation.

3 You are at home. Decide what you are doing at the moment.

4 Phone a friend at home. Ask him/her what he/she is doing now. Does he/she want to go for a coffee? If yes, decide on a time and place to meet. You start this conversation.

b) Decide what you want to say in each conversation. Use language from the box or your own ideas.

> Hello, can I speak to … , please?
> Hello, is that … ?
> Speaking.
> This is … from … .
> It's … .
>
> Can I talk to you about … ?
> Call me on my mobile.
>
> Would you like to … ?
> Yes, good idea.
> Shall we meet at … ?
> Let's meet at … .
> See you then. Bye.

c) Work with your partner. Take turns to phone each other.

Pair and Group Work: Student/Group C

3B 🔟 p25

a) Work on your own. Choose the correct words in the phrases.

	name	name
1 go to the cinema *at /every* month		
2 watch TV *in/on* the afternoons		
3 visit your family *in/at* the weekend		
4 stay in *at/on* Sunday evenings		
5 go out *at/every* Saturday evening		

b) Make questions with *you* with phrases 1–5 in **a)**.

1 Do you go to the cinema every month?

c) Ask other students in the class your questions. Find two people who answer *yes* for each question. Write their names in the table.

d) Tell the class about the people in your table.

Filip and Lena both go to the cinema every month.

6B 🔟 p49

a) Work on your own. Choose five to eight of these events in your life. Write the year/month when these things happened on the timeline.

- born
- start/leave school
- start/leave university
- get married
- have a child
- meet your best friend(s)
- meet your first girlfriend/boyfriend
- go to live in a different town/city
- start your first job/a new job
- meet your husband/wife

b) Work in pairs. Take turns to tell your partner about your timeline. Ask questions to get more information.

> I met my husband in 1998.   Where did you meet him?

c) Tell another student three things about your partner's life.

19...   NOW

4B 🔟 c) p33

MARK Susie's very nice. We both like the same things – watching TV and doing sport. Also, she has lots of cats and I really like cats. She doesn't like rock music very much but that's OK. Yes, I'd like a second date with her. Yes, please!

SUSIE Mark? Yes, I like him. We both do a lot of sport – I like swimming and he likes football. And we both watch a lot of TV and DVDs, so that's a good thing. Do I want to see him again? Yes, why not? Maybe we can go dancing next time.

10A 🔟 p79

a) You have these problems. Check you understand them. Then write one more problem.

1 I can't find a job.
2 I need to find somewhere to live very quickly.
3 I want to learn more English vocabulary.
4 _____

b) Work with students A and B. Take turns to ask for and give advice. Whose advice is the best, do you think?

> I can't find a job. What should I do?

> (I think) you should ...

> (Don't) go ...

> Well, you shouldn't ...

Vocabulary

V0.1 Colours p4

red   green   blue   yellow   white   black   grey

V0.2 The alphabet p4

Aa Bb Cc Dd Ee
Ff Gg Hh Ii Jj Kk
Ll Mm Nn Oo Pp
Qq Rr Ss Tt Uu
Vv Ww Xx Yy Zz

/eɪ/	/iː/	/e/	/aɪ/	/əʊ/	/uː/	/ɑː/
Aa	Bb	Ff	Ii	Oo	Qq	Rr
Hh	Cc	Ll	Yy		Uu	
Jj	Dd	Mm			Ww	
Kk	Ee	Nn				
	Gg	Ss				
	Pp	Xx				
	Tt	Zz				
	Vv					

V0.3 Days of the week  p5

Monday /ˈmʌndeɪ/
Tuesday /ˈtjuːzdeɪ/
Wednesday /ˈwenzdeɪ/
Thursday /ˈθɜːzdeɪ/
Friday /ˈfraɪdeɪ/
Saturday /ˈsætədeɪ/
Sunday /ˈsʌndeɪ/

TIPS! • You can check phonemic symbols (/eɪ/, /iː/, etc.) on p159.
• ee = *double e*, A = *capital A*, a = *small a*.

Real World

RW0.1 Saying hello and goodbye p4 p5

Hello, my name's Marco.

Hi, I'm Lin.

Nice to meet you.

Nice to meet you too.

Goodbye/Bye, Lin.

Goodbye/Bye. See you on Thursday.

Yes, see you.

RW0.3 Names p4 p5

What's your name?
(My name's/It's) Claire.

What's your first name?
It's Pablo.

What's your surname?
Ruano.

How do you spell that?
R–U–A–N–O.

RW0.2 Classroom instructions p5

Match the instructions to pictures a)–l).

1 *f* Look at page ten.
2 *h* Answer the questions.
3 ☐ Fill in the gaps.
4 ☐ Open your book.
5 ☐ Read the article.
6 ☐ Match the words to the pictures.
7 ☐ Check your answers.
8 ☐ Work in pairs.
9 ☐ Work in groups.
10 ☐ Listen and practise.
11 ☐ Don't write.
12 ☐ Close your book.

RW0.4 I can p5

I can say the alphabet.
a b c d e f …

I can't say the alphabet.
a b f h … k?

a

b

c HELLO HELLO

d

e

f

g

h

i Weather
Match the words to pictures a)–k).
1 e hot
2 d warm
3 ☐ cold
4 ☐ wet
dry

j a) Fill in the gaps with 'm, 're or 's.
POSITIVE
1 I'm from Italy. (= I am)
2 You're in room C. (= you are)
3 He from Mexico. (= he is)
4 She from Australia. (= she is)
5 It Maria Favia. (= it is)

k

l

Language Summary 1

V1.1 Countries, nationalities and languages

(1A 3 p6)

countries *I'm from …*	nationalities *I'm …*	languages *I speak …*
Brazil	Brazilian	Portuguese
Australia	Australian	English
Argentina	Argentinian	Spanish
the USA	American	English
Germany	German	German
Italy	Italian	Italian
Mexico	Mexican	Spanish
Russia	Russian	Russian
the UK	British	English
Spain	Spanish	Spanish
Poland	Polish	Polish
Turkey	Turkish	Turkish
China	Chinese	Chinese
Japan	Japanese	Japanese
France	French	French

V1.2 Numbers 0–20 (1B 1 p8)

0 = zero/nought /nɔːt/	7 = seven	14 = fourteen
1 = one /wʌn/	8 = eight /eɪt/	15 = fifteen
2 = two /tuː/	9 = nine	16 = sixteen
3 = three /θriː/	10 = ten	17 = seventeen
4 = four	11 = eleven	18 = eighteen
5 = five	12 = twelve	19 = nineteen
6 = six	13 = thirteen /θɜː'tiːn/	20 = twenty

V1.3 Jobs (1B 5 p8)

Match the jobs to pictures a)–p).

1. ☐ a doctor
2. ☐ a musician /mju:'zɪʃən/
3. ☐ an engineer /endʒɪ'nɪə/
4. ☐ a shop assistant
5. ☐ a cleaner
6. ☐ a police officer
7. ☐ a waiter/a waitress
8. ☐ an accountant
9. ☐ an actor/an actress
10. ☐ a builder
11. ☐ a teacher
12. [a] a manager /'mænɪdʒə/
13. ☐ a housewife
14. ☐ a lawyer /'lɔɪə/
15. ☐ unemployed /ʌnɪm'plɔɪd/
16. ☐ retired /rɪ'taɪəd/

TIPS! • *What do you do? = What's your job?*
• We use *a* or *an* with jobs: *I'm a lawyer.* not ~~I'm lawyer~~.
• *unemployed* and *retired* are adjectives. We say:
I'm unemployed. not ~~I'm an unemployed~~.

V1.4 *a* and *an* (1B 6 p8)

● We use *a* with nouns that begin with a consonant sound. (The consonants are *b, c, d, f,* etc.): *I'm a student.*
● We use *an* with nouns that begin with a vowel sound. (The vowels are *a, e, i, o, u*): *He's an actor.*

TIP! • We use *a* with nouns that begin with a /j/ sound: *a university* /juːnɪ'vɜːsɪti/.

V1.5 Numbers 20–100 (1C 1 p10)

20 = twenty	26 = twenty-six	50 = fifty
21 = twenty-one	27 = twenty-seven	60 = sixty
22 = twenty-two	28 = twenty-eight	70 = seventy
23 = twenty-three	29 = twenty-nine	80 = eighty
24 = twenty-four	30 = thirty	90 = ninety
25 = twenty-five	40 = forty	100 = a hundred

V1.6 Personal possessions (1) (1D 1 p12)

Do you remember these things? Check on p12.

a diary	a coat	a watch	a bag
a suitcase	an umbrella	a camera	a bike/bicycle
a wallet	a CD player	/'kæmrə/	/'baɪsɪkl/
a shoe /ʃuː/	an ID (identity) card	a dress	false teeth

V1.7 Plurals (1D 2 p12)

	singular	plural
most nouns: add *-s*	a bag a shoe a suitcase	bags shoes suitcases /'suːtkeɪsɪz/
nouns ending in *-ch, -sh, -s, -ss, -x* or *-z*: add *-es*	a wat**ch** a dress	wat**ches** /'wɒtʃɪz/ dress**es** /'dresɪz/
nouns ending in consonant + *y*: *-y* → *-ies*	a diar**y**	diar**ies**
irregular plurals	a man a woman a child a person a tooth	men women /'wɪmɪn/ children people /'piːpl/ teeth /tiːθ/

V1.8 *this, that, these, those* (1D 7 p13)

	here ↓	there ↗
singular	this (umbrella)	that (CD player)
plural	these (watches)	those (false teeth)

Grammar

G1.1 *be*: positive and *Wh-* questions (1A **7** p7)

POSITIVE		WH- QUESTIONS
I'm from Italy.	(I'm = I am)	Where am I?
You're in room C.	(you're = you are)	Where are you from?
He's from Mexico.	(he's = he is)	Where's he from?
She's from Australia.	(she's = she is)	Where's she from?
It's Maria Favia.	(it's = it is)	Where's it from?
We're from the USA.	(we're = we are)	What's your name?
They're from Spain.	(they're = they are)	Where are we?
		What are your names?
		Where are they from?

TIP! • *you* and *your* are singular and plural in English.

G1.2 Subject pronouns and possessive adjectives (1A **10** p7)

subject pronouns	I	you	he	she	it	we	they
possessive adjectives	my	your	his	her	its	our	their

TIPS! • We use subject pronouns with **verbs**: *I am a teacher. They live in Rome.*
• We use possessive adjectives with **nouns**: *My name's Rupert Giles. It's her book.*

G1.3 *be*: negative, *yes/no* questions and short answers (1B **9** p9)

NEGATIVE

● We make negatives with *not*.

I'm not a teacher.
You/We/They aren't from Australia. (aren't = are not)
He/She/It isn't famous. (isn't = is not)

YES/NO QUESTIONS	SHORT ANSWERS	
Am I late?	Yes, I am.	No, I'm not.
Are you from Spain?	Yes, you are.	No, you aren't.
Is he/she a musician?	Yes, he/she is.	No, he/she isn't.
Is it from the USA?	Yes, it is.	No, it isn't.
Are we in room 5?	Yes, we are.	No, we aren't.
Are you from Sydney?	Yes, you are.	No, you aren't.
Are they French?	Yes, they are.	No, they aren't.

TIP! • We can also make negatives and negative short answers with 's or 're + *not*: *You're not from Australia. He's not famous. No, you're not. No, she's not*, etc.

Real World

RW1.1 Introducing people (1A **2** p6)

Elena, this is Roberto.

Hello, Elena. Nice to meet you.

And you.

RW1.2 Asking people to repeat things (1C **9** p11)

Could you say that again, please?
I'm sorry?
Sorry, could you repeat that, please?

RW1.3 Asking for personal details (1C **10** p11)

What's your surname?
What's your first name?
What's your nationality?
What's your address?
What's your postcode [US: zip code]?
What's your home phone number?
What's your mobile number?
What's your email address?

Are you married?
How old are you?

TIPS! • In phone numbers:
0 = *oh* and 44 = *double four*.
• In email addresses we say:
. = *dot*, @ = *at*, M = *capital M*.
• If you aren't married, you can say:
No, I'm single.
• We say: *I'm thirty-two (years old).*
not *I have thirty-two (years old).*
or *I'm thirty-two years.*

Language Summary 2

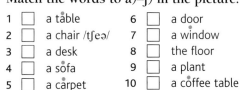

V2.1 Adjectives (1)

2A ❶ p14

Match the adjectives to pictures a)–n).

1	new	*h* old	8	fast ☐ slow
2	good ☐	bad ☐	9	young ☐ old ☐
3	cheap /tʃiːp/ ☐	expensive ☐	10	right /raɪt/ ☐ wrong /rɒŋ/ ☐
4	beautiful ☐	ugly ☐	11	nice *m*
5	easy ☐	difficult ☐	12	important ☐
6	big ☐	small ☐	13	great /greɪt/ ☐
7	long ☐	short ☐	14	favourite /ˈfeɪvrɪt/ ☐

V2.2 Adjectives with *very*   2A ❷ p14

- We put adjectives **after** the verb *be*: *She's **old**.*
- We put adjectives **before** a noun: *It's a **small** bag.*
- We put *very* **before** adjectives: *He's a very **happy** child.*
- Adjectives **aren't** plural with plural nouns: *Those are my **new** shoes.*

V2.3 Personal possessions (2)   2A ❽ p15

a computer

videos /ˈvɪdiəʊz/

CDs

a video recorder [US: a VCR]

a TV/television

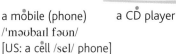

a DVD player

DVDs

a mobile (phone) /ˈməʊbaɪl fəʊn/ [US: a cell /sel/ phone]

a CD player

a laptop

a radio /ˈreɪdiəʊ/

a personal stereo

a digital /ˈdɪdʒɪtl/ camera

V2.4 Family   2B ❷ p16

♂ male	♀ female	♂♀ male and female
father (dad)	mother (mum)	parents /ˈpeərənts/
son /sʌn/	daughter /ˈdɔːtə/	children (kids)
brother /ˈbrʌðə/	sister	–
husband	wife (plural: wives)	–
grandfather	grandmother	grandparents
grandson	granddaughter	grandchildren
uncle	aunt /ɑːnt/	–
cousin /ˈkʌzən/	cousin	cousins

TIPS! • *parents* = mother and father only, *relatives* = all the people in your family.
• *brothers* = men/boys only. We ask: *How many brothers and sisters have you got?*
• *boyfriend/girlfriend* = a man/woman you have a romantic relationship with.
• We use *How many ... ?* to ask about a number: *How many children have you got?*

V2.5 Time words   2C ❶ p18

60 seconds = 1 minute /ˈmɪnɪt/
60 minutes = 1 hour /aʊə/
24 hours = 1 day
7 days = 1 week
12 months /mʌnθs/ = 1 year

TIP! • We say *two and a half hours* not
~~*two hours and a half*~~.

V2.6 Things in a house   2D ❶ p20

Match the words to a)–j) in the picture.

1 ☐ a table	6 ☐ a door
2 ☐ a chair /tʃeə/	7 ☐ a window
3 ☐ a desk	8 ☐ the floor
4 ☐ a sofa	9 ☐ a plant
5 ☐ a carpet	10 ☐ a coffee table

V2.7 Prepositions of place   2D ❷ p20

in   on   by

under   behind   in front of

VERY GOOD.

Grammar

G2.1 *have got*: positive and negative (2A **5** p15)

POSITIVE

I/you/we/they**'ve got** (= have got)

he/she/it**'s got** (= has got)

NEGATIVE

I/you/we/they **haven't got** (= have not got)

he/she/it **hasn't got** (= has not got)

G2.2 *have got*: questions and short answers

(2A **10** p15)

QUESTIONS

Have I got any letters today?

Have you got a computer?

Has he/she/it got a DVD player?

Have we got any CDs?

Have they got any cheap TVs?

What have you got in your bag?

What has he/she got in his/her bag?

SHORT ANSWERS

Yes, I have.	No, I haven't.
Yes, you have.	No, you haven't.
Yes, he/she/it has.	No, he/she/it hasn't.
Yes, we have.	No, we haven't.
Yes, they have.	No, they haven't.

TIPS! • We don't use *got* in short answers.

• We use *any* in plural negatives and questions with *have got*: *We haven't got any CDs. Have I got any letters?*

G2.3 Possessive *'s* (2B **6** p17)

● We use *name* + *'s* for the possessive: *Kate is Lisa's sister.* not ~~Kate is the sister of Lisa~~. *Pat is Chris and Emma's grandmother.*

TIPS! • For plural nouns, the apostrophe (') is **after** the *s*: *My parents' names are Pat and Bill.*

• *'s* can mean the possessive, *is* or *has*:
Bill is Lisa's father. (*'s* = possessive)
Kate's her sister. (*'s* = is)
She's got a brother. (*'s* = has)

• We use *whose* to ask which person/people a thing belongs to: *Whose mobile phone is that? It's Tom's.*

Real World

RW2.1 Telling the time (2C **2 3** p18)

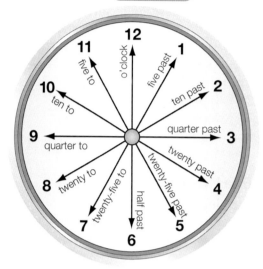

TIPS! • We can say *quarter past/to six* or *a quarter past/to six*. We don't say ~~fifteen past six~~. For other times, we say *minutes*: *nineteen minutes past six* not ~~nineteen past six~~.

• We can also say the time like this: *six fifteen, two thirty, ten forty, six nineteen*, etc. But for 6.05 we say: *six oh five* not ~~six five~~.

• In American English, 10.05 = *five after ten*.

RW2.2 Talking about the time (2C **5** p18)

QUESTIONS ABOUT THE TIME

A What time is it?   B It's five o'clock.

A What's the time, please?   B It's about half past two.

A Excuse me. Have you   B Yes, it's eight fifteen.
   got the time, please?

PREPOSITIONS OF TIME

● We use *at* for times: *My English class is **at** ten.*

● We use *from … to* for length of time: *My son's class is **from** seven **to** nine thirty.*

TIPS! • a.m. = 0.00–12.00   midday/noon = 12.00
            p.m. = 12.00–24.00   midnight = 24.00

RW2.3 Asking about prices (2C **10** p19)

● We use *How much …?* to ask about prices.

(How much is (that)/(the concert)?)   (It's ten dollars.)

(How much are (the tickets)/ (these books)?)   (They're six pounds fifty.)

£20 = twenty pounds

£7.50 = seven pounds fifty

40p = forty p /piː/

£29.99 = twenty-nine ninety-nine

€9 = nine euros /ˈjʊərəʊz/

€6.50 = six euros fifty

$35 = thirty-five dollars

50c = fifty cents /sents/

Language Summary 3

Vocabulary

V3.1 Daily routines (3A ❶ p22)

Match the words/phrases to pictures a)–o).

1 ☐ get up
2 ☐ go to bed
3 ☐ have breakfast /'brekfəst/
4 ☐ have lunch /lʌntʃ/
5 ☐ have dinner
6 ☐ start work /wɜːk/
7 ☐ start classes
8 ☐ finish work
9 ☐ finish classes
10 ☐ leave home
11 ☐ get home
12 ☐ *g* work
13 ☐ *h* study
14 ☐ sleep
15 ☐ live

V3.2 Free time activities (1) (3B ❶ p24)

Match the phrases to pictures a)–l).

1 ☐ go out
2 ☐ *e* stay in
3 ☐ eat out
4 ☐ go for a drink
5 ☐ go to the cinema
6 ☐ go to concerts
7 ☐ go shopping
8 ☐ phone friends/ my family
9 ☐ visit friends/ my family
10 ☐ have coffee with friends
11 ☐ do sport
12 ☐ watch TV

TIP! • We say: *Do you want to go for a drink?* not *Do you want to drink something?*

V3.3 Time phrases with *on, in, at, every* (3B ❾ p25)

on	in	at	every
+ day	**+ part of the day**	**+ time**	week
Saturday	the morning	nine o'clock	Thursday
Thursday	the afternoon	half past three	day
Mondays	the evening		month
Monday mornings	the week	night	night
Sunday afternoon		the weekend	morning

TIPS! • When we talk about routines, we can use the singular or plural of days, parts of the day and *the weekend*: *I play tennis on (Monday/Mondays), in (the evening/evenings), at (the weekend/weekends)*.

• We don't use a plural with *every*: *every week* not ~~every weeks~~.

• Notice we say *in the morning/afternoon/evening* but *at night*.

V3.4 Months (3C ❹ p26)

January /'dʒænjʊəri/   April /'eɪprəl/   July /dʒʊ'laɪ/   October
February /'februəri/   May   August /'ɔːgəst/   November
March   June /dʒuːn/   September   December

V3.5 Dates (3C ❺ p26)

1st = first /fɜːst/   8th = eighth /eɪtθ/   20th = twentieth
2nd = second   9th = ninth /naɪnθ/   21st = twenty-first
3rd = third /θɜːd/   10th = tenth   22nd = twenty-second
4th = fourth /fɔːθ/   11th = eleventh   23rd = twenty-third
5th = fifth   12th = twelfth /twelfθ/   24th = twenty-fourth
6th = sixth   13th = thirteenth   30th = thirtieth /'θɜːtiə
7th = seventh   14th = fourteenth   31st = thirty-first

TIPS! • We say: *the fifth of May* or *May the fifth*. We write: *5th May* or *May 5th*.

• In the UK, *1.9.07* = *1st September 2007* (day/month/year).
In the USA, *1.9.07* = *9th January 2007* (month/day/year).

V3.6 Frequency adverbs (3D ❶ p28)

always   usually   often   sometimes   hardly ever   never

100%   0%

V3.7 Word order of frequency adverbs (3D ❸ p28)

• Frequency adverbs go **after** the verb *be*: *I'm **always** happy when I get u*
• Frequency adverbs go **before** other verbs: *I **sometimes** get up before 9*

TIP! • We can only use *always, usually* and *often* in negative sentences: *I don't often go out on Sunday evenings.*

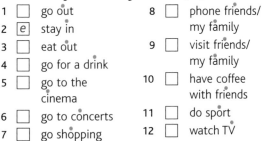

Grammar

G3.1 **Present Simple: positive (*I/you/we/they*)** 3A ❹ p22

I/You/We/They **get up** at five o clock.
I/You/We/They **get up** very early.
I/You/We/They **start** work at about 5.45.
I/You/We/They **have** an hour for lunch.

G3.2 **Present Simple: *Wh-* questions (*I/you/we/they*)**

3A ❽ p23

question word	auxiliary	subject	infinitive	
Where	do	I/you/we/they	live?	
Where	do	they	have	dinner?
What time	do	you	go	to bed?
When	do	you	get back	to the hotel?
What time	do	they	finish	work?
When	do	we	start	work?

G3.3 **Present Simple: negative (*I/you/we/they*)** 3B ❺ p24

subject	auxiliary	infinitive	
I/you/we/they	don't (= do not)	live	in England.
I	don't	go	out in the week.
We	don't	stay	in at the weekend.
They	don't	watch	TV in the day.

G3.4 **Present Simple: *yes/no* questions and short answers (*I/you/we/they*)** 3B ❼ p25

YES/NO QUESTIONS

auxiliary	subject	infinitive	
Do	I/you/we/they	live	in England?
Do	you	eat	out a lot?
Do	you	go	to concerts?
Do	they	watch	TV a lot?

SHORT ANSWERS

Yes, I/you/we/they do.	No, I/you/we/they don't.

G3.5 **Subject and object pronouns** 3D ❺ p29

subject pronouns	object pronouns
I	me
you	you
he	him
she	her
it	it
we	us
they	them

TIP! • In positive and negative sentences, subject pronouns come before the verb and object pronouns come after the verb: *I often phone <u>her</u> at 11 p.m.* **We** *don't usually see <u>him</u> in the mornings.*

Real World

RW3.1 **Phrases for special days**

3C ❷ p26

a birthday /ˈbɜːθdeɪ/ (Happy birthday!)

a wedding (Congratulations!)

the birth of a new baby (Congratulations!)

a New Year's Eve party (Happy New Year!)

a wedding anniversary (Happy anniversary!)

RW3.2 **Suggestions** 3C ❿ p27

asking for suggestions		making suggestions		responding to suggestions
What shall we	get him? buy him? give her?	Let's	get him a book. buy him a DVD. give her a CD.	✓ That's a good idea. ✓✗ I'm not sure. ✗ No, I don't think so.
		What about	a DVD?	

TIP! • We use the infinitive after *What shall we …?* and *Let's: What shall we* **do** *tonight? Let's* **go** *to the cinema.*

Language Summary 4

Vocabulary

V4.1 Free time activities (2)

4A ❶ p30

Match the phrases to pictures a)–k).

1. ☐ read /riːd/ books/magazines
2. ☐ watch DVDs/videos
3. ☐ play tennis
4. ☐ take photos
5. ☐ go skiing /ˈskiːɪŋ/
6. ☐ go swimming
7. ☐ go running /ˈrʌnɪŋ/
8. ☐ go dancing
9. ☐ listen /ˈlɪsən/ to music
10. ☐ listen to the radio
11. ☐ watch sport on TV

V4.2 Things you like/don't like **4B ❶ p32**

Match the words/phrases to pictures a)–o).

1. ☐ reading
2. ☐ football
3. ☐ travelling
4. ☐ cats
5. ☐ shopping for clothes /kləʊðz/
6. ☐ computer games
7. ☐ animals
8. ☐ dancing
9. ☐ cooking
10. ☐ dance music
11. ☐ rock music
12. ☐ jazz
13. ☐ Italian food
14. ☐ Chinese food
15. ☐ fast food

V4.3 *like/love/hate* **4B ❷ p32**

☺	I love ...
☺	I really like ...
☺	I like ...
☺	I quite like ...
☺	... is/are OK.
☹	I don't like ...
☹	I hate ...

V4.4 Verb+*ing* **4B ❸ p32**

verb + verb+*ing*	verb + noun
I love **reading**.	I love **rock music**.
I really like **travelling**.	I like **books**.
Shopping for clothes is OK.	I quite like **Italian food**.
I don't like **dancing**.	I don't like **computer games**.
I hate **cooking**.	I hate **football**.

TIPS! • We don't use *the* to talk about things we like/don't like in general:
I love books. (= books in general). *He doesn't like cats.* (= cats in general).

• We often use *very much* with *like*. We put it after the noun or verb+*ing*:
I like reading very much. not ~~I like very much reading~~.

V4.5 Food and drink (1) (4C 4 p34)

a cheese and tomato sandwich /'sænwɪdʒ/

a tuna mayonnaise /meɪə'neɪz/ sandwich

a coffee

a bottle of beer

a bottle of red wine

a glass of white wine

a bottle of sparkling mineral water

a bottle of still mineral water

a cheeseburger and chips

a burger /'bɜːgə/ and chips [US: French fries]

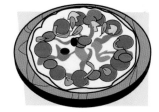

a mixed /mɪkst/ salad

a tuna salad /'sæləd/

a chicken /'tʃɪkɪn/ salad

a pizza

V4.6 Food and drink (2) (4D 1 p36)

Match the words to pictures a)–t).

1. ☐ biscuits /'bɪskɪts/
2. ☐ milk
3. ☐ an apple
4. ☐ rice
5. ☐ toast /təʊst/
6. ☐ bread
7. ☐ sausages /'sɒsɪdʒɪz/
8. ☐ fish
9. ☐ eggs
10. ☐ coffee
11. ☐ soup /suːp/
12. ☐ cheese
13. ☐ vegetables /'vedʒtəblz/
14. ☐ a banana /bə'nɑːnə/
15. ☐ orange juice /'ɒrɪndʒ dʒuːs/
16. ☐ tea
17. ☐ jam /dʒæm/
18. ☐ meat /miːt/
19. ☐ fruit /fruːt/
20. ☐ cereal /'sɪərɪəl/

V4.7 Countable and uncountable nouns (4D 5 p36)

COUNTABLE NOUNS

- Countable nouns can be plural: *biscuits*, *apples*.
- We use *a* or *an* with singular countable nouns: *a biscuit*, *an apple*.
- We don't use *a* or *an* with plural countable nouns: *biscuits* not *a biscuits*, *apples* not *an apples*.

UNCOUNTABLE NOUNS

- Uncountable nouns aren't usually plural: *milk* not *milks*, *rice* not *rices*.
- We don't use *a* or *an* with uncountable nouns: *milk* not *a milk*, *rice* not *a rice*.

TIP! • Some nouns can be countable and uncountable: *I like coffee.* (uncountable = coffee in general)
Can I have a coffee, please? (countable = a cup of coffee)

Language Summary 4

G4.1 Present Simple: positive and negative (*he/she/it*)
(4A 5 p31)

POSITIVE

- In positive sentences with *he/she/it* we add *-s* or *-es* to the infinitive.

subject	infinitive + *-s* or *-es*	
He/She/It	work**s**	in Antarctica.
Paul	watch**es**	a lot of sport on TV.

NEGATIVE

- In negative sentences with *he/she/it* we use *doesn't* (= *does not*) + infinitive.

- In negative sentences with *I/you/we/they* we use *don't* (= *do not*) + infinitive (see G3.3).

subject	auxiliary + *not*	infinitive	
He/She/It	doesn't (= does not)	like	the job very much.
Alison	doesn't	talk	to him very often.

G4.2 Present Simple positive: spelling rules (*he/she/it*)
(4A 6 p31)

spelling rule	examples	
most verbs: add *-s*	play**s**	like**s**
	read**s**	listen**s**
verbs ending in *-ch, -sh, -s,* *-ss, -x* or *-z*: add *-es*	watch**es** /ˈwɒtʃɪz/	
	fini**sh**es /ˈfɪnɪʃɪz/	
verbs ending in consonant + *y*: *-y* → *-ies*	stud**ies**	
the verbs *go* and *do*: add *-es*	goe**s**	doe**s** /dʌz/
the verb *have* is irregular	ha**s**	

G4.3 Present Simple: questions and short answers (*he/she/it*)
(4B 7 p33)

- We use *does* in questions with *he/she/it*.
- We use *do* in questions with *I/you/we/they*.

QUESTIONS

question word	auxiliary	subject	infinitive	
	Does	he/she/it	like	animals?
What	does	she	do	in her free time?
	Does	she	watch	TV a lot?
	Does	she	like	films?
What music	does	she	like?	

SHORT ANSWERS

Yes, he/she/it does. | No, he/she/it doesn't.

TIP! • We don't repeat the verb in short answers:
Yes, she does. not ~~Yes, she likes~~.
No, she doesn't. not ~~No, she doesn't like~~.

G4.4 *have* or *have got*? (4B 7 p33)

- We can use *have* or *have got* to talk about possessions and family:
  She's got two dogs. = She has two dogs.
  I haven't got any children. = I don't have any children.
  Have you got a car? = Do you have a car?

- We can only use *have* to talk about meals and other activities:
  I don't have breakfast. not ~~I haven't got breakfast~~.
  We often have coffee with friends. not ~~We often have got coffee with friends~~.
  Do you want to have a game of tennis? not ~~Do you want to have got a game of tennis?~~

RW4.1 Requests and offers (4C 8 p35)

- We use *I'd/We'd like* and *Can I/we have ... ?* for requests (we want something).
  I'd like = I would like; We'd like = we would like.

  I'd like a bottle of water, please. | Can I/we have the bill, please?

- We use *Would you like ...?* for offers (we want to give something or help someone).

  Would you like to order now? | What would you like to drink?

TIPS! • We use a noun after *Can I/we have ...?*: *Can we have **a bottle of wine**?*
• We use a noun or an infinitive with *to* after *Would you like ...?* and *I'd/We'd like*:
*Would you like **a drink**? I'd like **to order**, please.*

Language Summary 5

Vocabulary

V5.1 Places in a town/the country

5A ① p38

Match the words to pictures a)–t).

1 □ a square /skweə/
2 □ a park
3 a a market
4 □ a bus station /'steɪʃən/
5 □ a station
6 □ a lake
7 □ a beach /biːtʃ/
8 □ the sea /siː/
9 □ a river
10 □ a museum /mjuː'ziːəm/
11 □ an airport
12 □ mountains /'maʊntɪnz/
13 □ a road /rəʊd/
14 □ a café
15 □ a bar
16 □ a shop
17 □ a flat [US: an apartment]
18 □ a house
19 □ a hotel
20 □ a bed and breakfast

TIP! • a station = a train station.

V5.2 Rooms and things in a house

5B ① ② p40

Do you remember the things in the flat in Park Street? Check on p40.

rooms	furniture /'fɜːnɪtʃə/ and other things in a house
in the kitchen /'kɪtʃɪn/	a cooker, a sink, a fridge /frɪdʒ/, a table, four chairs, a washing machine /mə'ʃiːn/
in the living room	a coffee table, two plants, a sofa, two armchairs
in the bathroom	a bath /bɑːθ/, a shower, a toilet, a washbasin /'wɒʃbeɪsən/
in the bedrooms	a double /'dʌbl/ bed, a single bed, a chair, a desk, a plant
on the balcony	a table, three plants, two chairs

V5.3 Shops 5C ② p42

Fill in the gaps with these words.

a supermarket a bookshop a bank a dry cleaner's a chemist's /'kemɪsts/ [US: a pharmacy] a kiosk a newsagent's /'njuːz,eɪdʒənts/ a butcher's /'bʊtʃəz/ a baker's a department store a greengrocer's /'griːngrəʊsəz/ a post office

1 You buy food in _a supermarket_ .
2 You buy fruit and vegetables in _____ .
3 You buy meat in _____ .
4 You change money in _____ .
5 You buy things for the house in _____ .
6 You buy bread in _____ .
7 You buy medicine in _____ .
8 _____ cleans your expensive clothes.
9 You buy books in _____ .
10 You post letters at _____ .
11 You buy newspapers at _____ or in _____ .

TIP! • We use in or at with shops: You buy meat in/at a butcher's. But we say: at a kiosk not in a kiosk.

V5.4 one and ones 5C ⑤ p42

• We use **one** in place of a singular noun: How much is this **sofa**? This **one**?
• We use **ones** in place of a plural noun: A kilo of **apples**, please. The green **ones**?

Language Summary 5

V5.5 Things to buy 5C **7** p43

Match the words to pictures a)–n).

1. ☐ stamps
2. ☐ cigarettes
3. ☐ a map
4. ☐ phone cards
5. ☐ batteries
6. ☐ a film
7. ☐ envelopes /'envələups/
8. ☐ postcards
9. ☐ tissues /'tɪʃuːz/
10. ☐ a magazine
11. ☐ a lighter
12. ☐ a bottle of water
13. ☐ a newspaper
14. ☐ chocolate /'tʃɒklət/

V5.6 Clothes 5D **1** p44

Match the words to pictures a)–s).

1	☐	trousers /'trauzəz/	9	☐ trainers
2	☐	shorts	10	☐ a jacket /'dʒækɪt/
3	☐	jeans /dʒiːnz/	11	☐ a hat
4	☐	a dress	12	☐ a tie
5	☐	shoes	13	☐ boots
6	a	a suit /suːt/	14	☐ a shirt /ʃɜːt/
7	☐	a skirt /skɜːt/	15	☐ socks
8	☐	a jumper /'dʒʌmpə/	16	☐ a T-shirt
			17	☐ a top
			18	☐ a coat
			19	☐ a cap

V5.7 Plural nouns 5D **3** p44

look plural but can mean *one thing*	can be singular or plural
jeans	a shoe/shoes
shorts	a sock/socks
trousers	a boot/boots
	a trainer/trainers

TIPS! • We can use *a pair of* ... with both types of plural noun: *I've got a new pair of shoes/jeans.*

• The word *clothes* /kləuðz/ is always plural. If we want to use the singular, we can say *an item of clothing.*

132

Grammar

G5.1 **_there is/there are_** (5A **7** p39)

	singular	plural
POSITIVE	**There's** a beautiful lake.	**There are** lots of things to do.
NEGATIVE	**There isn't** a park near our flat.	**There aren't** any restaurants.
QUESTIONS	**Is there** a hotel?	**Are there** any cheap places to stay?
SHORT ANSWERS	Yes, **there is.**/No, **there isn't.**	Yes, **there are.**/No, **there aren't.**

TIPS! • We use _any_ in negatives and questions with _there are._
• We can also make negative sentences with _no_: _There are no shops._ = _There aren't any shops._

G5.2 **_How much ... ?/How many ... ?_** (5B **4** p40)

HOW MANY ... ?

● We use _How many ... ?_ with **plural countable** nouns (_tables, bedrooms, people, chairs,_ etc.):
How many bedrooms are there? How many people are in this room?

HOW MUCH ... ?

● We use _How much ... ?_ with **uncountable** nouns (_furniture, money, space, time,_ etc.):
How much space is there in the flat? How much furniture have you got?

TIP! • When we ask about prices we say: _How much is that? It's £10._

G5.3 **_some, any, a_** (5B **8** p41)

● We usually use **some** in **positive** sentences with plural countable nouns and uncountable nouns.
● We usually use **any** in **negatives** and **questions** with plural countable nouns and uncountable nouns.
● We use _a_ (or _an_) in **positive** sentences, **negatives** and **questions** with singular countable nouns.

	singular countable nouns	plural countable nouns	uncountable nouns
POSITIVE	There's **a** cooker.	There are **some** chairs.	I'd like **some** information.
NEGATIVE	There isn't **a** TV.	We haven't got **any** children.	I haven't got **any** money.
QUESTIONS	Has it got **a** shower?	Are there **any** shops?	Is there **any** furniture?

Real World

RW5.1 **Shop language** (5C **10** p43)

SAYING WHAT YOU WANT

I'll have these ones, please.

Have you got any big bottles of water?

Can I have four stamps for Europe, please?

ASKING ABOUT PRICES

How much are the phone cards?

How much is that?

Language Summary 6

Vocabulary

V6.1 Adjectives (2) (6A 2 p46)

Match the words to pictures a)–k).

1	happy	[h] unhappy
2	poor	☐ rich
3	hot	☐ cold
4	friendly /'frendli/	☐ unfriendly
5	noisy	☐ quiet /kwaɪət/
6	short	☐ tall
7	boring	☐ interesting /'ɪntrəstɪŋ/
8	well	☐ ill
9	clean	☐ dirty /'dɜːti/
10	intelligent	☐ stupid
11	crowded /'kraʊdɪd/	☐ empty

V6.2 Years (6A 10 p47)

1953 = nineteen fifty-three   1900 = nineteen hundred
1970 = nineteen seventy   2000 = two thousand
1895 = eighteen ninety-five   2005 = two thousand and five

V6.3 Life events (6B 1 p48)

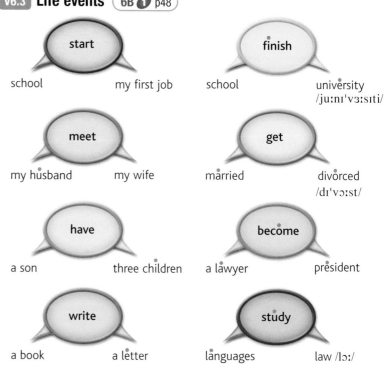

start		finish	
school	my first job	school	university /juːnɪ'vɜːsɪti/
meet		**get**	
my husband	my wife	married	divorced /dɪ'vɔːst/
have		**become**	
a son	three children	a lawyer	president
write		**study**	
a book	a letter	languages	law /lɔː/

V6.4 Weekend activities (6C 2 p50)

work every evening/all day   **go away** for the weekend/for a couple of days
clean the car/the house   **sleep** for eight hours/until 11 a.m.
write a report/an email   **be** ill/tired /taɪəd/
do the washing/the shopping   **have** a wonderful time/a bad cold

V6.5 Adjectives with *very, really, quite, too* (6D 5 p52)

It's **quite** big.   It's **very/really** big.   It's **too** big.

- *Too* has a negative meaning. It means *more than you want*.
- *Very*, *really*, *quite* and *too* come **after** the verb *be* and **before** adjectives.

TIP! • We don't use *too* to mean *very very*: *She's really happy.* not *She's too happy.*

Grammar

G6.1 *was/were/wasn't/weren't* 6A ④ p46

POSITIVE	NEGATIVE
I was	I wasn't (= was not)
you/we/they were	you/we/they weren't (= were not)
he/she/it was	he/she/it wasn't

TIPS! • We say: *When/Where were you born? I was born in 1987/Paris.*

• The past of *there is/are* is *there was/were.*

G6.2 Questions and short answers with *was/were*

6A ⑧ p47

QUESTIONS

question word	*was/were*	subject	
When	was	I/he/she/it	in London?
Where	were	you/we/they	yesterday?
When	was	Margaret's 13ᵗʰ birthday?	
	Were	her friends	there?
Where	was	the party?	
	Was	the weather	good?

YES/NO QUESTIONS	SHORT ANSWERS
Was I/he/she/it good?	Yes, I/he/she/it was. No, I/he/she/it wasn't.
Were you/we/they at the party?	Yes, you/we/they were. No, you/we/they weren't.
Was there a lot of food?	Yes, there was. No, there wasn't.
Were there parties in every street?	Yes, there were. No, there weren't.

G6.3 Past Simple regular and irregular verbs: positive

6B ④ p48

• We use the Past Simple to talk about the past. We know **when** these things happened.

• The Past Simple is the same for all subjects: *I/You/He/She/It/We/They played tennis yesterday.*

regular verbs: spelling rule	examples	
most regular verbs: add *-ed*	start**ed** work**ed** stay**ed**	finish**ed** want**ed**
regular verbs ending in -e: add *-d*	liv**ed**	hat**ed**
regular verbs ending in consonant+ *y*: *-y* → *-i* and add *-ed*	stud**ied**	marr**ied**
regular verbs ending in consonant + vowel + consonant: double the last consonant	stop**ped**	

TIP! • There are no rules for irregular verbs. There is an Irregular Verb List, p159.

G6.4 Past Simple: *Wh-* questions 6B ⑧ p49

question word	auxiliary	subject	infinitive	
Where	did	I/you/he/she/it/ we/they	go	last weekend?
Where	did	Albert Einstein	come	from?
When	did	the Wright brothers	fly	the first plane?
Where	did	Mother Teresa	live	for most of her life?

TIP! • Notice the difference between Present Simple questions and Past Simple questions: *Where **do** you live?* (Present Simple), *Where **did** you live?* (Past Simple).

Real World

RW6.1 Showing interest 6C ⑤ p51

I'm happy for you.	*I'm sorry for you.*	*I'm surprised.*	*I'm not surprised.*
Oh, great! Oh, nice.	Oh, dear. What a shame.	Wow! You're joking! Really?	Oh, right.

RW6.2 Continuing a conversation 6C ⑧ p51

QUESTIONS YOU CAN ASK SOMEONE WHO ...

... WENT TO THE CINEMA	... STAYED AT HOME ALL WEEKEND	... WAS ILL	... WENT AWAY FOR THE WEEKEND
What did you see? What was it like? Who did you go with?	What did you do?	What was wrong? Are you OK now?	What was it like? Where did you go? Who did you go with? Where did you stay?

Language Summary 7

V7.1 Types of film
7A ➊ p54

action films | thrillers | horror films | science-fiction (sci-fi /'saɪfaɪ/) films

cartoons | love stories | comedies | historical dramas

TIP! • The American English word for *film* is *movie*: *action movies*, etc.

V7.2 Types of music 7B ➊ p56

rap | rock music | pop music | classical music | opera | jazz | dance music | reggae /'reɡeɪ/ | rock'n'roll

V7.3 Question words 7B ➍ p56

question word	meaning	example
Who	a person	**Who**'s that man over there? It's Michael.
Where	a place	**Where** did you go last week? To Germany.
When	a time	**When** does the lesson start? At two o'clock.
Why	a reason	**Why** are you late? Because I missed the bus.
Whose	possessive	**Whose** shoes are these? They're Susan's.
Which	a thing (from a small number of possible answers)	**Which** do you like, the red shirt or the blue shirt? The red shirt.
What	a thing (from many possible answers)	**What** do you want to do tonight? Let's watch a DVD.
How many	a number	**How many** people are there in your class? Twelve.
How long	a period of time	**How long** did you work in Russia? For two years.
How old	age	**How old** is your teacher? She's about thirty.

TIPS! • We often answer *Why … ?* questions with *Because … .*

• We often answer *How long … ?* questions with *For* + period of time: *For six hours.*

• We also use *What time … ?* to ask about time and *How much … ?* to ask about prices.

V7.4 Irregular Past Simple forms 7C ➎ p58

lose /luːz/ (lost) | find (found) | take (took)

say (said /sed/) | fall (fell) | break /breɪk/ (broke)

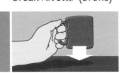

choose (chose) | win (won) | put (put)

tell (told)

TIP! • For other irregular Past Simple forms, see the Irregular Verb List, p159.

V7.5 *a, an* and *the* 7D ➍ p60

• We use *a/an* to talk about things or people for the first time: ***An** old man in **a** long coat sat near him.*

• We use ***the*** when we know which thing or person: ***The** old man had a big black dog.*

• We use ***the*** when there is only one thing or person in a particular place: *He sat in **the** front row.*

TIP! • We also use ***the*** in some fixed phrases: *go to **the** cinema/**the** theatre, in **the** morning/afternoon/evening, at **the** weekend, **the** news,* etc.

Grammar

G7.1 Past Simple: negative (7A ❹ p55)

- To make the Past Simple negative of *be*, we use *wasn't* or *weren't* (see G6.1).
- To make the Past Simple negative of all other verbs, we use *didn't* + infinitive.

subject	auxiliary	infinitive	
I/You/He/She/It/We/They	didn't (= did not)	study	very much.

TIP! • We use *didn't* for all subjects (*I, you, we, they,* etc.).

G7.2 Past Simple: *yes/no* questions and short answers (7A ❿ p55)

YES/NO QUESTIONS

auxiliary	subject	infinitive	
Did	I/you/he/she/ it/we/they	make go	a lot of money? to the same school?

SHORT ANSWERS

Yes, I/you/he/she/it/we/they did.
No, I/you/he/she/it/we/they didn't.

G7.3 Past time phrases (7B ❷ p56)

AGO

- We use *ago* to talk about a time in the past. We use it with the Past Simple: *I went to Mexico two years ago.* (= two years before now).

LAST

- We use *last* to say the day, week, etc. in the past that is nearest to now: *I went dancing last Saturday.* (= the Saturday before now).
- We use *last* with **days** (*last Tuesday*), **months** (*last March*) and in these phrases: *last night, last week, last weekend, last month, last year, last century.*

TIPS! • We say *last night*, but *yesterday morning/afternoon/evening* not ~~last morning~~, etc.

• We don't use a preposition with *last*: *last weekend* not ~~in last weekend~~, *last month* not ~~at last month~~.

IN

- We use *in* with **years** (*in 2005*) and **months** (*in May*).
- We use *in the* with **decades** (*in the nineties*) and **centuries** (*in the twenty-first century*).

TIPS! • We can use *on* with **days** (*on Monday*) to mean *last: I met him on Monday.* = *I met him last Monday.*

• We use *at* with **times** (*at ten o'clock*).

G7.4 Question forms (7B ❻ p56)

QUESTION FORMS: ALL VERBS EXCEPT BE

- We use the auxiliary *did* in Past Simple questions (see G6.4), and the auxiliary *do* or *does* in Present Simple questions (see G3.2 and G4.3).

PAST SIMPLE

question word	auxiliary	subject	infinitive	
When What	did did	Madonna Sting	make do	her first record? before he became a singer?

PRESENT SIMPLE

question word	auxiliary	subject	infinitive	
Where Which instrument	do does	U2 Elton John	come play?	from?

TIP! • We can also make Present Simple questions with *have got: What car has he got?* (see G2.2). In the Past Simple we say: *Did you have a car?* not ~~Did you have got a car?~~

QUESTION FORMS: BE

- For the verb *be*, we don't use *do, does* or *did* to make questions (see G1.1 and G6.2).

	question word	be	subject	
PAST SIMPLE	How old How long	was were	Shakira the Beatles	when she released *Magic*? together?
PRESENT SIMPLE	Where What How old	am is are	I? your name? they?	

Real World

RW7.1 Talking about the news (7C ❽ p59)

- To start a conversation about the news, we can say:

Did you hear about that plane crash?

Did you read about the couple on Everest?

No, where was it?

No, what happened?

- To respond to good, bad and surprising news, we can say:

good news	bad news	surprising news
Oh, that's good.	Yes, isn't it awful? Oh, dear. Are they OK? Oh no, that's terrible.	Really? You're joking!

TIP! • *news* is a singular noun. We say: *The news is terrible.* not ~~The news are terrible.~~

Language Summary 8

Vocabulary

V8.1 Holiday activities (8A **2** p62)

Match the words/phrases to pictures a)–r).

1 ☐ go for walks
2 ☐ go fishing
3 ☐ go sightseeing /ˈsaɪtsiːɪŋ/
4 ☐ go shopping
5 ☐ go to the beach
6 ☐ go skiing
7 ☐ go swimming
8 ☐ go cycling /ˈsaɪklɪŋ/
9 ☐ go on boat trips
10 ☐ sunbathe /ˈsʌnbeɪð/
11 ☐ have picnics
12 ☐ stay in a hotel
13 ☐ stay with friends/family
14 ☐ camp
15 ☐ rent a car
16 ☐ rent a bike
17 ☐ travel by public transport
18 ☐ go on holiday
[US: go on vacation]

V8.2 Adjectives to describe places

(8B **1** p64)

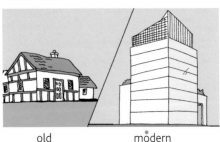

old   modern

dangerous   safe
/ˈdeɪndʒərəs/

TIP! • We can also use these adjectives to describe places (see V6.1): *noisy/quiet*, *clean/dirty*, *boring/interesting*, *friendly/unfriendly*, *crowded/empty*.

V8.3 Verb collocations (8D **4** p68)

book	rent	get	stay
a flight /flaɪt/	a motorbike	to your/our place	in (Canada)
a hotel room	a car	a taxi	with you/us
a table (at a restaurant)	an apartment	a bus	in a hotel

TIP! • *a flight* is a journey by plane: *Have a good flight!*

Grammar

G8.1 *can/can't* for possibility   8A 6 p63

- We use **can** to say that something is possible.
- We use **can't** to say that something isn't possible.
- For positive sentences, we use:
  subject + **can** + infinitive.
- For negative sentences, we use:
  subject + **can't** + infinitive (can't = cannot).
- **can** and **can't** are the same for all subjects (*I, you, he, they,* etc.).

POSITIVE	subject + *can* + infinitive: *I/You/He/She/It/We/They can go for long walks.*
NEGATIVE	subject + *can't* + infinitive: *I/You/He/She/It/We/They can't stay there.*
WH- QUESTIONS	question word + *can* + subject + infinitive: *What can I/you/he/she/it/we/they do there?*
YES/NO QUESTIONS	*can* + subject + infinitive: *Can I/you/he/she/it/we/they stay on the island?*
SHORT ANSWERS	*Yes, I/you/he/she/it/we/they can.* *No, I/you/he/she/it/we/they can't.*

TIPS! • We also use *can* for ability, making requests and offers.

ability	She can speak French. I can't decide where to go.
requests	Can you help me? Can I borrow it?
offers	Can I help you?

G8.2 Comparatives   8B 5 p64

- We use comparatives to compare two places, people or things: *Phuket is hotter than Bangkok. Bangkok is more crowded than Phuket.*
- When we compare two things in the same sentence we use *than* after the comparative: *The Sawadee Hotel is bigger **than** the Kata Hotel.*

type of adjective	spelling rule	comparative
most **1**-syllable adjectives	add *-er*	small**er** old**er** but! dry → drier
1-syllable adjectives ending in *-e*	add *-r*	safe**r** nice**r**
1-syllable adjectives ending in consonant + vowel + consonant	double the last consonant and add *-er*	hot**ter** big**ger** but! new → newer
2-syllable adjectives ending in *-y*	*-y* → *-i* and add *-er*	nois**ier** happ**ier**
2-syllable adjectives not ending in *-y*	put *more* before the adjective	**more** crowded **more** common
adjectives with **3** syllables or more	put *more* before the adjective	**more** expensive **more** interesting
irregular adjectives	*good* *bad* *far*	better worse further/farther

TIPS! • The opposite of *more* is *less*: *The holiday in Phuket is more expensive. The holiday in Bangkok is less expensive.*
• We can also use *more* with nouns: *There are more rooms in the Sawadee Hotel.*

Real World

RW8.1 Planning a day out   8C 5 p67

asking people what they want to do	saying what you want to do
What do you want to do (tomorrow)? Where would you like to go? Do you want to (go to Regent's Park)?	I'd like to (go to the beach). I want to (go to Chessington). I'd rather (stay at home).

- I'd = I would.
- We use *I'd rather* to say I want to do this more than something else.
- After *would rather* we use the infinitive (*go, do,* etc.): *I'd rather **rent** a bike.*
- After *would like* and *want* we use the infinitive with *to* (*to go, to do,* etc.): *I'd like **to go** swimming. I want **to rent** a car.*

TIP! • *would like* is more polite than *want.*

Language Summary 9

V9.1 Work 9A ❶ p70

Match the words to pictures a)–i).

1 ☐ a customer
2 ☐ a report
3 g notes
4 ☐ a letter
5 ☐ a message
6 ☐ a contract
7 a a company
8 ☐ a meeting
9 ☐ a conference

V9.2 Types of transport 9B ❶ p72

a car

a plane

a train

a taxi [US: a cab]

a bus

a tram

a bike

a scooter

a boat

a motorbike

V9.3 Travelling verbs/phrases 9B ❷ p72

go by bike = cycle
go by car = drive
go on foot = walk
go by boat = sail
go by plane = fly
go by train/tube/bus = take the train/tube/bus

TIPS! • We say *go by bike, train,* etc., but *go on foot* not ~~go by foot~~.

• We can say *the tube* or *the underground* in British English: *the London underground.* The American English word is *subway*: *the New York subway.*

V9.4 Indoor and outdoor activities 9D ❶ p76

Match the verbs/phrases to pictures a)–p).

1 ☐ swim
2 ☐ ski
3 ☐ type
4 ☐ surf
5 ☐ windsurf
6 ☐ sail
7 ☐ sing
8 ☐ cook
9 ☐ drive
10 ☐ speak another language
11 ☐ use a computer
12 ☐ ride a horse
13 ☐ ride a motorbike
14 ☐ play tennis
15 ☐ play chess
16 ☐ play a musical instrument

TIP! • We use *can/can't* to talk about ability:
I can type.
I can't ride a horse.
(See G8.1.)

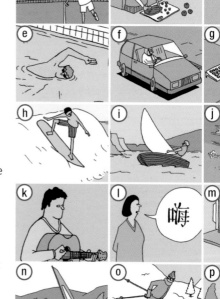

V9.5 Adverbs and adjectives 9D ❹ p76

• We use **adjectives** to describe nouns. They usually come **before** the noun:
*She is an **excellent** driver.*

• We use **adverbs** to describe verbs. They usually come **after** the verb:
*She speaks French **fluently**.*

spelling rule	adjective	adverb
most adverbs: add *-ly* to the adjective	beautiful fluent bad	beautifully fluently badly
adjectives ending in *-y*: *-y* → *-i* and add *-ly*	easy happy	easily happily
irregular adverbs	good fast hard	well fast hard

Grammar

G9.1 Present Continuous: positive and negative (9A p70)

- We use the Present Continuous to talk about things **happening now**:
  I'm waiting for a taxi. They're sitting in your office.

POSITIVE		NEGATIVE	
I'm ('m = am)		I'm not	
you/we/they're ('re = are)	verb+*ing*	you/we/they aren't (= are not)	verb+*ing*
he/she/it's ('s = is)		he/she/it isn't (= is not)	

verb+*ing*: spelling rules	examples	
most verbs: add -*ing*	play → playing look → looking	study → studying go → going
verbs ending in -e: take off -*e* and add -*ing*	smoke → smoking live → living	write → writing
verbs ending in consonant + vowel + consonant: double the last consonant and add -*ing*	sit → sitting stop → stopping	run → running

TIP! • We can also make negatives with *'re* or *'s* + *not*: *Danny's not doing anything. They're not looking very happy,* etc.

G9.2 Present Continuous: questions and short answers (9A ⑩ p71)

QUESTIONS

question word	auxiliary	subject	verb+*ing*	
Where	is	Frank	calling	from?
	Is	the taxi	moving?	
What	are	Janet and Danny	doing?	
Where	are	they	having	the meeting?

YES/NO QUESTIONS	SHORT ANSWERS	
Am I working here today?	Yes, I am.	No, I'm not.
Are you watching TV at the moment?	Yes, you are.	No, you aren't.
Is he/she/Janet answering the phone?	Yes, he/she is.	No, he/she isn't.
Are we going now?	Yes, we are.	No, we aren't.
Are they having the meeting now?	Yes, they are.	No, they aren't.

TIP! • We can also make negative short answers with *'re* or *'s* + *not*: *No, you're not. No, she's not,* etc.

G9.3 Present Simple or Present Continuous? (9B ⑥ p73)

- We use the **Present Simple** to talk about things that happen every day/week/month, etc.
- We use the **Present Continuous** to talk about things happening now.
- We use *am*, *are* and *is* in **Present Continuous** questions (see G9.2).
- We use *do* and *does* in **Present Simple** questions (see G3.2 and G4.3).
- We usually use the **Present Simple** with these words: *usually, sometimes, always, often, normally, hardly ever, never, every day/week/month,* etc.
  I normally go to work by train.
  I visit my grandparents every month.
- We usually use the **Present Continuous** with these words: *now, today, at the moment.*
  He's watching TV now.
  I'm driving to work today.
  What are you doing at the moment?

Real World

RW9.1 Talking on the phone (9C ⑤ p75)

asking to speak to people	saying who you are
Hello, can I speak to (Emily), please? Hello, is that (Chris Morris)?	This is (Emily Wise), from (3DUK). It's (Katrina). Speaking.

calling people back	other useful phrases
Can I call you back? I'll call you later. Can you call me back?	I got your message. Call me on my mobile. Hold on a moment, I'll get him/her.

TIPS! • We say *It's (Katrina).* not ~~*I'm (Katrina)*~~.

• *I'll = I will.*

Language Summary 10

Vocabulary

V10.1 Health (10A ❶ p78)

Match the phrases to pictures a)–j).

1. [h] do exercise
2. [ ] lose weight /weɪt/
3. [ ] stop smoking
4. [ ] get stressed /strest/
5. [ ] get fit
6. [ ] go to the gym
7. [ ] have a heart attack /əˈtæk/
8. [ ] eat fried food
9. [ ] drink alcohol
10. [ ] high/low in fat

V10.2 How often ... ? and frequency expressions (10A ❺ p79)

- We use *How often ... ?* to ask about frequency:
  How often do you go to the theatre?
  How often does your brother phone you?
  How often did you visit your grandfather?

once	a day		day
twice	a week		week
three times	a month	every	month
four times	a year		year
ten times	an hour		weekend
etc.	etc.		etc.

V10.3 Appearance (10B ❷ p80)

age	height /haɪt/	body	general appearance	race
He's/She's ... young middle-aged /mɪdlˈeɪdʒd/ old	He's/She's ... tall short	He's/She's ... fat overweight /əʊvəˈweɪt/ thin slim	He's/She's ... beautiful good-looking attractive	He's/She's ... white black Asian /ˈeɪʒ

eyes	hair /heə/		
He's/She's got ... blue eyes brown eyes green eyes	He's/She's got ... long/short hair dark/fair /feə/ hair blonde /blɒnd/ hair grey hair	He's got ... a beard /bɪəd/ a moustache /mʊsˈtɑːʃ/	He's ... bald /bɔːld/

overweight   slim   blonde hair   grey hair   a beard   a moustache   bald

TIPS! • *Middle-aged* = the time in your life between young and old.
- *Overweight* is more polite than *fat*. *Slim* is more attractive than *thin*.
- *Beautiful*, *attractive* and *good-looking* all mean the same.
Beautiful is usually for women. *Good-looking* is usually for men.
Attractive can be for both men and women.
- *Asian* = from a country in Asia: India, Thailand, Japan, etc.
- We say *long hair* not ~~long hairs~~ and *long dark hair* not ~~dark long hair~~.

V10.4 Character (10B ❻❼ p81)

A **generous** /ˈdʒenərəs/ person likes giving people money and presents.
It's difficult for a **shy** person to talk to new people.
A **lazy** person doesn't like working and enjoys watching TV all day.
A **kind** /kaɪnd/ person likes doing things to help other people.
A **funny** person makes people laugh a lot.
Selfish people usually think about themselves, not other people.
An **outgoing** person is friendly and likes meeting new people.
When **reliable** /rɪˈlaɪəbl/ people promise to do something, they always do it.

V10.5 Health problems (10C ❷ p82)

I've got ...	a stomach ache /ˈstʌmək eɪk/ a temperature /ˈtemprətʃə/ a headache /ˈhedeɪk/ a toothache /ˈtuːθeɪk/ a sore throat /sɔː ˈθrəʊt/ a cold a cough /kɒf/
I feel ...	ill terrible sick better
My ... hurts.	back arm foot leg

TIPS! • We can also say: *I'm ill/sick/better.*, but not ~~I'm terrible.~~
- In British English *I'm sick.* usually means *I'm ill.*, while *I feel sick.* usually means *I want to be sick.*
- We can say *I've got a stomach ache/a toothache.* or *I've got stomach ache/toothache.* but not ~~I've got headache.~~

V10.6 **Treatment** (10C **3** p82)

go	to bed	stay	at home
	home		in bed
	to the doctor		
	to the dentist		
take	the day off		
	some painkillers		
	some cough medicine /'medisən/		
	some antibiotics /æntibaɪ'ɒtɪks/		

V10.7 **Seasons** (10D **1** p84)

spring   summer   autumn   winter
                   [US: fall]

TIP! • We use *in* with seasons: *in (the) winter*.

V10.8 **Weather** (10D **4** p85)

Match the words to pictures a)–k).

1 e   hot
2 d   warm
3 ☐ cold
4 ☐ wet
5 ☐ dry
6 ☐ raining
7 ☐ snowing
8 ☐ windy /'wɪndi/
9 ☐ cloudy /'klaʊdi/
10 ☐ sunny
11 ☐ 34° (degrees)

(What's the weather like?)   (It's very hot and sunny.)

V10.9 **Word building** (10D **6** p85)

noun	adjective	verb
rain	rainy	rain
snow	snowy	snow
wind	windy	–
cloud	cloudy	–
sun	sunny	–

Noun: *There's not much **wind** today.*
Adjective: *I love **sunny** days.*
Verb: *Look! It's **snowing**!*

Grammar

G10.1 **Imperatives** (10A **3** p79)

- We often use imperatives to give very strong advice.
- The positive imperative is the same as the infinitive (*go, do,* etc.): *Stop smoking. Do more exercise.*
- The negative imperative is *don't* + infinitive (*don't go, don't do,* etc.): *Don't eat a lot of salt.*

TIP! • We also use imperatives to give orders: *Go home!* and instructions: *Don't write anything.*

G10.2 ***should/shouldn't*** (10A **8** p79)

- We use *should/shouldn't* to give advice.
- We use *should* to say something is a **good** thing to do: *You should do more exercise.*
- We use *shouldn't* to say something is a **bad** thing to do: *You shouldn't eat so much red meat.*
- After *should* and *shouldn't* we use the infinitive: *He should stop smoking.* not *He should to stop smoking.*

TIPS! • To ask for advice, we can say: *What should I do?*

• In spoken English, *should/shouldn't* is more common than the imperative for advice.

G10.3 **Questions with *like*** (10B **10** p81)

- We use **What's** (= *What is*) **he/she like?** to ask for a general description. We often ask this when we don't know the person. The answer can include character and physical appearance: *She's really friendly and outgoing. And she's very beautiful.*
- We use **What does he/she look like?** to ask about physical appearance only: *She's tall and slim, and she's got long dark hair.*
- We use **What does he/she like doing?** to ask about people's likes and free time interests: *She likes dancing and going to restaurants.*

TIPS! • *How is he/she?* asks about health, not personality: *How's Buffy? She's fine, thanks.*

• We don't use *like* in answers to questions with *What's he like? He's kind.* not *He's like kind.* and *What does she look like? She's very tall.* not *She's like very tall.*

Real World

RW10.1 **Talking about health** (10C **5** p83)

asking about someone's health	expressing sympathy	giving advice
How are you?	Oh, dear.	Why don't you (go home)?
Are you OK?	That's a shame.	You should (take the day off).
What's wrong?	I hope you get better soon.	Drink lots of water.
What's the matter?		

TIPS! • Only use the imperative to give advice to people you know well: *Go home and go to bed!*

• After *Why don't you ... ?* we use the infinitive: *Why don't you **see** a doctor?*

Language Summary 11

V11.1 **Verb collocations** (11A **2** p86)

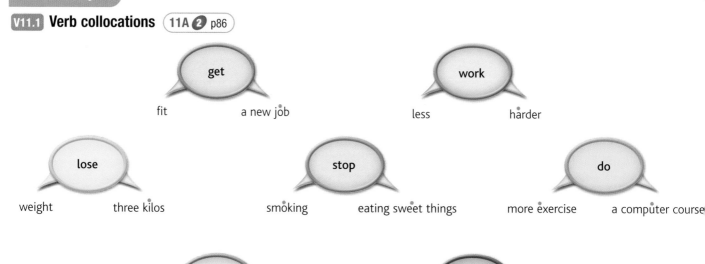

get — fit, a new job

work — less, harder

lose — weight, three kilos

stop — smoking, eating sweet things

do — more exercise, a computer course

have — a holiday, fun

move — to another country, house

V11.2 **Studying** (11B **1** p88)

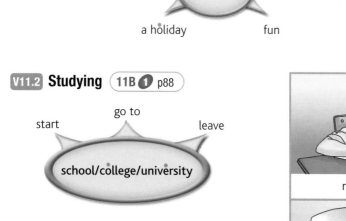

go to — start, leave

school/college/university

take — revise for, pass, fail

an exam

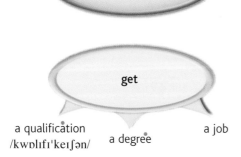

get

a qualification /kwɒlɪfɪˈkeɪʃən/, a degree, a job

TIP! • We *get a degree* when we finish university. *A qualification* is more general: we *get a qualification* when we pass any official exam, for example, when you leave school, finish a training course, etc.

revise for an exam

take an exam

fail an exam

pass an exam

get a degree

V11.3 **Verb patterns** (11D **5** p93)

• After some verbs only one verb form is possible:

> I **want** to spend more time with my family.

> They **love** living in the city.

+ infinitive with *to*	+ verb+*ing*
want (to do)	love (doing)
need (to do)	hate (doing)
would like (to do)	enjoy (doing)
would love (to do)	like (doing)

TIPS! • These verbs can also be followed by nouns or pronouns: *You don't need **a car**.* (noun) *He hates **it**.* (pronoun)

• It is also possible to use the infinitive with *to* after *like*, *love* and *hate*, but verb+*ing* is more common in British English.

Grammar

G11.1 *be going to*: positive and negative (11A **5** p86)

> I'm going to do a computer course.

> I'm not going to eat sweet things anymore.

- These sentences talk about the **future**.
- The people decided to do these things **before** they said them.
- We use *be going to* + infinitive for **future plans**.

subject	auxiliary (+ *not*)	*going to*	infinitive	
I	'm/'m not	going to	work	harder.
You/We/They	're/aren't	going to	have	a holiday next year.
He/She/It	's/isn't	going to	lose	ten kilos.
We	're	going to	get	fit.
Val	's	going to	stop	smoking.
I	'm	going to	do	more exercise.
I	'm not	going to	eat	sweet things anymore.

TIP! • With the verb *go*, we usually say *I'm going to Spain.* not *I'm going to go to Spain.* But both are correct.

G11.2 *be going to*: Wh- questions (11A **9** p87)

question word	auxiliary	subject	*going to*	infinitive	
What	am	I	going to	do?	
Where	are	you/we/they	going to	live	next year?
When	's (is)	he/she/it	going to	arrive?	
What	are	you	going to	do	all day?
Where	are	you	going to	stay?	
What	are	you	going to	eat?	

G11.3 *might* or *be going to* (11B **4** p89)

- We use *be going to* to say a future plan is **decided**: *I'm going to meet Tony in town.*
- We use *might* to say something in the future is **possible**, but **not decided**: *I might go for a drink with Peter or I might go to Jane's party.*
- After *might* we use the infinitive: *We might **go** and **see** a film.*

TIPS! • *might* is the same for all subjects (*I, you, he, they*, etc.).
• To make questions with *might*, we usually use *Do you think ... ?*:
Do you think he might come to the party?

G11.4 *be going to*: yes/no questions and short answers (11B **10** p89)

YES/NO QUESTIONS

Am I going to be late?
Are you going to get a job?
Is he/she going to sell his car?
Are we going to move house?
Are they going to study in the UK?

SHORT ANSWERS

Yes, I am.	No, I'm not.
Yes, you are.	No, you aren't.
Yes, he/she is.	No, he/she isn't.
Yes, we are.	No, we aren't.
Yes, they are.	No, they aren't.

TIP! • We can also use *I might* as a short answer: *Are you going to stay?* *(Yes,) I might.*

Real World

RW11.1 Directions (11C **3** p90)

Match the phrases to pictures a)–i).

1. ☐ turn right
2. ☐ turn left
3. ☐ go over the bridge /brɪdʒ/
4. ☐ go past the pub
5. ☐ go along this street
6. ☐ it's on the/your left
7. ☐ it's on the/your right
8. ☐ it's opposite /ˈɒpəzɪt/
9. ☐ it's next to

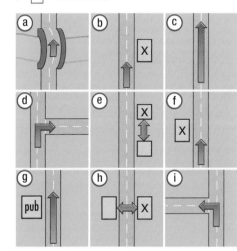

RW11.2 Asking for and giving directions (11C **7** p91)

ASKING FOR DIRECTIONS

Excuse me. Is there (a newsagent's) near here?
Where's (the police station)?
Do you know (the Park Hotel)?

GIVING DIRECTIONS

There's one in (Berry Street).
Go along this road and turn right/left.
Go past the pub.
Go over the bridge.
The newsagent's is on the/your right/left.
It's opposite (the supermarket).
It's next to (the Internet café).
It's over there.
You can't miss it.

IF YOU CAN'T GIVE DIRECTIONS

Sorry, I don't know.
Sorry, I don't live around here.

Language Summary 12

Vocabulary

V12.1 Big and small numbers (12A p94)

- For numbers with a decimal point(.) we say *point*:
  - 0.6 = *nought point six* or *zero point six*
  - 3.25 = *three point two five*

TIPS! • 0 = *nought* /nɔːt/ or *zero* (or *oh* when we say phone numbers).
- In English we write 7.5 not ~~7,5~~. We use a decimal point (.) not a comma (,).
- We can use *one* or *a* with *hundred*, *thousand* and *million*:
  - 100 = *a hundred* or *one hundred*
  - 1,000 = *a thousand* or *one thousand* /'θaʊzənd/
  - 1,000,000 = *a million* or *one million*

- For long numbers we use *and* after *hundred* (but not after *thousand* or *million*):
  - 156 = *a hundred **and** fifty-six*
  - 650,000 = *six hundred **and** fifty thousand*
  - But 2,300 = *two thousand, three hundred* not ~~two thousand and three hundred~~

- We don't add a plural *-s* to *hundred*, *thousand* and *million*:
  - 45,270 = *forty-five thousand, two hundred and seventy*
  - 70,000,000 = *seventy million* not ~~seventy millions~~
  - But we can say: *There were hundreds of people there.*

V12.2 Things and places at an airport
(12C **5** p99)

Match the words/phrases to pictures a)–m).

1. ☐ a passport
2. ☐ a boarding /'bɔːdɪŋ/ card
3. ☐ hand luggage /'lʌgɪdʒ/
4. ☐ a ticket
5. ☐ sharp items
6. ☐ pack your bags
7. ☐ passengers
8. ☐ a flight /flaɪt/ number
9. ☐ a gate
10. ☐ a check-in desk
11. ☐ a window seat
12. ☐ a middle seat
13. ☐ an aisle /aɪl/ seat

(a) (b) (c) (d) (e) (f) (g) (h)
BA 901
(i) gate 12 (j)
(k) (l) (m)

Grammar

G12.1 Superlatives (12A p95)

- We use **superlatives** to compare three or more things.
- We use **comparatives** (*bigger*, *more expensive*, etc.) to compare two things (see G8.2).

type of adjective	spelling rule	superlative
most **1**-syllable adjectives	add *-est*	long**est** fast**est** but! dry → driest
1-syllable adjectives ending in *-e*	add *-st*	safe**st** nice**st**
1-syllable adjectives ending in consonant + vowel + consonant	double the last consonant and add *-est*	wet**test** big**gest** but! new → newest
2-syllable adjectives ending in *-y*	*-y* → *-i* and add *-est*	earl**iest** happ**iest**
2-syllable adjectives <u>not</u> ending in *-y*	put *most* before the adjective	**most** boring **most** common
adjectives with **3** syllables or more	put *most* before the adjective	**most** expensive **most** interesting
irregular adjectives	*good* *bad* *far*	best worst furthest/farthest

TIPS! • We say: *The best place in the world.* not ~~of the world~~ or ~~for the world~~.
- Before superlatives in sentences we use:

the
*Mount Wai'ale'ale is probably **the** wettest place in the world.*
***The** best bottle of wine cost £12,300.*

possessive *'s*
*It was the **world's** most expensive meal.*
*He's my **sister's** oldest relative.*

possessive adjectives
*Mat's **my** best friend.*
*It was **his** most important book.*

- *the* + superlative is the most common form.

Grammar

G12.2 Present Perfect: positive and negative (12B ③ p96)

- We use the Present Perfect to talk about experiences in life until now. We don't say when they happened: *I've been to about forty countries. I've stayed in some of the world's best hotels.*
- We use the Past Simple if we say when something happened: *Two weeks ago I went to Mexico. Last month I spent five days in Barbados.*

TIP! • We can't use the Present Perfect if we say a time: *I went to England in 2003.* not *I've been to England in 2003.*

POSITIVE

subject	auxiliary	past participle	
I/You/We/They	've (= have)	had met	lots of other jobs. some interesting people.
He/She/It	's (= has)	been	to Mexico.

NEGATIVE

subject	auxiliary + *not*	past participle	
I/You/We/They	haven't (= have not)	had	a holiday.
He/She/It	hasn't (= has not)	been	to the USA before.

TIP! • We often make negative Present Perfect sentences with *never*: *I've never been to Australia.*

PAST PARTICIPLES

- For **regular verbs**, add *-ed* or *-d* to the infinitive: *work → worked, live → lived*, etc. The Past Simple and past participles of regular verbs are the same (see G6.3).
- For **irregular verbs**, there are no rules. Look at the past participles in the Irregular Verb List, p159.

TIP! • *go* has two past participles, *been* and *gone*. When we use the Present Perfect to talk about experience we usually use *been*: *I've been to Italy.* (*I am back in my country now.*)

G12.3 Present Perfect: *Have you ever ... ?* questions and short answers (12B ⑦ p97)

- We use the **Present Perfect** to ask about people's experiences. If the answer is *yes*, we use the **Past Simple** to ask for (or give) more information:
  Have you ever been to Australia? Yes, I have.
  Did you have a good time? Yes, I did.

QUESTIONS

auxiliary	subject	(*ever*)	past participle	
Have	I/you/we/they	ever	worked	in a restaurant?
Has	he/she/it	ever	been	to the UK?

SHORT ANSWERS

Yes, I/you/we/they have.	No, I/you/we/they haven't.
Yes, he/she/it has.	No, he/she/it hasn't.

TIP! • *ever* + Present Perfect = any time in your life until now. We often use it in questions.

Real World

RW12.1 At the airport (12C ⑥ p99)

THINGS YOU HEAR AT THE CHECK-IN DESK

Can I have your ticket and your passport, please?
How many bags have you got?
Did you pack your bags yourself?
Have you got any sharp items in your hand luggage?
Would you like a window seat or an aisle seat?
Here's your boarding card. You're in seat (16A).
Gate (12).
It leaves at (13.20).
Enjoy your flight.

THINGS YOU CAN SAY AT THE CHECK-IN DESK

(I'd like) a window seat/an aisle seat, please.
Which gate is it?
Is the flight on time?

RW12.2 Saying goodbye (12C ⑧ p99)

Have a	nice weekend! nice holiday! good trip!	You too. Thanks, I will.
See you	in two weeks. next year. on the next course.	Yes, see you.
Send me/us	an email. a postcard.	Yes, of course.

Recording Scripts

R0.4

A H J K | B C D E G P T V | F L M N S X Z |
I Y | Q U W | O R

R0.5

yellow | please | green | class |
teacher | student | welcome

R0.6

Open your book. | Look at page ten. | Match
the words to the pictures. | Read the article. |
Answer the questions. | Check your answers. |
Listen and practise. | Work in pairs. | Work
in groups. | Fill in the gaps. | Don't write. |
Close your book.

R0.7

PABLO Hello. Sorry I'm late.

TEACHER No problem. What's your
first name?

P It's Pablo.

T What's your surname?

P Ruano.

T How do you spell that?

P R–U–A–N–O.

T Welcome to the class, Pablo.

P Thank you.

R0.8

A

ISABEL Hello, is this the English class?

TEACHER Yes, it is.

I Oh, good. I'm sorry I'm late!

T No problem. What's your first name?

I Isabel.

T How do you spell that?

I I–S–A–B–E–L.

T And what's your surname?

I It's Boutron.

T And how do you spell that?

I B–O–U–T–R–O–N.

T Thanks, Isabel. Welcome to the class.

B

PAVEL Hello, sorry I'm late.

TEACHER No problem. What's your name?

P My name's Pavel.

T Is that your first name?

P Er, yes.

T How do you spell that, please?

P P–A–V–E–L.

T And what's your surname, Pavel?

P Stepanov.

T OK ... and how do you spell that?

P S–T–E–P–A–N–O–V.

T S–T–E–P–A–N–O–V. Thanks. Welcome
to the class, Pavel.

P Thank you.

R0.11

ANSWER Thursday.

R1.4

ANSWERS 3 Italy 4 the USA 5 Mexico;
Australia; Spain

R1.7

My name's Carol. | What are your names? |
Our names are Joe and Susan. | What are
their names? | His name's David. |
Her name's Molly.

R1.8

A

RECEPTIONIST Hello. What are your
names, please?

KAREN My name's Karen Jansen.

R Hmm. How do you spell your surname,
please?

K It's J–A–N–S–E–N.

R Ah. Right.

PETER And I'm Peter Iveson. That's
I–V–E–S–O–N.

R OK. And where are you from?

P We're from the UK.

R OK ... here are your name cards.

P Thank you very much.

B

RECEPTIONIST Good morning, sir. What's your
name, please?

MURAT My name's Murat Demirlek.

R OK ... um how do you spell your
surname?

M D–E–M–I–R–L–E–K.

R D–E–M–I–R–L–E–K. Um, right. And
where are you from?

M I'm from Turkey.

R OK, here's your name card. Enjoy the
conference.

M Thank you very much.

C

RECEPTIONIST Hello, are you here for the
conference?

DOROTA Yes, my name's Dorota Koprowska.

R And how do you spell your surname,
please?

D K–O–P–R–O–W–S–K–A.

R K–O–P–R–O–W–S–K–A ... . Um and
where are you from?

D I'm from Poland.

R Here's your name card.

D Thank you very much.

R1.9

A

A Welcome to our hotel, Mrs Johnson.
You're in room 19.

B Thank you.

B

A Hello, Tom. Where are you?

B I'm in my room. It's number 427.

C

A Good afternoon, Mr and Mrs Richards.
You're in room 15.

B Thank you very much.

D

A Peter, what's our room number?

B 319.

A Oh yes, of course.

E

A Good evening, Mr Jones. Room 316?

B Yes, that's right. Thank you.

R1.11

A

A What's the number of their hotel?

B It's 01622 654331.

B

A ... and Tina's in London. Her mobile
number is 07931 516087.

C

A What's our new phone number?

B Er ... wait a minute ... it's 01902 785664.

A Oh yes, that's right.

D

A Hi, Tim! What's your number in Spain?

B It's ... er ... 0034 96 3922 959.

A So that's 0034 ... 96 ...

B ... 3922 959.

A OK. Thanks.

R1.13

ANSWERS 1 engineer; lawyer 2 musician
3 doctor; teacher

R1.14

I'm not a teacher. | We aren't from Australia. |
He isn't famous. | Are you from Spain? |
Yes, I am. | No, I'm not. | Is he a musician? |
Yes, he is. | No, he isn't. | Are you from
Sydney? | Yes, we are. | No, we aren't.

R1.18

CLERK Right, I need some personal details.

DAVID OK.

C What's your surname, please?

D It's Holmes.

C And how do you spell that?

D H–O–L–M–E–S.

C OK. What's your first name?

D David.

C And what's your nationality?

D I'm British.

C OK. What's your address?

D It's 57 Green Road, Birmingham, B22 4LJ.

C **Could you say that again, please?**

D Yes, it's 57 Green Road, Birmingham.

C That's G–R–double E–N, like the colour?

D Yes, that's right.

C And the postcode again, please?

D Yes, it's B22 4LJ.

C OK. What's your home phone number?

D It's 0121 787 6544.

C **I'm sorry?**

D 0121 787 6544.

C And what's your mobile number?

D It's 07810 056678.

c 07810 05 …
D … 6678.
C Right. And the last question … what's your email address?
D It's d holmes at webmail dot com.
C **Sorry, could you repeat that, please?**
D Yes, it's d holmes at webmail dot com.
C OK, thanks a lot. Now, what do you …

R1.22

1 this → What's this? → What's this in English?
2 these → What are these? → What are these in English?
3 that → What's that? → What's that in English?
4 those → What are those?

R2.2

I've got an old car. | You've got a great CD player. | He's got a lot of CDs. | She's got a red dress. | We've got a new DVD player. | They've got a dog. | I haven't got a lot of CDs. | She hasn't got a car.

R2.3

INTERVIEWER Hello.
BILL Hello?
I Have you got time to answer some questions? It's a product survey about cameras, computers, that sort of thing.
B Yes, OK.
SALLY Sure.
I Thanks. Right, first question – have you got a computer?
B Yes, I have. I've got an old laptop.
I And what about you? Have you got a laptop, too?
S No, I haven't got a computer.
I OK. And have you got a mobile phone?
S Yes, of course! *Everyone's* got a mobile phone!
B Well, I haven't. They're expensive.
I And have you got a digital camera?
S Er, no, I haven't. I've got a normal camera, but not a digital one.
I And you, sir?
B Yes, I've got a new digital camera.
I And have you got a personal stereo?
B Yes, I have.
S No, I haven't. I've got a CD player at home, but not a personal stereo.
I OK. And have you got a DVD player?
S No, I haven't.
I What about you, sir?
B Yes, I've got a very good DVD player.
S Yes, but his TV isn't very good!
B No, I'm here to buy a new one.
I Well, we've got some beautiful new TVs and they're very cheap at the moment.

R2.5

ANSWERS LISA 2 children 4 son 5 father
6 mother 7 brother MAX 9 sisters
11 grandchildren 12 granddaughters
13 grandson SALLY 15 uncle 16 cousins
18 grandfather 19 grandmother

R2.8

Sally's → Lisa is Sally's aunt. | Anna's → Max is Anna's husband. | Bill's → Pat is Bill's wife. | Pat's → Chris is Bill and Pat's grandson. | Chris's → Emma is Chris's sister. | Max's → Sally is Anna and Max's daughter.

R2.9

KATE Tim, come and /ən/ look at /ət/ these photos of /əv/ my family.
TIM OK.
K Right … This is my sister, Lisa, and /ənd/ her /hə/ husband, Tom.
T Lisa's a /ə/ doctor, isn't she?
K Yes, that's right.
T What about Tom?
K He's a /ə/ jazz musician. He's very good.
T Oh, right. How many children have /həv/ they got?
K Two. A /ə/ girl and /ən/ a /ə/ boy. Look, here's a /ə/ photo of /əv/ them /ðəm/.
T Hmm. How old are they?
K Er, Emma is seven, I think and /ən/ Chris is about ten months old.
T They're beautiful.
K Yes, they are. And /ənd/ this is my brother, Max. He's a /ə/ lawyer.
T And who's that?
K That's Max's wife, Anna. She's from /frəm/ Italy, but /bət/ her /hər/ English is very good.
T Wow! She's nice.
K Yes, she is. She's an /ən/ actress, actually. And that's their daughter, Sally. She's sixteen.
T Right.
K And these are /ə/ my parents. Mum's a /ə/ teacher – she teaches French – and Dad's retired.
T How old are they?
K Mum's sixty-three and Dad's seventy-three.
T OK.
K And that's Fred, my favourite member of /əv/ the /ðə/ family.
T Sorry, where?
K There.
T Oh, the /ðə/ dog!
K Yes, he's great!

R2.10

1
A What time is it?
B It's five o'clock.
2
A What's the time, please?
B It's about half past two.
3
A Excuse me, have you got the time, please?
B Yes, it's eight fifteen.
A Thanks a lot.
B You're welcome.

R2.12 R2.14

A
Hello, you have reached the Lewisham Gallery information service. We're open Mondays to Fridays from 10 a.m. to 5.30 p.m. and on Saturday and Sunday from 10 a.m. to 4.30 p.m. Currently the exhibition is Modern Art in [end of R2.12] Europe and admission is £7, or £5 for students and children. For more information call the Ticket Office on 020 8960 2424.

B
TICKET SELLER … OK, so that's 2 tickets for the Mary Colgan concert at the Camden Apollo on Friday the 5th of April at 7.30 p.m.
CUSTOMER Yes. That's right. How much are the tickets? [end of R2.12]
TS They're £19.50 and £17.50.
C £19.50 and £17.50?
TS Yes, that's right.
C OK, 2 tickets at £19.50 please.

C
Welcome to the Ritz Cinema information and booking line. Here are the films showing at this cinema from Friday April the 5th to Thursday April the 11th. *Sons and Daughters*, certificate 12, showing at 3.25, 5.40 and 8.50 p.m. *Good Times, Bad Times*, certificate 15, showing at 2.50, 5.10 and 8.30 p.m. To hear these times again, say "yes please" after the tone. [end of R2.12] Ticket prices for all performances are £6.50 for adults and £4 for children under 16. To book tickets, say "yes please" after the tone.

R2.16

TOM Lisa, where's my suitcase?
LISA Here it is, under the sofa.
T And have you got my keys?
L No, Tom, of course I haven't. They're on the desk. By the computer.
T OK, thanks. And where's my mobile phone?
L Oh, I don't know. Look, there it is, under my coat. There, on the sofa!
T Thanks.
EMMA Mum, where are my new shoes?
L They're under the chair by the window.
E And where's my bag?
L Oh, Emma. It's by the door. Where it always is.
E Thanks, Mum.
T Right. Are you ready, Emma?
E Yes.
L Have you got your school books?
E Yes, they're in my bag. Look.
T Oh no! Where's my passport?
L It's on the table by the window. In front of the plant.
T Oh yes, thanks.
L Bye, darling. See you on Sunday.
T Bye, sweetheart.
L Right … hmm … where's the baby?

149

Recording Scripts

R3.2

INTERVIEWER When do you finish work?
SAM Most days we finish at about 9 o'clock.
I   You start at 5.45 and you finish at 9!
S   Yes, it's a long day. But some days I sleep for an hour or two in the afternoon.
I   And when do you have dinner?
S   At about half past 9, after we finish work. We have dinner together and we talk about the day.
I   What time do you get back to the hotel?
S   At about half past 10.
I   And what time do you go to bed?
S   At 11 o'clock. And then I sleep for 6 hours.
I   So, *do* you have a glamorous life?
S   Not when I'm at work, no – definitely not.

R3.4

ANSWERS 2 What do you do in the evenings?
3 Do you eat out? 4 And what do you do at the weekends? 5 Do you go to concerts?

R3.5

ROBERT Hello, Tanya!
TANYA Oh, hello. It's Robert, isn't it? You work in … er …
R   In our King Street office. I'm the manager there.
T   Oh, that's right, yes.
R   Good party, isn't it?
T   Yes, very nice.
R   Er, Tanya. Do you go for a drink after work? On Fridays, maybe?
T   No, I don't.
R   What do you do in the evenings?
T   Well, I don't go out very much in the week.
R   OK. Do you eat out?
T   No, I don't. Restaurants are very expensive round here.
R   Right. And what do you do at the weekends?
T   Well, on Saturday afternoons I go shopping. But I don't go out on Saturday evenings. I stay in and watch TV.
R   Right. Er … do you go to concerts?
T   Er, yes, I do.
R   Well, um … there's a good concert on Friday. Do you want to come with me?
T   Er … thanks, but there's a problem – well 3 problems, actually!
R   Oh?
T   I'm married! *And* I've got 2 children!
R   Oh …

R3.7

1
A   It's nearly midnight. Come on, everybody!
PEOPLE 10, 9, 8, 7, 6, 5, 4, 3, 2, 1 …
A   Happy New Year, Chris!
B   You too!

2
A   Is it a boy or a girl?
B   It's a girl!
C   Congratulations!

3
A   Happy anniversary, darling.
B   Happy anniversary, dear. Oh, what nice flowers!
A   So, 50 years … a long time.
B   Yes, a *very* long time!

4
A   Happy birthday, Sheena.
B   Oh, thank you.
A   How old are you now?
B   Er … 22 … again!

5
A   Hello.
B   Hello, Uncle John. Guess what – we're getting married!
A   Congratulations! That's wonderful news.

R3.9

1   I'm 30 today.
2   We've got a new baby boy.
3   Today is our 40th wedding anniversary.
4   We're getting married!
5   10, 9, 8, 7, 6, 5, 4, 3, 2, 1 …

R3.12

ANSWERS 1 April 2 July 3 May

R3.13

1
A   When do you start your English course?
B   September the fifth.

2
A   When's your birthday?
B   The thirteenth of December.
A   Oh, that's on Tuesday!

3
A   When's Mother's Day?
B   This year it's on March the fourteenth.
A   Oh, that's next week.

4
A   When do your courses finish?
B   They all finish on the second of July.

5
A   Excuse me. What's the date today?
B   It's, er, October the twentieth.
A   Thanks a lot.

6
A   When's Jim and Mary's wedding day?
B   I think it's the first of February.
A   Oh no! That's today!

R3.15

ANSWERS 1 tenth 2 birthday 3 book 4 DVD
5 DVD 6 good 7 watch

R3.16

What shall we get him for his birthday? |
Let's get him a book. | I'm not sure. |
Let's buy him a DVD. | That's a good idea. |
What about a Star Trek DVD? | No, I don't
think so.

R3.17

TANYA Do you think I'm a happy person in the morning?
SIMON Sometimes. Why?

T   It's a questionnaire. "Are you an early bird or a night owl?" But I don't have a lot of energy … so that's b).
S   What are the other questions?
T   Here, look. Question 2, well, that's easy. I hardly ever get up before 9 at the weekend.
S   Yes, that's true.
T   Right, question 3. Yes, I often watch films late at night.
S   But you never see the end!
T   Yes, that's true! So that's c). Next question – parties.
S   Oh that's easy. You never stay to the end.
T   True, I never stay to the end, so it's c). Question 5 … well, I usually see friends in the afternoon, I think. Right, the last one. Yes, I'm always happy to talk to friends when they phone before 8.
S   What! I always answer the phone.
T   Yes, *you* answer the phone, then *I* talk to my friends. So, it's a). Right, what's my score then?

R4.1

VICKY Hi, Alison. How are you?
ALISON Hello, Vicky. I'm fine, and you?
V   Fine, thanks. Is Paul here?
A   Paul? Oh no, he's got a new job. He works in Antarctica now.
V   No!
A   Yes, he works at a weather station there. He's got a job as an engineer.
V   Wow! Does he like it?
A   Yes and no. He doesn't like the job very much. The people on the weather station all work 6 days a week, but then they have 3 months off a year and the money's good.

R4.2

ALISON The people at the weather station all work 6 days a week, but then they have 3 months off a year and the money's good.
VICKY Hmm, that's good. What about his free time?
A   Well, you know Paul. He's usually quite active. He doesn't read a lot and he doesn't listen to the radio. So it's a bit difficult for him.
V   So what does he do?
A   Well, they have a TV there, so he watches a lot of sport. And he goes skiing and running. Oh, and he takes a lot of photos. They're very good!
V   Right.
A   *And* he goes swimming.
V   In Antarctica?!
A   Well, only on New Year's Day. *Everyone* goes swimming then – but only for about a minute!
V   Hmm. Do you talk to him a lot?
A   No, he doesn't phone much, it's expensive. But he emails a lot.
V   And what do *you* think about his job?

R4.4

live in → They live in Toronto. |
works at → She works at the airport. |
She's always → She's always very happy. |
a lot of → He buys her a lot of presents. |
watch it → She doesn't watch it.

R4.7

What does she do? | Does she like rock music? | What food does she like? | Does she like sport? | Does she have any animals? | What does she do on Saturday evenings?

R4.8

MESSAGE Sorry, I can't come to the phone right now. Please leave a message after the tone.

JACK Hi, Emma. This is Jack. It's 6 o'clock. I'm at the airport. See you in about 2 hours. Oh, don't worry about food. We can eat out. See you soon. Bye.

R4.9

JACK Hello?

EMMA Hi, Jack. It's Emma. I got your message. Where are you now?

J I'm in a taxi, about 20 minutes from your flat.

E Oh, good.

J Where do you want to eat?

E Shall we go to the Chinese restaurant again?

J No. Let's go somewhere different this time.

E OK. There's a new restaurant on Queen Street.

J You mean The Jazz Café?

E Yes. It's very nice, I think.

J Is it expensive?

E No, I don't think so. It's quite cheap and the food's very good.

J OK. Let's go there.

E OK. See you there at 8 o'clock then.

J Bye.

E Bye.

R4.11

ANSWERS 1 Would you like to order now?
2 What would you like to drink? 3 Would you like red or white? 4 Would you like anything else?

R4.12

Would you like to order now? | Would you like anything else? | I'd like a tuna salad, please. | Can I have a cheeseburger and chips, please? | We'd like a bottle of mineral water, please. | Can we have the bill, please?

R4.13

1 Would you like to order now? a)
2 Can I have a chicken salad, please? b)
3 What would you like to drink? b)
4 Can we have a bottle of red wine? a)
5 Would you like anything else? b)
6 I'd like a Neapolitan pizza, please. a)

R4.15

ANDY Morning, Kevin!

KEVIN Hi, Andy.

A Ah, have we got a new breakfast menu?

K Yes. The students say they want lots of different breakfasts – you know, from different countries.

A OK. Tell me what they want and I can write it on the board.

K Right … the Japanese usually have rice and fish and soup, and they drink green tea.

A And green tea. OK. What about a Brazilian breakfast?

K Well, Carlos says he has bread and cheese, orange juice and coffee. He says that's a typical breakfast in Brazil.

A Orange juice and coffee. Well, that's easy. And what do the Spanish have?

K Well, that's another easy one. In Spain they have biscuits or toast, or a sandwich. But they always have coffee.

A OK. Biscuits, toast, sandwich, coffee – got that.

K And some students say they want a full English breakfast. You know – eggs, sausages, toast, jam and tea.

A So that's eggs, sausages, toast, jam and tea. Right.

K OK, let's start cooking.

A Actually, it's time for my break!

R5.2

A

A Do you know any good places to go on holiday in England?

B Well, we always go to Keswick, in the Lake District. It's lovely.

A Really?

B Yes. There's a beautiful lake near the town and it's a good place for walking. There are lots of mountains.

A It sounds great. Are there any cheap places to stay?

B Yes, there are. B-and-Bs are quite cheap.

A B-and-Bs?

B Bed-and-breakfasts.

A Oh, right. What was the name of the town again?

B

A Where are you from, Vanessa?

B I'm from a small village in Ireland called Eyeries. My family still lives there.

A Is it nice?

B Yes, it's beautiful. It's by the sea and there's only one road. And all the houses are different colours!

A It sounds nice. Is there a hotel?

B No, there isn't. And there aren't any restaurants! But there are 3 or 4 little shops.

A And where in Ireland is it? …

C

TONY Hi, Aunt Rosie!

ROSIE Hello, Tony! How are you?

T I'm fine, thanks.

R And how's life in New Zealand? Do you like living in Auckland?

T Yes, I love it here. There are lots of things to do in the evening and lots of great restaurants.

R And where's your new flat?

T It's in a place called Mission Bay. There's a nice beach here and the people are very friendly. I play football with a group of New Zealanders every weekend.

R Oh, great. And do you still go running?

T Yes, of course. There isn't a park near our flat, but I run on the beach every morning. And how are things with you and Uncle Frank?

R5.5

JOHN Hello. Rent-A-Home. My name's John. How can I help you?

ALEX Hi. I'd like some information about the flat in Park Street, please.

J Of course. What would you like to know?

A Er, firstly, is there any furniture?

J Yes, there are some chairs, a sofa, beds – it's fully furnished. But, er, there isn't a TV.

A Oh, that's OK. And the bedrooms – are they big?

J Er, well, one bedroom's very big, but the other is, er, quite small. It's OK for a child.

A That's OK. The flat's for me and my wife. We haven't got any children.

J Right.

A And the bathroom. Has it got a shower?

J Yes, there's a shower and a bath. It's very nice.

A OK. Now, what else … Oh yes, what's in the kitchen?

J There's a cooker, a fridge and a washing machine. And I think there are some chairs and a table.

A Right. And are there any shops near the flat?

J Yes, there are some shops only 5 minutes away. And it's near the station.

A That's very good for £700 a month.

J Actually, It's, er, £800 a month.

A But your advert says 700.

J I'm sorry, that's a mistake, it's 800. But it is a beautiful flat. Would you like to see it?

A Er, yes … OK.

J Great! What about this afternoon at 3?

R5.6

ANSWERS 2 some 3 any 4 some 5 any
6 some 7 some 8 any 9 a 10 any 11 some
12 some 13 a

R5.7

ANSWERS 2 600 3 550 4 think 5 apples
6 green 7 red 8 bananas

Recording Scripts

R5.9

SHOP ASSISTANT Hello, can I help you?
ALEX Hi. Have you got any batteries?
SA Yes, they're there.
A Oh, yes. I'll have these ones, please. And have you got any big bottles of water?
SA No, sorry, we haven't.
A Oh, OK. How much are the phone cards?
SA They're £10 and £20.
A OK, I'll have a £10 one. Oh, and, um, these postcards, please.
SA Do you need any stamps?
A Yes, can I have 4 stamps for Europe, please?
SA Sure. Here you are. Anything else?
A No, that's all, thanks. How much is that?
SA That's £22.70, please.
A Thanks.
SA Here's your change and your receipt.
A Thanks very much. Bye.
SA Bye.

R6.2

REBECCA Grandma, when were you born?
GRANDMA Oh, I was born in 1940.
R And where were you on your 13th birthday?
G I was in London. I remember that birthday party very well.
R Why? Was it good?
G Yes, it was.
R Where was the party?
G It was in the street.
R In the street!
G Well, it was June 2nd 1953, the same day as Queen Elizabeth's coronation. The weather wasn't very good, but there were parties in every street in the country.
R Wow! Were they big parties?
G Yes, they were.
R And was there any food?
G Oh yes, there was. There were lots of chicken sandwiches and tea and beer. My family was very poor, but that year my birthday party was wonderful.
R Were your friends with you?
G No, they weren't. They were at other street parties with their families. But I was very happy because there were about 300 people at *my* party.

R6.4

I was /wəz/ in London. | There were /wə/ parties in every street. | The weather wasn't /wɒznt/ very good. | My friends weren't /wɜːnt/ with me. | Was /wəz/ it good? | Yes, it was /wɒz/. | No, it wasn't /wɒznt/. | Were /wə/ they big parties? | Yes, they were /wɜː/. | No, they weren't /wɜːnt/. | Where was /wəz/ the party? | When were /wə/ you born?

R6.5

ANSWERS 1 18th July 2 1943 3 1957 4 two
5 eighteen 6 four 7 1996

R6.9

1
JANE Hi. How was your weekend?
HENRY Terrible. I was really ill on Saturday.
J Oh, dear. What was wrong?
H I had a really bad cold.
J What a shame. Are you OK now?
H Yes, much better, thanks. And how was your weekend?
J Oh, very quiet. I stayed at home.
H Oh, right. What did you do?
J Not much. I slept a lot, did the washing and watched TV, you know, the usual. But I went to the cinema yesterday afternoon.
H What did you see?
J *Night and Day*.
H Oh yes. What was it like?
J It was good. I really liked it.
H I want to see that. It sounds good.

2
MICK Hi. How are you?
SARAH I'm very well, thanks. I went away for the weekend. To Italy!
M Wow! Where did you go?
S We went to Rome – it was wonderful!
M Oh, great! Who did you go with?
S My friend, Ingrid.
M And where did you stay?
S We stayed with some old friends from university.
M Oh, nice.
S What about you? How was your weekend?
M Oh, busy. I worked all weekend.
S Really? What did you do?
M I wrote the report you wanted. It took me 10 hours.
S You're joking! Did you finish it?
M Yes, here it is.
S That's great! Thanks, Mick.

R6.12

I met him on a Monday
And my heart stood still
Da do ron ron ron, da do ron ron
Somebody told me that his name was Bill
Da do ron ron ron, da do ron ron

Yes, my heart stood still
Yes, his name was Bill
And when he walked me home
Da do ron ron ron, da do ron ron

I knew what he was doing
When he caught my eye
Da do ron ron ron, da do ron ron
He looked so quiet but my oh my
Da do ron ron ron, da do ron ron

Yes, he caught my eye
Yes, my, oh my
And when he walked me home
Da do ron ron ron, da do ron ron

He picked me up at seven
And he looked so fine
Da do ron ron ron, da do ron ron
Someday soon I'm going to make him mine
Da do ron ron ron, da do ron ron

Yes, he looked so fine
Yes, I'll make him mine
And when he walked me home
Da do ron ron ron, da do ron ron

R6.13

Listening Test (See Teacher's Book)

R7.1

He didn't have any brothers or sisters. | He didn't like it there. | He didn't study very much. | He didn't get his 'licence to kill' until nineteen fifty. | He wasn't a very good student. | He wasn't married for long.

R7.2 R7.4

PRESENTER Good afternoon and welcome to "On the Page". Today's first guest is the writer, Will Forbes.
WILL Hello.
P Now, Will, you're the author of a new book about Ian Fleming, the man who wrote the James Bond books.
W Yes, that's right.
P We all know about James Bond, of course, but what can you tell us about Ian Fleming?
W Well, what's interesting is that Ian Fleming's life was quite similar to James Bond's.
P Really? [end of R7.2] Did Ian Fleming work for the British Secret Service too?
W Yes, he did. He joined the navy as an Intelligence Officer in 1939. Bond was also in the navy, of course.
P Did Fleming have a 'licence to kill'? Double oh six, maybe?
W No, he didn't. But his job *was* very important.
P Did he work for the Secret Service after the war?
W No, he worked for a newspaper as a journalist and then he became a writer.
P And what about his early life? Did Fleming and Bond go to the same school?
W Yes, they did, actually. They both went to Eton and were both very good at sports.
P Hmm … so Ian Fleming *was* James Bond.
W Yes, in a way.
P When did Ian Fleming write the first Bond book?
W He wrote *Casino Royale*, the first Bond book, in 1952.
P Did he make a lot of money?
W No, he didn't. He died in 1964 – only 2 years after the first Bond film.
P Well, thank you for coming to talk to us, Will. That was Will Forbes, whose new book, *The Man behind Bond*, is …

R7.3

1 Did Ian Fleming work for the British Secret Service too? 2 Did Fleming have a 'licence to kill'? 3 Did he work for the Secret Service after the war? 4 Did Fleming and Bond go to the same school?

5 When did Ian Fleming write the first
Bond book? 6 Did he make a lot of money?

R7.5

Did you go to the cinema last week? |
Did you see a Bond film last year? | Did you
watch a film on TV last weekend? | Did you
want to be an actor when you were a child? |
Yes, I did. | No, I didn't.

R7.6

ANSWERS 2 rock music 3 reggae 4 opera
5 rock'n'roll 6 jazz 7 dance music
8 classical music 9 pop music

R7.7

WOMAN Hey, do you want to do this quiz?
It's called "Are you a musical genius?".
MAN Yes, OK. Read me the questions.
W Right, the first one. When did Madonna
make her first record? Was it in the 70s,
80s, or 90s?
M Er, the 70s I think, about 1979?
W Correct. Number 2. Where do U2 come
from?
M That's easy. They're from Ireland.
W Yes, that's right. Question 3. What did
Sting do before he became a singer?
Was he a teacher, a writer or an actor?
M Er … an actor?
W No, sorry! He was a teacher. The next,
one's easy, though. Which of these
instruments does Elton John play?
M The piano.
W Correct. Number 5. How long were the
Beatles together? Was it for 5, 10 or 15
years?
M Hmm, let me think … 15 years?
W No, only 10 years. From 1960 to 1970.
Right, the next one! How old was
Colombian singer Shakira when she
released her first album, *Magic*? Was she
13, 17, or 22?
M I've got no idea, but my guess is 13.
W Yes, that's right. Well done. Number 7.
Who was the first singer to have a
number one album and film in the USA
at the same time? Was it Eminem,
Jennifer Lopez or David Bowie?
M I don't know – David Bowie?
W No, it was Jennifer Lopez, in 2001.
The film was called *The Wedding Planner*
and the album was *J-Lo*. Next one.
How many people were in the Swedish
group, Abba?
M 4 – 2 women and 2 men.
W Correct. Whose real name is or was
Faroukh Bulsara? Was it a) George
Michael, b) Bob Dylan, or c) Freddie
Mercury?
M Well, I know it's not Bob Dylan … was it
George Michael?
W No, it was Freddie Mercury. Right, the
last question. Why didn't Elvis Presley
make any records between 1958 and
1960?

M Ah, I know this. He was in the army.
W Correct. So your final score is … 6 out of
10. Sorry.
M Why?
W Well, I got 10 out of 10.
M I don't believe you!
W I did! Look!

R7.8

ANNOUNCER It's one o'clock and here's Teresa
Ross with the news.
NEWSREADER Over a hundred people died
in a plane crash in China last night.
The plane was on its way to Thailand
but crashed only minutes after it left
the airport.
Terry and Carla Ellis, who want to
become the first British husband and
wife to climb Mount Everest, are
missing, only three days after they
started their climb. Helicopters are now
looking for the two climbers.
In India there are floods in many parts of
the country, after five days of heavy rain.
Yesterday thirty-two people died in
floods near Calcutta.
And finally, supermarket manager Joe
Hall won over thirteen million pounds in
last night's lottery – thanks to his
dog! Joe told reporters today that his
dog, Max, chose the numbers!
That's the news this Thursday lunchtime.
And now over to Wendy Simmons for
the travel news.

R7.10

1
A Did you read about the man who won
this week's lottery?
B No. How much did he win?
A Over 13 million pounds.
B Really?
A Yeah, but that's not the best bit. His dog
chose the numbers for him!
B You're joking!
A Yes, apparently he wrote the numbers on
envelopes and …

2
A Have you got family in India?
B Yes, why?
A Did you hear about the floods?
B Yes, isn't it awful? I saw it on the news
last night.
A Is your family alright?
B Yes, they're fine. They don't live in that
part of India.

3
A Did you hear about that plane crash?
B No, where was it?
A Somewhere in China. Over a hundred
people died.
B Oh no, that's terrible.
A Yes, I know. I've got a friend who works
in China and she says …

4
A Did you read about the couple on
Everest?
B No, what happened?
A One of them fell and they lost their radio.
B Oh dear. Are they OK?
A Yes, a helicopter found them yesterday.
B Oh, that's good.
A Yes, the husband broke his leg, but …

R7.11

Did you hear about that plane crash? |
No, where was it? | Did you read about the
couple on Everest? | No, what happened? |
Oh, that's good. | Yes, isn't it awful? | Oh,
dear. Are they OK? | Oh no, that's terrible. |
Really? | You're joking!

R7.12

WOMAN Do you know any good jokes?
MAN No, but Tom's good at telling jokes.
W OK, Tom, Tell us a joke.
TOM OK, let me think … right, here's one …
One day Mike … [**see p60**] … Yes, it
was amazing. He hated the book.

R8.1

JAMES Rachel?
RACHEL Yes?
J Can /kən/ you help me?
R Sure, what's the problem?
J I want to go to the USA on holiday,
but I can't /kɑːnt/ decide where to go
– any ideas?
R Well, how about San Francisco? We
went there last year and had a great time.
J That's an idea. What can /kən/ you do
there?
R Well, there's Golden Gate Bridge of
course, and Golden Gate Park. It's a
really big park – you can /kən/ go for
long walks or just relax in the Japanese
Tea Garden. It's beautiful there.
J Uh-huh.
R And there are the cable cars – they're
really good. You can /kən/ go by cable car
to a place called Nob Hill, where you can
/kən/ see the whole city. Then you can
/kən/ walk to Chinatown, which has lots
of good places to eat.
J Hmm, that sounds good.
R And there's also a place called
Fisherman's Wharf. That's really popular
with tourists. There are lots of shops,
cafés and street musicians, and some
wonderful seafood restaurants. We went
there for dinner every night.
J Right.
R And from there you can /kən/ go on
a boat trip to Alcatraz. You know, the
island where the prison is.
J Oh, I'd like to go there. What a great
place to stay!
R No, you can't /kɑːnt/ stay on the island,
there aren't any hotels. You can /kən/
only go for the day. I think I've still got

Recording Scripts

a book and a brochure about San Francisco at home.

J Can /kən/ I borrow them?

R Of course you can /kæn/. I'll give them to you tomorrow.

J Thanks a lot. San Francisco, here I come!

R8.3

ANSWERS 1a) 2b) 3b) 4a) 5b)

R8.4

Can you go swimming there? | Yes, you can. | No, you can't. | Can you stay there? | Yes, you can. | Can you rent a car? | No, you can't. | What can you do there? | You can go for walks. | You can go on boat trips. | You can't stay on the island. | You can't camp there.

R8.5

LUKE Well, it's a week in Phuket or a week in Bangkok. Where do you want to go, Monica?

MONICA Hmm, it's difficult. Phuket's more beautiful than Bangkok.

L But maybe Bangkok's more interesting.

M Yes, maybe. But Phuket looks better than Bangkok – look at the photos. It's beautiful!

L Yes, but Bangkok's a fantastic city. There's lots to do there. We can go sightseeing, visit Buddhist temples, go to markets, er, go shopping.

M Maybe. But Bangkok's more crowded.

L Well, all capital cities are crowded.

M And the people in Phuket are probably friendlier. They usually are in smaller places.

L But Phuket's more expensive.

M Yes, but I love the beach. I'm happy to spend every day there.

L Yes, but you know I'm not really a beach person. It's boring after a couple of days.

M But you can go for walks, or you can rent a motorbike and go round the island.

L I still think Bangkok's more interesting than Phuket.

M Phuket's probably safer too. Especially at night. And it's quieter. I want to *relax*, Luke. It's a holiday!

L But we can go to a beach near Bangkok, you know, just for a day or two. And next year we can ...

R8.7

TERRY Hi Luke, how are you?

LUKE Hi, Terry. I'm fine, thanks. Just back from holiday, actually.

T Where did you go?

L Er, we went to Thailand, a place called Phuket. It's an island.

T Yes, I know. But I thought you didn't like beach holidays.

L Me? Oh yes, I *love* the beach. It was my choice, actually. Monica wanted to go to Bangkok!

T Really?

R8.8

FATHER **What do you want to do tomorrow?**
                /dʒə/   /tə/   /ə/

MOTHER **Well, I'd like to go to the beach.**
            /aɪd/   /tə/ /tə ðə/

SON Oh no. Not the beach again.
    I'd rather go somewhere different.
    /aɪd/   /ə/   /ə/

F He's right. We went to the beach last weekend.

M **Would you like to go to London, then?**
   /wʊdʒə/   /tə/ /tə/ /ə/

F Yeah, that's a good idea.

M We can spend the day at Regent's Park. It's really beautiful in summer and there's lots to do there.

F **Do you want to do that?**
  /dʒə/   /tə/

S Do what, Dad?

F **Do you want to go to Regent's Park?**
  /dʒə/   /tə/ /tə/ /ə/

S Sounds boring.
    I'd rather stay at home.
    /aɪd/   /ə/   /ət/

M It isn't boring. You can go on bike rides, go to concerts and there's a really good open air theatre there.

S Mmm.

F **So where would you like to go?**
             /wʊdʒə/   /tə/

S I want to go to Chessington.

F Oh, I don't think so. It's a long way.

S But my friends went there last week. There are lots of animals and some great rides. It sounds fun.

F But you can see animals in Regent's Park – that's where London Zoo is! Look, your Mum's right, the park sounds good. Let's go there. You can bring a friend with you.

S Yeah, OK. Can I ask Jason?

M Fine. Tell him to be at the station tomorrow at 9.

R8.9

A Would you like to go to the beach?

B I'd rather stay at home.

A Do you want to go to the theatre?

B I'd rather go to the cinema.

A What do you want to do tomorrow?

B I'd like to go to London.

A Where would you like to go?

B I want to go to the park.

R8.10

Holiday! Celebrate!
Holiday! Celebrate!

CHORUS

If we took a holiday
Took some time to celebrate
Just one day out of life
It would be, it would be so nice

If we finally spread the word
We're going to have a celebration
All across the world
In every nation
It's time for the good times
Forget about the bad times, oh yeah
One day to come together
To release the pressure
We need a holiday

CHORUS

We can turn this world around
And bring back all of those happy days
Put your troubles down
It's time to celebrate
Let love shine
And we will find
A way to come together
Can make things better
We need a holiday

CHORUS

Holiday! Celebrate!
Holiday! Celebrate!

CHORUS

Holiday! Celebrate!
Holiday! Celebrate!

R9.1

FRANK Janet? It's Frank.

JANET Frank! Where *are* you?

F I'm at the station. The train was late. I'm waiting for a taxi.

J But we've got that meeting with the Tamada brothers at 10 o'clock!

F Yes, I know. Are they there yet?

J Yes, they're sitting in your office.

F Oh no!

J And they aren't looking very happy.

F Hold on ... here's a taxi. Start the meeting without me, but take notes. Oh and Janet?

J Yes?

F Remember – this is *my* contract!

J Of *course* it is, Frank ... bye! Liz?

LIZ Yes?

J Where's Adriana?

L Adriana? Oh, she's working at home today.

J Oh, dear. I need someone to take notes at the Tamada meeting.

L Well, I'm not doing anything important at the moment. Do you want me to do it?

J Actually, I want you to finish those reports.

L Well, Danny isn't doing anything. I can ask him.

J OK, thanks.

R9.2

I'm waiting for a taxi. | They're sitting in your office. | They aren't looking very happy. | She's working at home today. | I'm not doing anything important. | Danny isn't doing anything.

R9.4

FRANK Hello, Liz, it's Frank.
LIZ Hi, Frank. Where are you calling from?
F I'm in a taxi. There was an accident or something. We're not moving.
L Oh, dear.
F Look, Janet isn't answering her phone. What's she doing?
L She's talking to the Tamada brothers. And Danny's taking notes.
F Oh, right. Where are they having the meeting?
L Er ... in Janet's office.
F In *Janet's* office? Oh no! Liz, please go and tell Janet *not* to sign that contract.
L OK, Frank. See you soon. And hurry up!

R9.5

FRANK Hi, Liz. Are they still in Janet's office?
LIZ Yes, they are. Good luck!
F Right ... Hello, everybody. Sorry I'm late.
JANET Er, hello, Frank. Mr Tamada and I are just signing the contract.
F No, you're not, Janet. *I'm* signing the contract.
J OK, Frank. It's all yours.
F I'm so sorry I wasn't here when you arrived. You see, there was an accident and ...

R9.7

Are you still working? | Are you having a nice time? | What are you doing? | Are the kids doing their homework? | What are they doing?

R9.8

PRESENTER ... are meeting later this afternoon. And now for more on today's transport strike, let's go to our reporter Amy Peters.
AMY Hi, Michael. I'm in the centre of the city and the traffic isn't moving at all. Excuse me, sir. What do you think of the strike?
FIRST MAN Well, I'm not very happy about it. I usually go to work by train, but I'm driving today. And it's taking a very long time.
A Right. When did you leave home?
FM About a quarter past 6 – that's 3 hours ago.
A Wow! How long is your journey, usually?
FM Er, it's about 40 minutes, that's all.
A Well, good luck! And here's someone on a bike. Hello, madam, are you going to work?
WOMAN Yes, I am.
A Do you cycle to work every day?
W Yes, I do. It's cheaper than the tube.
A And how long is your journey, usually?
W It's about half an hour, but it's taking longer today, of course, because of all the traffic.
A Thanks. Excuse me, sir. Are you walking to work today?

SECOND MAN Yes, I am. It's quicker than driving, I think. But I'm getting very tired!
A And how do you normally get to work?
SM I take the tube – or sometimes the bus.
A Do you have a message for the people on strike?
SM Yes, I do. Go back to work!
A Well, as you can hear, Michael, many people on their way to work aren't enjoying their journey.
P Thanks Amy. That was Amy Peters, reporting on today's transport strike.

R9.10

think of → think of the strike? → What do you think of the strike? | It's about → It's about forty minutes → It's about forty minutes, that's all. | And it's → And it's taking a → And it's taking a very long time. | someone on a → someone on a bike → Here's someone on a bike. | I'm in → I'm in the centre of → I'm in the centre of the city. | The traffic isn't → moving at all → The traffic isn't moving at all.

R9.13 **R9.14**

1

MESSAGE Hello, this is Alan Wick's voicemail. I'm sorry I can't take your call at the moment. If you leave a message, I'll get back to you. Thanks for calling. [end of R9.13]
EMILY Hello, it's Emily Wise here, from the contracts office at 3DUK. Can we meet tomorrow morning, at about 10? I need to talk to you about the new contract with Morris Computers. Can you call me back? Thanks. Bye.

2

MESSAGE Welcome to the NRL voicemail service. I'm sorry, but the person you called is not available. Please leave your message after the tone. [end of R9.13]
EMILY Hi, Katrina, it's Emily. Would you like to meet for coffee after work? Call me later – I'm at the office. Bye!

3

MESSAGE Thank you for calling the King's Theatre. Please choose one of the following 3 options. For ticket information, press 1. To book tickets by credit card, press 2. For any other enquiries, press 3. [end of R9.13] You are in a queue. Please hold. Your call will be answered as soon as possible.
TICKET SELLER Hello, King's Theatre.
EMILY Oh, hi. Are there any tickets available for *Say Cheese!* on Saturday?
TS Yes, there are.
E How much are they?
TS They're £27.50 and £22.
E £27.50 and £22. OK, thanks a lot. Bye.
TS Goodbye.

4

[R9.13 only] I'm sorry. there's no one available to take your call. Please try later.

R9.15

ANSWERS 2 Hold on a moment, I'll get her. 3 Hi. It's Katrina. 4 I got your message. 5 Hello, is that Chris Morris? 6 Speaking. 7 This is Emily Wise, from 3DUK. 8 Can I call you back? 9 If it's after 5, call me on my mobile. 10 I'll call you later.

R9.17

ANSWERS 2 This is 3 Can I call 4 Call me on 5 call you 6 It's 7 Can I speak 8 Hold on 9 got

R9.18

Calling out around the world
Are you ready for a brand new beat?
Summer's here and the time is right
For dancing in the street
They're dancing in Chicago
Down in New Orleans
In New York City

CHORUS
All we need is music, sweet music
There'll be music everywhere
They'll be swinging, swaying and records playing
Dancing in the street, oh
It doesn't matter what you wear, just as long as you are there
So come on, every guy, grab a girl, everywhere, around the world
They'll be dancing, they're dancing in the street

This is an invitation across the nation
A chance for folks to meet
There'll be laughing, singing and music swinging
Dancing in the street
Philadelphia, PA, Baltimore and DC now
Can't forget the motor city

CHORUS

Way down in LA, every day
They're dancing in the street ...

R10.1

DOCTOR Hello, Mr Taylor.
MR TAYLOR Hello, doctor.
D Right, is everything OK?
T Er, I think so.
D Good. First let's check your weight. Over here, please. Mmm.
T How much do I weigh?
D 93 kilos.
T Really?
D Yes. Do you do much exercise?
T Er, no, not really. I go swimming about once a month, that's all.
D And what do you usually eat?
T I eat a lot of meat and vegetables. You know, business lunches – but I sometimes have salad. And, er, we eat a lot of pizzas at home.
D And do you usually eat red meat, or chicken or fish?

Recording Scripts

T Oh, I suppose I eat red meat about 4 times a week. And we usually have chicken on Sunday.
D Do you smoke?
T No, I don't. I gave up 2 years ago.
D That's good. And what about alcohol? Do you drink a lot?
T No, not much.
D Do you drink every day?
T Er, yes, but only 1 or 2 beers. And maybe a glass of wine with a meal.
D Hmm. Well, your diet's not too bad, but you shouldn't eat so much red meat. Have chicken or fish instead, it's better for you. And I'm not sure about all those pizzas!
T OK.
D And you should do more exercise, maybe 3 times a week. But you probably know that.
T Er, yes. I'll try.
D Right, let's listen to your heart.

R10.3

TINA OK, Leo. I've got four people for the *Break* poster. See what you think.
LEO Right. Where's the first one? Hmm, he's not bad.
T Yes, I quite like him. He looks friendly, the type of person who buys a lot of chocolate.
L I can see that!
T Yes, he's a bit overweight, isn't he? Is that a problem?
L Er, I'm not sure. Who else have you got?
T Well, there's him.
L He's better, maybe. He's tall and good-looking.
T He's very good-looking – but I don't know about the hair.
L Yes, you've got a point there. Who's next?
T What about her?
L She's nice. Tall, slim, nice hair and very attractive.
T Yes, she's beautiful – but do we want a beautiful person on this poster? Do beautiful people eat chocolate?
L Not very often, probably. But everyone wants to be beautiful *and* eat chocolate! Is that all of them?
T No, there's one more.
L She's – well, she's a bit older, isn't she?
T Yes, but maybe that's good. People her age buy a lot of chocolate. And she's attractive – she looks very friendly and happy, I think.
L Yes, she does.
T And people eat chocolate because they want to be happy.
L Yes, you're right. Well, let's choose.
T OK. Do we want a man or a woman?

R10.4

TINA OK. Do we want a man or a woman?
L I think that we want a woman, not a man.
T Why's that?
L Well, women buy more chocolate than men. So they want to see a woman on the poster.
T Yes, good point.
L And people know that chocolate makes you fat – but everyone wants to be thin.
T So we want someone slim.
L And people always think they're young – so they want to see young people on posters.
T Which means …
L … Zoë.
T OK. Zoë. Fine. Shall I ask her to come for a meeting?
L Yes, good idea. Right, what else do we need to talk about?

R10.5

TINA Hi, Leo. I hear you've got a new girlfriend.
LEO Er, yes, I have.
T What's she like?
L Well, she's really friendly and outgoing. And she's very beautiful.
T I see. What does she like doing?
L Well, she likes dancing and going to restaurants. The same things as me, really.
T OK. What does she look like?
L Well, she's tall and slim, and she's got long dark hair.
T Leo?
L Yes?
T What's your new girlfriend's name?
L It's, er, Zoë. You know, from the poster.
T Oh, really?

R10.6

1 What's she like?
2 What does she look like?
3 What's he like?
4 What does she like doing?
5 What does he look like?
6 What are they like?

R10.8

I've got a stomach ache. | I've got a temperature. | I've got a headache. | I've got a toothache. | I've got a sore throat. | I've got a cold. | I've got a cough. | I feel ill. | I feel terrible. | I feel sick. | I feel better. | My back hurts. | My arm hurts. | My foot hurts. | My leg hurts.

R10.10

ANSWERS 2b) 3b) 4a) 5a) 6b)

R11.1

1
MEG Happy New Year, Jack!
JACK Thanks, Meg. And happy New Year to you.
M Any New Year's resolutions?
J Yes, I have, actually. I'm not going to work until ten every night. I'm going to work less and have more fun. And I'm going to have a holiday this year.
M Good! Where are you going?
J Oh, I don't know. Somewhere I can relax.
M Good idea.
J And what about you? Have you got any plans for the New Year?
M Yes, I'm going to move to Australia.
J Wow! When did you decide that?
M Oh, a couple of months ago.
J That's great. Are you going to sell your house? …

2
ED Hello, David. Hi, Val.
DAVID Hi, Ed. Happy New Year!
E Happy New Year to you too!
VAL Have you got any New Year's resolutions?
E Yes, I'm going to do a computer course.
D Oh, right. Why computers?
E I want to get a new job. The one I've got now is really boring.
D Right. Well, good luck with that.
E Thanks. And what about you? Any New Year's resolutions?
D Yes, we're going to get fit and Val's going to stop smoking.
V Yes, I am. And David's going to lose weight. Well, he says he is.
D Yes, I want to lose eight kilos. I'm going to do more exercise – and I'm not going to eat sweet things any more.
WOMAN Chocolate cake, anyone?
D Not for me, thank you.
W Oh, go on. It's really good!
D Well, er, just a little, thank you. But this really is the last.

R11.2

I'm going to work less and have more fun. | I'm going to have a holiday this year. | She's going to move to Australia. | He's going to do a computer course. | We're going to get fit. | I'm not going to work every night. | He's not going to eat sweet things.

R11.4

TIM Wow, Debbie, that was a difficult exam. And I really revised this time.
DEBBIE Do you think you passed, Tim?
T I don't know. The first part was OK, but the last question was really difficult.
D Yes, for me too. So how are you going to celebrate tonight?
T I'm not sure. I might go for a drink with Peter, or I might go to Jane's party. What about you?

D Well, first I'm going to go home and sleep.

T Yes, good idea.

D Then I'm going to meet Tony in town. After that, I don't know. We might go to a club, but I'm not sure what Tony wants to do. He might just want to go home and watch a video.

T Well, I'm sure of one thing.

D What's that?

T That's the last exam I'm ever going to take! What are you going to do this evening, Sid?

SID Well, Clare and I might go out with some friends, or we might go to the cinema.

T That sounds good. There's a really good film on at the Ritzy.

R11.5

I might go for a drink with Peter. | I might go to Jane's party. | We might go to a club. | We might watch a video. | We might go out with some friends. | We might go to the cinema.

R11.7

ANSWERS 2a) 3a) 4b) 5b) 6b)

R11.8

TIM Are you going to get a job, Sid?

SID No, I'm not. I'm going to do a business course in the USA.

T Really?

S Yes, if I can find the money.

T Are you going too, Clare?

CLARE Yes, I am. I'm going to study law.

T Wow! How are you going to pay for it all?

C Good question. We're going to talk to the bank tomorrow, actually.

S Are you going to stay here, Tim? I mean in the UK?

T Yes, I am. I'm going to get a job. No more studying for me.

S Mmm. And you haven't got a car, have you?

T No, why?

S Well, I'm going to sell my car. Do you want to buy it?

T Yes, I might. How much do you want for it?

S Oh, about $30,000!

T Yeah. You mean the cost of a business course!

S Well, and the plane tickets.

T You don't need to do a course, Sid. You're already a businessman!

R11.9

ANGELA Hello, Craven Holiday Homes, can I help you?

SUE Oh, hello, I'm phoning about your advert for Benton House. Is it available in September?

A Yes, it is. When would you like to stay there?

S From September 12th for 2 weeks.

A Er, yes, it's available then. Would you like to book it?

S Er, how much is it?

A 2 weeks in September, er, that's £650.

S Oh, that's a bit expensive. Is Hill Place cheaper?

A Yes, that's £570.

S And is it available for those 2 weeks?

A Let me check … Oh, it's available the first week, but not the second. Sorry.

S Right … OK, can I book Benton House, please?

A Certainly. Can I have your name, please?

S Yes, my name's Sue Daniels.

A And do you have an email address, Mrs Daniels?

S Yes, it's s daniels at freemail dot com.

A Right. I'll email you directions. It's very easy to find.

S Thank you very much.

R11.10

1 Go along Abbott Street and it's on the right, next to the bus station.

2 Go along the High Street, past the station, and it's on the left, opposite the department store.

3 Go along the High Street, past the department store, and turn right. Go along North Road and it's on the left.

4 Go along Abbott Street and turn right by the river. That's West Street. Go along that street for about 100 metres and it's on the right.

R11.13

CHORUS
Going to the chapel
And we're going to get married
Going to the chapel
And we're going to get married
Gee, I really love you
And we're going to get married
Going to the chapel of love

Spring is here, the sky is blue
Birds all sing, as if they knew
Today's the day we'll say "I do"
And we'll never be lonely any more

Because we're …
CHORUS

Bells will ring, the sun will shine
I'll be his and he'll be mine
We'll love until the end of time
And we'll never be lonely any more

Because we're …
CHORUS

R12.1

1 sixteen million
2 four point two three
3 five hundred thousand
4 seven thousand, six hundred and fifty
5 three hundred and ninety
6 nought point one
7 a hundred and seventy-two
8 ninety-eight thousand, five hundred

R12.2

ANSWERS a) 82 b) 335 c) 11.68 d) 0.01 e) $120,000 f) 85 g) £44,007 h) £12,300

R12.6

LUCY Are you enjoying the food?

STEVE Yes, it's wonderful. Guy's a great cook. How's business?

L Oh, it's fine. Busy, you know. I really need a holiday.

S Yes, me too.

L But you're always on holiday!

S No, I'm not. People always say that. I work very hard when I'm travelling.

L Yeah, right. Have you ever been to Rio de Janeiro?

S Yes, I have.

L When did you go there?

S 4 or 5 years ago.

L And did you enjoy it?

S Oh, yes, I had a great time. The people are really friendly and the beaches are beautiful.

L I'd like to go there on holiday. It sounds fun.

S I'd like to go to Australia. Have you ever been there?

L Yes, I have, actually. I went there about 8 years ago, with a boyfriend.

S And did you have a good time?

L Yes, we travelled around in an old car and camped on the beaches. It was fantastic.

S Mmm, it sounds great.

GUY Is the food OK, Steve?

S Yes, very good, as usual. Guy, have you ever been to Australia?

G No, I haven't. I never leave this restaurant!

R12.7

A Have you ever worked in a restaurant?

B Yes, I have.

A Have you ever been to the UK?

B No, I haven't.

A Have you ever met anyone from Ireland?

B Yes, I have.

A Have you ever seen a Japanese film?

B No, I haven't.

R12.10

TRAVEL AGENT Welcome to Call-a-Flight. My name's Helen. How can I help you?

JOE Hello. I'm calling about flights to Boston.

TA When would you like to go?

J On 24th February. That's a Saturday.

TA When do you want to come back?

J Sunday 11th March.

TA How many people are travelling?

J Er, just me.

TA And from which airport?

J London Heathrow.

TA And what's your name, please?

J It's Joe. Joe Hunter.

TA OK, hold on a moment, I'll just check availability. Right. There's a British Airways flight that leaves London Heathrow at 13.20 on the 24th of February and arrives in Boston at 18.45.

J So that's leaving Heathrow at 13.20 and arriving in Boston at 18.45.

TA That's right. And the return flight leaves Boston at 5.15 on Sunday the 11th of March, arriving at London Heathrow at 08.20. That's the cheapest direct flight we have.

J So the return is on Sunday the 11th, leaving at 5.15 in the morning and er …

TA … arriving at London Heathrow at 8.20.

J OK. And how much is that?

TA Let me check. That's £259, including all taxes.

J OK, that's not too bad. Can I book that, please?

TA Yes, of course. How would you like to pay?

J By credit card, please.

TA And the number on the card?

R12.11

WOMAN Can I have your ticket and your passport, please?

JOE Yes. Here you are.

W How many bags have you got?

J Two.

W Did you pack your bags yourself?

J Yes, I did.

W Have you got any sharp items in your hand luggage?

J No, I haven't.

W And would you like a window seat or an aisle seat?

J A window seat, please.

W OK. Here's your boarding card. You're in seat 16A.

J Which gate is it?

W Gate 12.

J Is the flight on time?

W Yes, it is. It leaves at 13.20. Enjoy your flight.

J Thanks. Bye.

R12.13

ANNOUNCER Flight BA 901 to Boston is now boarding at gate 12.

JOE Well, that's my flight. Time to go.

WOMAN Have a good trip, Joe.

J Thanks, I will.

MAN And have a nice holiday.

J Thanks. See you in 2 weeks.

M AND W Yes, see you. Bye.

J Bye.

W Oh, Joe?

J Yes?

W Send me a postcard!

J Er, yes, I will.

R12.14

Listening Test (see Teacher's Book)

Answer Key

3D ❷ b) p28

Are you an early bird or a night owl?

1	a) 1 point	b) 2 points	c) 3 points
2	a) 2 points	b) 1 point	c) 3 points
3	a) 3 points	b) 1 point	c) 2 points
4	a) 3 points	b) 2 points	c) 1 point
5	a) 2 points	b) 1 point	c) 3 points
6	a) 1 point	b) 2 points	c) 3 points

5–7 points:
You're definitely an early bird. You probably get up very early and do lots of things before lunchtime. But you're probably not a good person to go to an all-night party with!

8–11 points:
You're not a night owl or an early bird – so you're probably an afternoon person! You probably get up early in the week and then sleep a lot at the weekend.

12–15 points:
You're definitely a night owl. You probably go out a lot in the evening and watch TV late at night. But you're probably not a good person to have breakfast with!

6B ❼ a) p49

History-makers

1 b) Albert Einstein came from Germany. He was born in Ulm in 1879.

2 a) Orville and Wilbur Wright flew the first plane on December 17th 1903 in the USA.

3 b) Mother Teresa lived in Calcutta, India, from 1931 until she died in 1997.

4 a) George Washington became the first President of the USA in April 1789.

5 a) Marco Polo first went to China in 1271 when he was only seventeen years old.

7B ❷ c) p56

1 Mozart wrote his first symphony **about 250 years ago**, in 1764.

2 Rickenbacker and Beauchamp made the first electric guitar **about 80 years ago**, in 1931.

3 The Beatles' first concert in the USA was **in February 1964**.

4 The first performance of an opera was **in the sixteenth century**, in 1598.

5 Elvis Presley's mother bought him his first guitar **in 1946**.

12A ❼ b) p95

The best quiz in the world!

1 **largest** (1 point)
b) (2 points)
Buenos Aires has a population of 13.8 million, Istanbul has 9.29 million people and about 8 million people live in New York.

2 **oldest** (1 point)
a) (2 points)
Mel Gibson was born in 1956, Brad Pitt was born in 1963 and Julia Roberts was born in 1967.

3 **most crowded** (1 point)
c) (2 points)
There are 17,000 people per km^2 in Monaco, in Singapore there are 5,400 and in Bangladesh there are 850.

4 **biggest** (1 point)
a) (2 points)
The USA is 9.1 million km^2, Brazil is 8.4 million km^2 and Australia is 7.6 million km^2.

5 **most expensive** (1 point)
b) (2 points)
In 2004 Tokyo was the most expensive city to live in, Moscow was third and New York was twelfth.

6 **youngest** (1 point)
b) (2 points)
Pelé was 17 when he scored in the World Cup final in 1958.

7 **most common** (1 point)
b) (2 points)
Chinese is the most common first language with about 900 million speakers.

8 **nearest** (1 point)
a) (2 points)
Mexico City (+20°) is nearest to the Equator, Rio de Janeiro is −23° and Madrid is +40°.

Phonemic Symbols

Vowel sounds

/ə/	/æ/	/ʊ/	/ɒ/	/ɪ/	/i/	/e/	/ʌ/
father ago	apple cat	book could	on got	in swim	happy easy	bed any	cup under
/ɜː/	/ɑː/	/uː/	/ɔː/	/iː/			
her shirt	arm car	blue too	born walk	eat meet			
/eə/	/ɪə/	/ʊə/	/ɔɪ/	/aɪ/	/eɪ/	/əʊ/	/aʊ/
chair where	near we're	tour mature	boy noisy	nine eye	eight day	go over	out brown

Consonant sounds

/p/	/b/	/f/	/v/	/t/	/d/	/k/	/g/
park soup	be rob	face laugh	very live	time white	dog red	cold look	girl bag
/θ/	/ð/	/tʃ/	/dʒ/	/s/	/z/	/ʃ/	/ʒ/
think both	mother the	chips teach	job page	see rice	zoo days	shoe action	television
/m/	/n/	/ŋ/	/h/	/l/	/r/	/w/	/j/
me name	now rain	sing think	hot hand	late hello	marry write	white we	you yes

Irregular Verb List

infinitive	Past Simple	past participle	infinitive	Past Simple	past participle
be	was/were	been	leave	left	left
become	became	become	lose /luːz/	lost	lost
begin	began	begun	make	made	made
break	broke	broken	meet	met	met
bring	brought /brɔːt/	brought /brɔːt/	pay	paid /peɪd/	paid /peɪd/
buy	bought /bɔːt/	bought /bɔːt/	put	put	put
can	could /kʊd/	been able	read /riːd/	read /red/	read /red/
catch	caught /kɔːt/	caught /kɔːt/	ride	rode	ridden
choose	chose /tʃəʊz/	chosen	run	ran	run
come	came	come	say	said /sed/	said /sed/
cost	cost	cost	see	saw /sɔː/	seen
cut	cut	cut	sell	sold	sold
do	did	done /dʌn/	send	sent	sent
drink	drank	drunk /drʌnk/	sing	sang	sung /sʌŋ/
drive	drove	driven	sit	sat	sat
eat	ate	eaten	sleep	slept	slept
fall	fell	fallen	speak	spoke	spoken
feel	felt	felt	spell	spelled/spelt	spelt
find	found	found	spend	spent	spent
fly	flew /fluː/	flown /fləʊn/	stand	stood	stood
forget	forgot	forgotten	swim	swam	swum /swʌm/
get	got	got [US: gotten]	take	took /tʊk/	taken
give	gave	given	teach	taught /tɔːt/	taught /tɔːt/
go	went	been/gone	tell	told	told
have	had	had	think	thought /θɔːt/	thought /θɔːt/
hear	heard /hɜːd/	heard /hɜːd/	understand	understood	understood
hold	held	held	wear	wore	worn
know	knew /njuː/	known /nəʊn/	win	won /wʌn/	won /wʌn/
learn	learned/learnt	learned/learnt	write	wrote	written

CD-ROM/Audio CD Instructions

Start the CD-ROM

- Insert the *face2face* CD-ROM into your CD-ROM drive.
- If Autorun is enabled, the CD-ROM will start automatically.
- If Autorun is not enabled, open **My Computer** and then **D:** (where D is the letter of your CD-ROM drive). Then double-click on the *face2face* icon.

Install the CD-ROM to your hard disk (recommended)

- Go to **My Computer** and then **D:** (where D is the letter of your CD-ROM drive).
- Right-click on *Explore*.
- Double-click on *Install face2face to hard disk*.
- Follow the installation instructions on your screen.

Listen and practise on your CD player

You can listen to and practise language from the Student's Book Real World lessons on your CD player at home or in the car:
R1.19 R1.20 R2.11 R2.13 R2.15 R3.8 R3.16 R4.11 R4.14 R5.7
R5.10 R6.10 R7.11 R8.9 R9.16 R9.17 R10.8 R10.11 R11.12 R12.12

What's on the CD-ROM?

- **Interactive practice activities**

Extra practice of Grammar, Vocabulary, Real World situations and English pronunciation. Click on one of the unit numbers (1–12) at the top of the screen. Then choose an activity and click on it to start.

- **My Activities**

Create your own lesson. Click on *My Activities* at the top of the screen. Drag activities from the unit menus into the *My Activities* panel on the right of the screen. Then click on *Start*.

- **My Portfolio**

This is a unique and customisable reference tool. Click on *Grammar, Word List, Real World* or *Phonemes* at any time for extra help and information. You can also add your own notes, check your progress and create your own English tests!

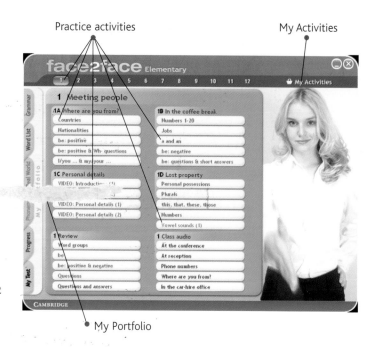

Practice activities   My Activities

My Portfolio

System specification

- Windows 98, NT4 with Service Pack 6, ME, 2000 or XP
- 128Mb RAM
- 500Mb hard disk space (if installing to hard disk)

Support

If you experience difficulties with this CD-ROM, please visit:
www.cambridge.org/elt/cdrom

Acknowledgements

The authors would like to thank all the team at Cambridge University Press for their tireless devotion to the *face2face* project. Special thanks for their support, enthusiasm and inspiration go to: Sue Ullstein (Commissioning Editor), Laurie Harrison (Electronic Project Manager), Rachel Jackson-Stevens, Lynne Rushton and Dilys Silva (Editorial team), Ruth Atkinson (Freelance editor), Alison Greenwood, Nicholas Tims and Lynn Townsend (CD-ROM team).

Chris Redston would like to thank the following people for their help and support during the writing of this book: Mark and Laura Skipper, Will Ord, Dylan Evans, Natasha Muñoz, Margie Baum, Joss Whedon, SMG, David B, John and Avis Hilder, his sisters, Anne and Carol, and his dear father, Bill Redston. Gillie Cunningham would like to thank Amybeth for her continued humour and patience, Richard Gibb for all his invaluable help and support, and Sue Mohamed for her constant encouragement.

The authors and publishers would like to thank the following teachers for the invaluable feedback which they provided:

Isidro Almendárez, Spain; David Barnes, Italy; Julia Blackwell, Germany; Mike Carter, Spain; Mike Delaney, Brazil; Jayne Freeman, Poland; Alison Greenwood, Italy; Ingrid Gürtler, Germany; Madeline Hall, Portugal; David Hill, Turkey; Krystal Jamet, France; Brenda Kent, UK; Hanna Kijowska, Poland; Justyna Kubica, Poland; Aleksander Kubot, Poland; Silvana Kuskunov, Argentina; Celia Martínez, Spain; Patricia Martínez, France; Rosa Mate, Spain; Michelle McKinlay, New Zealand; Paul Mitchell, Spain; Helen Paul, Germany; Dan Prichard, UK; Neide Silva, Brazil; Małgorzata Szulczyńska, Poland.

The authors and publishers are grateful to the following contributors:

Pentacorbig and Oliver Design: cover design
Pentacorbig: text design and page make-up
Hilary Fletcher: picture research, commissioned photography
Trevor Clifford: photography
Anne Rosenfeld: audio recordings

The authors and publishers are grateful to the following for permission to reproduce copyright material. All efforts have been made to contact the copyright holders of material reproduced in this book which belongs to third parties, and citations are given for the sources. We welcome approaches from any copyright holders whom we have not been able to trace but who find that their material has been reproduced herein.

For the text in 8C "Chessington World of Adventures," with permission of Tussauds Theme Parks Limited, www.chessington.co.uk; for the text in 8C, "Regent's Park," with permission of The Royal Parks. The information on Chessington World of Adventures and Regent's Park is accurate at the time of going to press and is subject to change at any time.

Da Do Ron Ron (When He Walked Me Home): words and music by Ellie Greenwich, Jeff Barry and Phil Spector © 1963 Trio Music Company (BMI). All Rights Reserved. Lyric reproduced by kind permission of Carlin Music Corp., London NW1 8BD. *Holiday*: words and music by Lisa Stevens and Curtis Hudson © 1983 Pure Energy Music Publishing Inc and House Of Fun Music Inc, USA. Warner/ Chappell Music Ltd, London W6 8BS. Reproduced by permission of International Music Publications Ltd. All Rights Reserved. Marathon Music International Limited, www.mmiuk.com for the sound recording, © Marathon Music.